Bound for the
Backcountry II

A History of Airstrips in the Wallowas, Hells Canyon, and the Lower Salmon River

Richard H. Holm Jr.

Bound for the Backcountry II
A History of Airstrips in the Wallowas, Hells Canyon, and the Lower Salmon River

By Richard H. Holm Jr.

To purchase copies of *Bound for the Backcountry II* please contact Richard H. Holm Jr. at boundforthebackcountry@gmail.com or visit www.coldmountainpress.com

Published by Cold Mountain Press
McCall, Idaho

Front cover: A Hillcrest Aviation Stinson 108-3 (N6327M) flying over the confluence of the Salmon and Snake rivers circa 1955. (Gustin family collection)

Back cover: Unloading Frank Hill's Cessna 180 (N42094) at the Lower Spencer Ranch airstrip in 1987. (R. Lorentz)

Cover and interior design by C Flinn Development Studio

ISBN: 978-0-692-30506-5

First Edition

Printed in the United States of America

CONTENTS

PREFACE

I first encountered Hells Canyon and its surrounding region as my interest grew in visiting and documenting historic fire lookouts. There was something about seeing the dramatic landscape from the lookouts along the Idaho side of the canyon – Horse Mountain, Kinney Point, Jackley Mountain, Heavens Gate, Cold Springs, and Grave Point. The landscape is almost indefinable. It is mysterious. Even from the great vantage of a fire lookout, the mind yearns to know what lies hidden behind the next ridge, drainage, or inaccessible pocket of timber and rock. The geology alone is unfathomable. I have never forgotten the first time I neared the top of the ridge at Heavens Gate, a carpet of early July wildflowers rolled out in front of me, and the massive Seven Devils loomed into view. The colossal peaks with their miniature frosty white capes of snow glistened in the countless cirques. The stature and presence of the mountain range is so grand that Native American lore expended centuries trying to explain its existence. Ever present to the west were the gigantic Wallowa Mountains – equally as impressive as the Seven Devils.

The aerial view of these alpine ecosystems is likewise breathtaking. As a pilot, I have often seen the isolated region in the four distinctive seasons. One of my earliest recollections of flying over the Devils was on a crisp sunny winter morning – scouting potential ski routes with friend Tor Andersen, who was longing to conquer the couloirs and chutes of the range. Later, I flew over the southern end of the area on scenic flights from McCall during the summer. The small, deep-blue, high mountain lakes and tarns cast against cirques

HOLM

Looking south at Hells Canyon with the Big Bar and Temperance Creek airstrips in the foreground and the Seven Devils in the distance.

1

of rock and snow all in the foreground of the ribboned greens and browns of the canyon seemed to never disappoint customers. The expression on their faces is still in my memory – noses pressed to the windows of the plane, gazing upon the rugged vistas with awe. Occasionally, one of them excited about what they were seeing, but not wanting to be distracted from the passing landscape, might half-motion to the other, to point out a lake or a noteworthy feature.

As the tourist season faded to early fall that year, I had another opportunity to see the region in a different light. By September fingerlings from the local hatchery were large enough to bag and assign to their new alpine homes. Delivery to the lakes in the southern end of the Hells Canyon National Recreation Area (NRA) is via airplane from McCall. Sitting behind pilot Steve Passmore in a Cessna 206, I was able to have an intimate view of the lakes as we skimmed fifty feet above the water to drop fish. Working our way through the enormous mountains at rock and treetop level from south to north, we reached the Dry Diggins and Bernard Lakes area – the last of our twenty-lake mission. Passmore slowed the plane and circled over Hells Canyon near the Dry Diggins Lookout. The maneuver let him position the airplane for an easy exit out of the next cirque, and time for me to load the hopper with fish. Set to go, he smoothly banked the plane to the east. At nearly idle power and full flaps, we sailed over the summit of Dry Diggins. Hints of the first frosts of autumn were evident on the flora of the mountaintop – slight hues of crimson and gold shown brightly against the specked granite brow. He then leveled the wings even with the catwalk of the lookout, and we plummeted straight for the lake. At the bottom of the dive over Bernard Lake, Passmore simultaneously shoved full power to the 206 and calmly asked me to pull the handle. As he initiated a steep ascending, 200-degree turn to the northwest, we arched partially across the canyon and headed south for home.

In contrast to the high altitude areas of the Wallowas and the Seven Devils, the lower reaches of the canyon present entirely different environments. Comparable but different, they are, beautiful in their own right. The first time I stepped out of an airplane onto the soft lush grasses of the canyon floor and was surrounded by spring wildflowers, I was simply amazed. At my feet were blooming prickly pear cacti. Beyond me, as far as the eye could see were penstemons, arrowleaf balsamroot, scarlet gilia, and tapertip. The bright colors of the flowering plants washed into the brilliant green vertical walls of the canyon. Weeks later, on another exploration of the area, I found that spring had crept up the slopes of Hells Canyon, to adjacent places like the unique island territory of Joseph Plains and its park-like settings of giant ponderosa pine. On the opposite side of the canyon, when we landed at Lord Flat, emerald green fields of wildflowers again greeted us.

Impressed with these remote lands of Idaho and Oregon, I originally planned to include them in separate chapters of *Bound for the Backcountry: A History of Idaho's Remote Airstrips*. But this unique region was so vastly different and rich with aviation history that it deserved its own book. This project turned out to be more expansive than I initially thought. The book covers the individual histories of more than forty landing sites, which are organized by drainage in three main chapters – the Eagle Cap Wilderness (Minam River), the middle Snake River (Hells Canyon Dam to Cache Creek), and the lower Salmon River (American Bar to the Snake River). Each airstrip is discussed by geographic location descending the drainage. This is a history book, not a guide, or a how-to-book. While the active, designated airstrips on federal and state land are generally open to the public, a good portion of the airfields chronicled within are on **PRIVATE** property. Readers should respect landowner rights and ask for permission prior to using their runways.

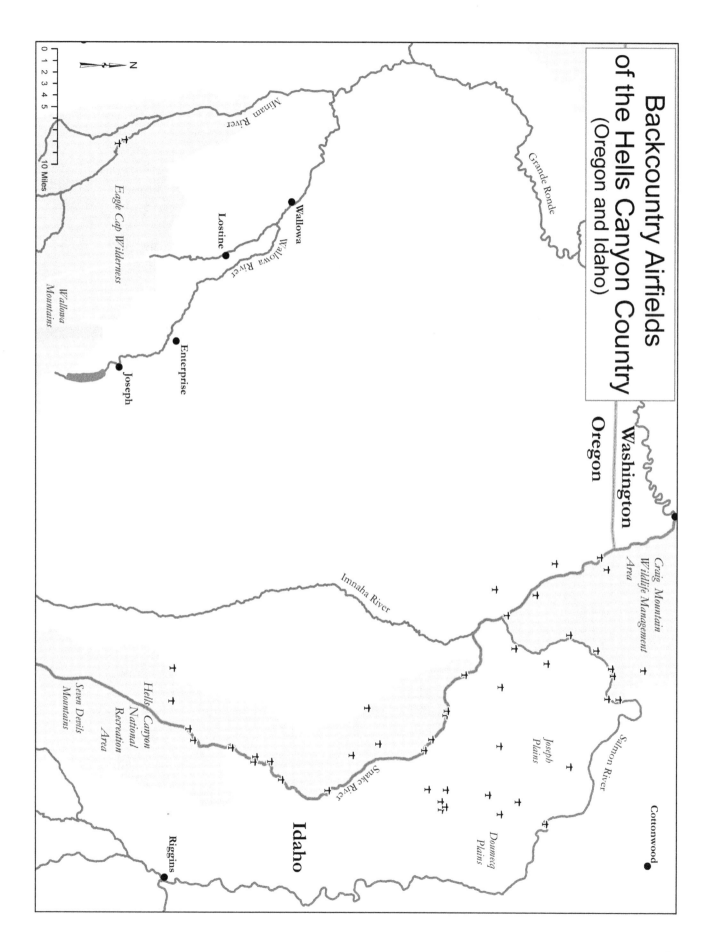

Backcountry Airfields
of the Hells Canyon Country
(Oregon and Idaho)

3

Acknowledgments

Every book is a journey — full of frustrations, joys, achievements, fascinating people, and new friendships. The history and stories recorded herein, are a tribute to the wonderful people who lived and worked in these remote regions, and to the many individuals who so diligently took the time to either help gather or provide me with irreplaceable information. I was fortunate and honored to have met and visited with two of the most accomplished pilots in the area, Bud Stangel and Ted Grote. Regrettably, I was not able to finish the manuscript before Bud's death in May 2014.

Through this project I'm grateful for many of the new people I became acquainted with who willingly shared their passion for the backcountry. I'm especially appreciative for the help given by Rusty Bentz and his family, who time and time again introduced me to people and places I would never have uncovered. To Cal Henry, Jerry Hughes, Tim Rivers, and Dick Stangel who patiently answered dozens of questions every time I called. To Polly Hollandsworth, Peggy Marek, and Donny Heckman who generously worked with me to access private ranch land and happily shared their family histories and childhood experiences of growing up on Joseph Plains. And finally to Joe Spence, who kindly contributed on multiple occasions his expansive familiarity and contacts with respect to the backcountry of eastern Oregon.

I'm also indebted to many old friends who have yet to tire of sharing their knowledge and history of the backcountry with me — among some of the more pestered — Cort Conley, Ron Gustin, and Chad Frei. Another is Bert Zimmerly Jr., who kindly granted me access to the documents of his family's pioneering aviation company Zimmerly Air Transport. Not wanting to always count on my own insignificant piloting abilities to explore locations in the book, I relied heavily on the help of two exceptional friends and professional pilots who donated their time, experience, and airplanes — Mike Dorris and Dick Williams. I hope the book lives up to their skills and extraordinary talents as pilots.

Additionally, I would like to thank the following people for their help and contributions to this publication: Bill Ables, Dennis Albers, Ed Allen, Tor Andersen, Dennis Baird, Josi Barinaga, Linda Barinaga, Justin Barrett, Steve Barrett, Wally and Myrna Beamer, Bryan Bentz, Darell Bentz, Bob Black, Gary Bledsoe, Arnie Brandt, Butch Brown, Jim Camp, Jay Cawley, Don Chapman, William Chetwood, Patty Clayton, Bob Cline, Norm and Joyce Close, Victor Coggins, Mick Courtney, Joe Corlett, Eleanor Dixon, Gayle Dixon, Earl Dodds, Jim Duran, Norma Jean Elmers, Brock Evans, Scott Findlay, Bill Fogg, Mike Foley, Craig

Fountain, Pete Fountain, Ron Fountain, Ron Grant, Nathan Goodrich, Dennis Grote, Dick Hammond, Clyde Hanson, Jerry Harlan, Bonnie Hathaway, George Hauptman, Carol Hawkins, Nora Hawkins, Ernie Heimgartner, Harold Heitstuman, Dave Helfrich, Bud Herr, Bob and Elaine Hitchcock, Todd Hitchcock, Carmen Hodges, Lew Hollandsworth, John Hollenbeak, Amy Holm, Rich and Ellen Holm, Frank and Carrie Hoyt, Greg Johnson, Joe Jordan, Anthony King, Tom Kovalicky, Ken Kuther, Gustave Lester, Mary Ann Lindsey, Randy and Nita Lorentz, Gunther and Donna Matsckhe, Buck and Chelsea Matthews, Jim Maxwell, Jerry McCauley Sr., John McKenna, Mary Ann McLaughlin, Sam McNeill, Teri Murphy, Boyd Norton, Joe Onaindia, Mike Pape, Bob Payne, Todd Pederson, Vickie Peterson, Jim and Janet Pope, Kathy Poston, Jim Renshaw, Bill Reynolds, Joe Rivers, Jean Rudolph, Cindy Schacher, Ned Schroeder, Art and Joyce Seamans, Glenn Shannon, Rex Shroyer, Anita Smith, Rod Snider, Dr. Adam Sowards, Ray Speer, Craig and Jane Spencer, Bill Stathem, Shawn Steen, Alex Stegner, Penn Stohr Jr., Sherron Stonecypher, Biden Tippett, Doug Tippett, Jack Trueblood, Ron Van Pool, Don Vogel, Doug Walberg, Bill Wilson, Dean Wilson, Gale Wilson, Mike Wilson, Ray Wilson, Rocke Wilson, Gary Willett, Patrick Williams, Wup Winn, Patti Wise, Bruce Womack, Mark Yates, and Steve Zanelli.

Chapter 1

EAGLE CAP WILDERNESS

I have often stopped here on a summer afternoon, enthralled by the view. Off to the west in the valley of the Minam is the great meadow of the Horse Ranch, where Red Higgins welcomes visitors at an airport in the wilderness. The light green of that meadow is the only break in the darkness of the conifers and basalt that line the valley – the only break, that is, except for an occasional glimpse of the blue water of the Minam itself . . . From a distance it seems impassable. The sharp cliffs, the precipitous mountainside, and the ravines that slash its surface in deep and ragged cuts seem indeed to be forbidding obstacles.

–William O. Douglas
Of Men and Mountains (1950)

Looking up the Minam River drainage with the upper portion of the Minam Lodge airstrip in the foreground and Red's Horse Ranch in the background.

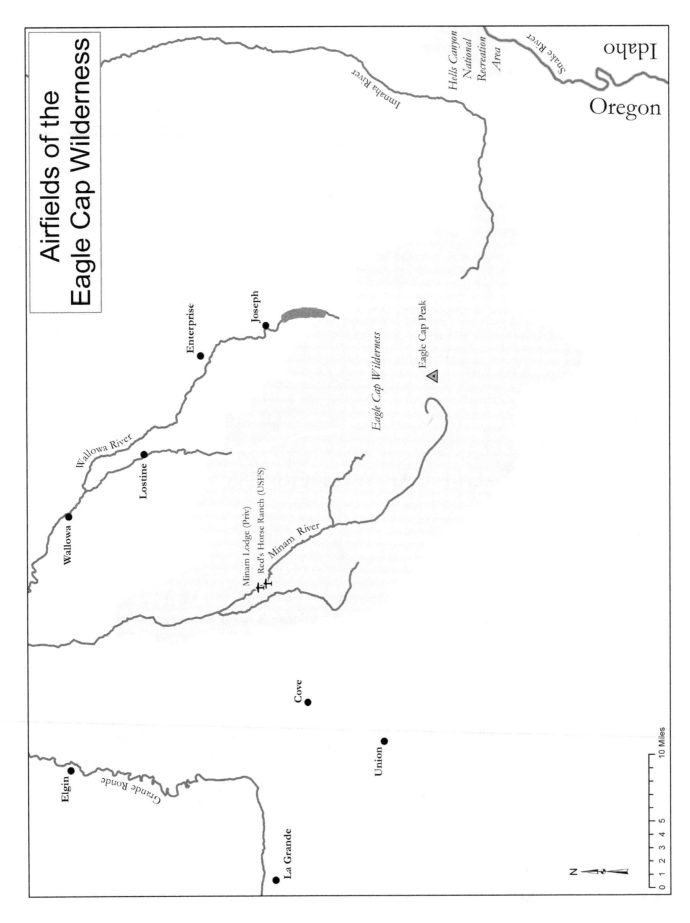

Airfields of the
Eagle Cap Wilderness

Idaho

Oregon

Snake River

Hells Canyon
National
Recreation
Area

Imnaha River

Enterprise

Joseph

Eagle Cap Wilderness

Eagle Cap Peak

Wallowa River

Lostine

Minam Lodge (Priv)
Red's Horse Ranch (USFS)

Minam River

Wallowa

Cove

Union

Elgin

Grande Ronde

La Grande

N

0 1 2 3 4 5   10 Miles

8

A pilot's view of the Wallowas near Eagle Cap Mountain.

Abutting the southwestern flank of the Hells Canyon NRA is the nearly 360,000-acre Eagle Cap Wilderness. The name of the remote central region is derived from Eagle Cap Mountain that stands as a sentinel among the other breathtaking Wallowa Mountains. Early descriptions of the territory suggest it was shaped roughly like a wagon wheel, with the Eagle Cap as the hub and various ridges running to it as spokes. The rugged wilderness is cut by five major drainages: the South Fork Imnaha River, Eagle Creek, the Lostine River, the Wallowa River, and the Minam River. The free-flowing Minam is home to the only backcountry airstrips in the Eagle Cap: Red's Horse Ranch and the Minam Lodge. These two locations are a favorite among aviation and outdoor enthusiasts of the region.

After approximately 8,000 years of Native American occupation, numerous landscape features bear names from their languages. Two pertinent examples are the words "minam" and "wallowa." Minam is the Nez Perce term for identifying a flowering carrot-like leaved plant belonging to the parsley family, more commonly known as "biscuitroot" (*Lomatium dissectum*). This spring plant, native to the drainages of the Wallowas, was part of the Indian diet, but was also used for medicinal purposes. Similarly, the term "wallowa" is also associated with the Nez Perce language and describes the tripod anchoring points for fish weirs that were used to enclose salmon for easier spearing.

Beginning at the turn of the twentieth century, stockmen used the river corridor and adjacent lands for grazing sheep, cattle, and range horses. Logging also played a brief role in land use on the Minam when two log splash dams were built in the early 1920s. The dams allowed winter timber harvests to float down the river in spring to a mill at the town of Minam. High water washed out the lower dam in 1928, four years after logging ended. In 1943, the Forest Service dynamited the upper dam located several miles above the Horse Ranch.

As time passed, the agency implemented more restrictive management policies and leaned on newly developed land designations to help preserve the remote area from further economic development. The first of many was designating the eastern Minam watershed as "primitive" in 1930 by creating the Eagle Cap Primitive Area. This area and additional acreage became a part of the National Wilderness Preservation System with the 1964 Wilderness Act. The Eagle Cap Wilderness gained more acreage in 1972 (73,410 acres) and again in 1984 (67,111 acres). The last expansion absorbed the two airfields, although they were both on private land at the time. Four years after the last wilderness increase, approximately forty-two miles of the fifty-one mile Minam was designated as a Wild and Scenic River.

Red's Horse Ranch

Early Years

The entrance to the Horse Ranch.

W. A. Adams first settled the 80-acre spread in the Minam Meadows area now known as "Red's Horse Ranch" or simply the "Horse Ranch," in October 1900. He built a small log cabin that still stands near the barn. Adams sold the remote parcel to Edwin and Matilda Millard the next year. Layfette Brazille acquired the ranch in 1911 and promptly moved it along to William A. Ogden. Ogden spent a decade bettering the property by adding a bunkhouse, barn, and another cabin. He also improved the land and domestic irrigation by further damming Millard Lake, situated about a mile and a half southeast of the main building complex. During Ogden's tenure he profited when the Minam Lumber Company logged in the area. He helped to care for the company's stock and provided housing for employees.

Biswells, Hudspeth, and an Airstrip

Ogden struggled to make ago of the place, but it ended up back in the hands of Brazille, who then sold it to Clarence Richards. Like Ogden, Richards could not hold on to it – the ranch reverted to Brazille. Myrtle and Marjorie Biswell of Baker City, Oregon, acquired the ranch in 1931. The Biswells were well versed in business and recognized the potential for creating one of the first dude ranches in the area, an idea that had recently become popular in the West. However, they also knew that they did not have the skills to carry the plan forward and turned to acquaintance, Ernest Hudspeth of Sumpter, Oregon. Hudspeth was an experienced horseman and packer who also owned his own stock. To entice his participation in the business, they offered him a half interest. He then brought in his two brothers Wallace and Greene, who also grew up riding horses. Under the ownership of this group the ranch became known as the "Big Minam Horse Ranch."

Improving the ranch and preparing for guests began as soon as the snow melted in the spring of 1931. In the beginning, their main customers were eastern Oregon businessmen who escaped to the remote getaway on weekend trips, reaching the place by horseback. Biswell, ever the entrepreneur, believed that a wider clientele could be attained if they could move people in and out of the ranch in a more efficient and less time-consuming manner than by horse. He consulted with Art Walker, a local aviator in Baker City, about building an airstrip in the meadow. The Hudspeths leveled and cleared a north-south runway. The same summer Walker was the first to land an airplane on the airstrip.

Even with a successful first year, Biswell could clearly see the tough lifestyle was not for him, and he sold his half interest to the Hudspeths in 1932. The brothers worked hard to keep the place going during the Great Depression, which often required them to seek outside employment in the logging industry to bring in extra cash. By the mid-1930s, the Hudspeths built four matching guest cabins along the river and improved the water system. Only one of these buildings survives, and it has been relocated to the lower meadow.

In 1935, tragedy struck the group when close friend and neighbor Clarence Richards killed Greene in a hunting accident on Chaparral Creek. Richards tried to save his friend, but could not stop the wound from bleeding. The accident was reported and a coroner was flown in to investigate.[1] No foul play was found. Greene's body was flown out and buried in the Baker City Mount Hope Cemetery. He left behind his wife Rachel and son Bill, both of whom remained actively involved with the ranch through the early 1940s.

Finally beating the economic downturn of the 1930s, the Hudspeths were faced with the difficulties of wartime America: shortages of rubber, gas rationing, and a general lack of patrons seeking recreation. By 1944, the Hudspeths sold the ranch to a group of former clients who organized as Big Minam Horse Ranch, Inc. The Hudspeth family moved to nearby Powder Valley and earned a living ranching. Wallace died in 1979 and Ernest in 1997. The two joined their brother in the Mount Hope Cemetery. Many of the Hudspeth's offspring have made annual journeys to visit the family's former Horse Ranch.

The faction that bought the ranch from the Hudspeths was comprised mainly of Portland businessmen. Some of the names involved were E. J. Christensen, Willard Pope, and R. E. Cavett. The men called the place the "Big Minam Horse Ranch" and hired a foreman to run it, but their ownership was short-lived. Throughout most of their brief occupancy the ranch was for sale. Evidence of this was clearly seen in *The Oregonian*, where the group advertised frequently for nearly a year starting in April 1945 through January 1946. During the war years when gas rationing and rubber shortages restricted family holiday travel, the Big Minam Horse Ranch tried to turn the dilemma into an advantage, and advertised that a stay with them was a vacation that did not require any gasoline. Ads read, "Primitive Paradise in the Wallowa Mountains of Oregon! The Switzerland of America – Vacation without gasoline – Hunting and Fishing."[2]

Red's Horse Ranch – The Higgins Years

Ralph A. "Red" Higgins and Jack Sanderson, also of Portland, eventually bought out the partners in 1946. Sanderson and his wife Maxine owned several retail stores in Portland, each called "Sandy's Camera Shop," a successful company started by Jack Sr. (aka "Sandy") in 1918. The family was known for its customer service and inventory and development of Kodak products. Higgins was born in Spokane, Washington, in 1909. He attended Willamette University, where he played football. After graduating he became a career firefighter in Portland, earning the rank of captain. He married Lois and the two had one daughter, Carol. Higgins spent his free time outdoors as a packer, mainly roaming south central Oregon. He and Sanderson enjoyed hunting together, and on a trip outside of their normal area they discovered the Horse Ranch. Sanderson's ownership was brief, but for Higgins the place became his life's passion. Henceforth the ranch became known as "Red's Horse Ranch," or simply, "Red's."

Higgins recognized from the beginning that for the ranch to be successful it required promotion and advertising. One of his first avenues to expand a customer base was his participation in the annual Sportsmen's Show that was held at the Pan Pacific Auditorium in Los Angeles. Here was a massive population of post-World War II city dwellers longing for an easy outdoors adventure. The event allowed likeminded vendors to gather and advertise their products – hunting, fishing, camping, dude ranch vacations, etc. And a salesman like Higgins could give a sales pitch on the spot to interested patrons.

Higgins's second approach to advertising was to gain the endorsement of two major newspapers, the *Los Angeles Times* and *The Oregonian*. The latter was one of the most read newspapers in the region, strategically centered in the most populated area of the state. During some years in the late 1940s, Red's Horse Ranch was featured or mentioned weekly from June through September. Journalists particularly enjoyed visiting the ranch for a western-style

Ralph "Red" Higgins demonstrating backcountry navigation skills.

The main lodge.

One of the many guest cabins built during the Higgins era with unique stone fireplaces.

vacation that could be turned into a business trip by jotting down a quick column about their experience. Unlike *The Oregonian*, the *Los Angeles Times* had a singular correspondent, Dick Hyland, who mentioned the Horse Ranch often from 1952 through 1958 in his weekly sports column, the "Hyland Fling." The combination of Hyland's support and the yearly marketing at the Sportsman's Show no doubt yielded the attention of some well-known guests such as Burt Lancaster, Sam Goldwyn Jr., Cornel Wilde, Jean Wallace, Kirk Douglas, Edgar Buchanan, and for several years the entire Los Angeles Rams football team that used the ranch for a spring training session. The splash of celebrity clientele of course heightened the notoriety of the place.

His final area of promotion targeted the booming postwar aviation industry. The airstrip at the ranch was the perfect facility to bring in a wide variety of customers. To get the weekend fliers to stop in, Higgins held large morning breakfast fly-ins – dubbed by some journalists as "buckaroo breakfasts." One of the early breakfast events held in 1947 attracted more than twenty-five privately-owned airplanes. Higgins and Sanderson worked with the Sportsman-pilots of Oregon to coordinate the event. Dozens of women pilots attended the fly-in; most noteworthy was Gloria Albertson, the 1947 University of Oregon Cover Girl and a runner-up in the Miss Portland beauty contest. For the trip, Albertson piloted a Western Skyways Stinson.[3]

For many years, the Sportsman-pilots of Oregon also organized an annual Labor Day weekend fly-in at the Horse Ranch. The occasion became increasingly popular as indicated by the number of planes reported each year: 1947 – thirty-eight planes, 1948 – eighty-two planes, and 1949 – eighty-some aircraft. In 1949, the "prop-hopping" pilots split the weekend into two stops. The first night was spent with hostess Bessie Halladay in Joseph, Oregon. Halladay, a member of the organization, managed the Joseph airport and operated a local flight service. Guests stayed at the Lazy T Dude Ranch adjacent to the airport – where they danced, fished, and rode horses. The next day and evening were spent at the Horse Ranch, where a special "airodeo" was held for "laughs," which included a wild cow milking contest and calf roping.[4] Higgins also hosted a yearly Independence Day gathering that featured pit barbecue cuisine popular with aviators.

The Los Angeles-based Upland Flying Club made annual trips to the Horse Ranch. The Upland fliers averaged about twenty airplanes per year,

A 1947 aerial of the Horse Ranch. Note the sketched in outline of the proposed pond to the right of the runway.

from 1946 through the 1960s.[5] In 1956, Higgins estimated about 350 guests arrived via airplane, while only 150 "old-fashion folk came in on horseback."[6]

How the customers discovered the ranch did not matter – undoubtedly once they were there, the scenery, atmosphere, hospitality, fishing, and quality hunting tended to promote it, and people returned year after year. In the summers pack trips could be taken to high mountain lakes; there was trout fishing on the Minam River, swimming, and relaxation. To help entertain young children, Higgins excavated two ponds circa 1947. Located between the river and the airstrip, they were then kept stocked for easy fishing. Beyond entertainment, the primary purpose of the ponds was to help drain the often-saturated airfield. Additionally, the excavation material was used to fill soft spots and expand the runway from 2,000' to the current 2,800'. During Higgins's tenure the field was rolled regularly with fifty-five gallon barrel drums filled with concrete that were pulled by horses or mules.

Shortly after purchasing the property, Higgins extensively remodeled the lodge and other older buildings. Moreover, he built several new structures, added indoor bathroom facilities, and created a western décor throughout the ranch. He undeniably transformed the place into one of the more impressive backcountry ranches in the Northwest. To tackle the large renovation cost-effectively, he opted to fly in most of the material. However, no flight service in eastern Oregon had an aircraft large enough to haul some of the items. Higgins looked across the Snake River to Idaho, and hired Johnson Flying

(top) Johnson Flying Service Ford Tri-Motor
landing at the Horse Ranch in spring 1947.
(bottom) Delivering a portion of the
21,000-pound freight load with the Tri-Motor.
(top opposite) Pilots Bob Johnson and Bob Fogg
with the Ford Tri-Motor at the Horse Ranch after
the mission was completed.
(bottom opposite) Looking downstream at the
expanded 2,800' runway.

FOGG FAMILY

FOGG FAMILY

16

Service for the job. This company, founded by Bob Johnson of Missoula, Montana, in 1928, became the largest commercial air carrier to ever operate in the backcountry of Idaho and Montana. It had a fleet of airplanes ranging from Piper Cubs to Cessnas to Travel Air 6000s to Ford Tri-Motors and even Douglas DC-3s. Johnson pioneered much of the early aerial forestry techniques, including the development of smokejumping. The company had a satellite operation, located in McCall, that was managed by Bob Fogg, who also served as the airport manager. When Higgins contacted Johnson Flying Service, Fogg and Johnson did not hesitate to book the charter, as they had used their Ford Tri-Motors on far tighter and shorter fields than the Horse Ranch.

With a plan in place, Johnson and Fogg met Higgins at the La Grande, Oregon, airport with a Ford Tri-Motor (NC9642) in late spring 1947. From La Grande, the pilots shuttled 21,000-pounds of freight divided into seven loads, in one day. Higgins figured it was the equivalent of one-month worth of horse packing. Impressed by the task, writer Paul Ewing reported, "In the cargo were 16-foot lengths of knotty pine to finish cabin interiors, 22-foot lengths of water pipe, a 900-pound kitchen range, two gas-operated refrigerators, 150 cases of canned goods, four tons of oats, saddles, pack gear and sports equipment ranging upward from bows and arrows. Costs average 2.5 cents per pound for air freight from La Grande to the ranch, but Higgins considers it cheap when compared with the cost of packing."[7]

Higgins, a dedicated horse and mule man, was impressed with what an airplane could do, especially for the price. Attracted by the airplanes coming and going from his ranch, he even took a few flying lessons in the winter of 1946–47.[8] According to his family, at one time he considered piloting a necessary skill to reach his ranch. Although he never earned his private pilot license, he did fly a small two-place airplane in and out of the ranch several times. According to his family, Higgins's flying days ended rather abruptly when he wrecked the plane at the ranch airstrip. From then on he relied on a saddle horse. In the last ten years of his life he actually refused to even ride on an airplane.[9]

During Higgins's lifetime there were several close calls, incidents, and accidents at the ranch with aircraft. As a young child, daughter Carol paid close attention to the arriving and departing planes. In fact, her first trip to the ranch was via a small door-less aircraft as an infant in her mother's arms. One of her distinct recollections tied to the backcountry and aviation was the wreckage of a single-engine airplane that was hauled off the south end of the airfield and left to decay. For years, she and her friends would climb in the fairly complete cockpit and take pretend flights from the Horse Ranch. Carol has scores of memories tied to airplanes and pilots who visited the ranch. One of the more unforgettable was a nighttime landing preformed by a pilot who had flown to the airstrip many times. Darkness had set in as he circled the field and he was able to communicate his intention to land. Folks on the ground scoured every nook and cranny of the place for Coleman Lanterns to mark the perimeter of the runway. With the airfield illuminated with the bright lanterns he made a safe landing.[10]

Another less-pleasant aircraft episode vividly ingrained in Carol's memory was the first fatality at the ranch. The accident occurred late in the day on Friday August 19, 1955. Three men from La Grande attempted a landing in unfavorable afternoon conditions and overshot the runway. The four-place plane crashed on the south end of the runway. Pilot Norman Kemp was killed instantly. The other two passengers, Wallace McGuire and Dean Cooper, were badly injured but survived.[11] Over the next several decades more accidents accumulated at the Horse Ranch and were mainly linked to pilot error, such as attempting upstream takeoffs.[12]

Tall Tales, A alleged DC-3, and a Bigfoot Sighting

On a lighter note, the Eagle Caps are similar to other backcountry areas and tend to draw-out the imagination of people telling and recollecting stories. As the seasons come and go in the rugged country these narratives have a propensity to become more exaggerated. According to Carol, longtime residents of the area attribute this trend to the river, by explaining, "If you drink the water from the Minam [River] you'll tell tales . . . some can be quite glorious, although maybe not entirely true." This yarn spinning has footing connected to the aviation history of the area. One of the more colorful stories tied to the ranch and aviation is John Wayne's visit. Articles re-accounting the history of the ranch and a few of its famous guests circulated in the 1980s. Enhancing the rumor of Wayne's visit was how he arrived. One Sunday *Oregonian* exposé in August 1984 interviewed a person who claimed Wayne flew in on a DC-3. The article explained, "[T]he late John Wayne once paid a surprise visit to Red's Horse Ranch . . . 'The Duke' arrived, the story goes, in his trademark larger-than-life style, by ordering his pilot to land an oversized DC-3 on Red's mountain-rimmed little airstrip."[13] The assumed wild visit has been a myth of the Minam for generations, but continues to perpetuate itself.[14]

One tall tale that Carol confirmed was half true was a Bigfoot sighting on the Minam that involved the Horse Ranch and aviation. The story began in the fall of 1958 with a group of La Grande businessmen consisting of Ray McFarland, Doug Holman, and Leonard Knight. After finishing a fulfilling Sunday morning breakfast at the ranch, the three men boarded McFarland's airplane and took a scenic detour, flying up the Minam before returning to civilization. Gaining as little altitude as necessary the men wanted to see if they could spot any elk in the area of Higgins's usual spike camps near Lost Chance Creek. It is unknown exactly what the group saw from the plane that day when they flew low over the camp, but apparently it was enough to conjure up a good story about their friend Mr. Red Higgins.[15]

Like any well thought-out practical joke, timing is important and the men waited until April Fool's Day the following year. For the prank they penned a carefully exaggerated tale about spotting a huge peculiar man-like creature in the Wallowas and submitted it to *The Observer*, the local La Grande newspaper. The sportsmen only expected to get a few laughs from area residents who would recognize the description of the hairy-man-beast as Red Higgins. Instead the article was picked up by the Associated Press and appeared in a dozen regional news outlets. Followers of Bigfoot and Sasquatch believed it was a real sighting. One version printed in the *Lewiston Morning Tribune* read, "Oregon Men Say 'Abominable Snowman' Seen In Wallowas." Describing Higgins, who always grew a large beard during hunting season, the men wrote, "It was the shock of my life. The best I can describe it is as half-man, half-beast. . . it was hairy, but patches of skin appeared. The hind legs were longer and it was tearing at the carcass of a small animal."[16] Of course Higgins, a charismatic entertainer and storyteller himself, thought the prank wonderfully played.

John Jobson – Writer and Horse Ranch Promoter

John Jobson was one of the most prolific outdoor writers to endorse and love Red's Horse Ranch. Jobson first became acquainted with Higgins in the mid-1950s as an outdoor writer for *Sports Afield*. As he was growing up his parents instilled in him a zeal for hunting and fishing. He also spent many summers on a ranch near the Sioux Indian Reservation in North Dakota, where he learned much about the tribal way of life. Infatuated with nature, Jobson's eclectic career began when he attended a lecture by well-known Arctic explorer Earl F. Hammond in Sioux Falls. Impressed by the voyager, he pursued a job with Hammond after high school as a helper on his Arctic Road Show. The show featured presentations and exhibits by the most famous explorers of the polar region. He worked five years for the outfit, roving the United States, and gradually earned the title of manager. Hammond taught him skills in writing, journalism, public speaking, and business. Most importantly Jobson's mentor introduced him to a network of people working for Hollywood movie studios. Through these connections he gained employment with Metro-Goldwyn-Mayer (MGM), RKO, and Fox as a prop manager and promoter.[17]

Jobson's talent for writing was soon discovered and he rose through the ranks, landing a position with movie mogul Nick Schenck at MGM's publicity department in New York City. In this position Jobson trekked around the country, from the New York and Philadelphia offices. In Philadelphia, he met and married Ann Marie D'Olio, his life's companion, who also shared the same passion for the outdoors. The two camped, fished, hunted, and hiked at any opportunity. He then started his own advertising business, and promptly signed MGM as his first client. Jobson successfully built the company and then sold it. During World War II the Jobsons moved to California where he took a job at Lockheed's Burbank aircraft manufacturing facility. After the war he returned to the drudgery of the Hollywood studios, aspiring to the position of head photographer at Corriganville Movie Ranch, where nearly every major studio filmed its westerns.[18]

A friend encouraged him to submit an article to a major outdoor magazine about a Colorado elk hunting experience. Surprisingly, the article was a hit. An introduction to Ted Kesting provided the next

(top) *Higgins and author John Jobson on a hunting trip in the Wallowas circa 1954.*
(bottom) *Bill Jenvey, Sam Hicks, Red Higgins, Erle Stanley Gardner, and John Jobson in the early 1960s.*

J. JOBSON

J. JOBSON

(top) The Jobsons called this cabin at the Horse Ranch home for one season in the 1950s.
(bottom) To illustrate Higgins's expert packing abilities author Jobson snapped this image of mules loaded with oversized items at the Horse Ranch.

encouragement directed to outdoor writing. Kesting, the editorial director of *Sports Afield* (1945–70), was the youngest editor of a major national publication in the United States when he was hired for the job at twenty-six. He was brought in to help modernize the magazine and liked what he saw in Jobson's writing. Jobson remained with the periodical for nearly thirty years (1950–79). He was appointed camping editor in 1962, replacing Colonel Weyland Townsend. Mystery writer Erle Stanley Gardner, now most remembered for his fictional character Perry Mason, was another budding author hired by Kesting. For the magazine, Gardner advocated gun owners' and hunters' rights. The trio became fast friends and regular visitors to the Horse Ranch. Jobson's Hollywood connections likely contributed greatly to the roster of famous guests at the ranch.[19]

One of Jobson's earliest outings to the Horse Ranch was an elk-hunting trip in 1954. For the occasion, he chartered an airplane to fly him and his party in. A report on the hunt, highlighting Higgins and the area, was published under the title "Fly In For Elk" in the January 1955 issue of *Sports Afield* – the first of many Jobson articles about the ranch. Over the next decade, a mutual admiration developed between Jobson and Higgins. For one whole season, the Jobsons lived in the far single-unit log cabin built by Higgins in 1948. Concerning the property and the extended stay, he wrote, "It's hard to decide which cabin we liked best, but a nice span of wilderness life was in one on the bank of the Big Minam River . . . We would sit on the porch on a cool evening and listen to the tinkle of the glass-clear Big Minam. We'd watch weary salmon – 300 [sic] long miles from the sea – Dolly Varden and steelhead trout. On a few larger rocks above water we observed the little gray water ouzels pump themselves up and down, then casually walk into the swift water and feed on the bottom . . . In the cliffs 300 yards or so back from the river, bull elk bugled in the frosty months of September and October. There were no phones, no roads, no radio, no TV, no city noise, no interruptions, no fret, fuss, or bother. Months slipped by. One way to fully enjoy life is in your own cozy log cabin under the big sky."[20]

The Jobsons moved in 1964 to Layton, Utah, where he died fifteen years later. His wife donated his personal papers and archives to the University of Idaho Special Collections in 1999. She died in December the same year. Amongst the hundreds of articles Jobson wrote, he only published one book – *The Complete Book of Practical Camping*.

Of all the people he met in his world travels, he expressed sincere gratitude for a mere ten in the acknowledgement portion of the book. Amid the scant number of names was, of course, Red Higgins. Throughout the book Jobson recalls noteworthy stories and suggestions from his travels and many regard Higgins – everything from navigation techniques to animal packing. Concerning packing Jobson observed, "The best packer I ever saw, anywhere, was the late Red Higgins, of Wallowa Mountains. He'd pack the Rose Bowl if you gave him a free hand. He easily carried lumber, big beams, king-size mattresses, steel fireplace units, shower stalls and once a cast iron cook stove for his upper elk camp."[21]

The Next Generation

Higgins died in October 1970 at age sixty-one. The sportsman community that had come to know Higgins and his legendary Horse Ranch was astonished by his death. Illustrating the disbelief, Jobson published Higgins's obituary in *Sports Afield* and spread the word to regional newspapers. In his letter to the papers Jobson wrote, "One of the best dude ranches in America, Red's was a favorite of well-known big game hunters, editors, politicians, movie stars, and other notables. It has often been written up in national magazines and featured on television . . . Friends remember Red as a great story teller who loved to perform around the fireplace in the main lodge, and a man who quit the rat race and went out and did what he wanted to do most for the last quarter century of his life."[22]

The unexpected loss caused Carol, who had just earned a masters degree in biochemistry, to take over the historic ranch at age twenty-three and forgo medical school. From the beginning, she had many big plans and successfully ran the ranch on her own for a few years. In September 1974, she married Merel Hawkins.

Merel also had a personal connection to the area since his family settled in northeastern Oregon in 1872. Merel began packing in the Wallowas and the Snake River region in 1954. He learned the trade from his father and great-uncle Roy Schaeffer, a well-known outfitter and packer. The Schaeffers owned the Lapover Dude Ranch located on the Lostine River, north of the present-day Turkey Flat Campground.[23]

Roy achieved a high rapport in the business and became well known though his association with client and friend Supreme Court Justice William O. Douglas. Following many years of guiding and packing for Douglas in the Wallowas, Schaeffer sold the Justice a few acres on the Lostine, where he built a summer cabin. Schaeffer's fame was boosted when Douglas wrote many times of his travels with him – which helped promote the Lapover Dude Ranch and his overall reputation. In Douglas's 1950 book, *Of Men and Mountains*, he dedicated an entire chapter cleanly titled "Roy Schaeffer" to his friend. Although the text is predominantly a narration of their horse riding, fishing, and camping experiences, Douglas's immense admiration for Schaeffer repeatedly shines through with observations such as, "Roy Schaeffer is the man I would want with me if I were catapulted into dense woods anywhere from Maine to Oregon. He knows Oregon best, but in any forest he would be king. For he is as much a part of the woods as the snowberry, the mountain ash, or the buck deer. The woods are part of him . . . Roy's strength is prodigious. His hands are like hams. Each of them is so strong it could crush a man. Taking hold of it is similar to grasping a wild steer by the horn. There are many stories of his feats and most of them have a Paul Bunyan touch."[24] While Douglas's writings included personal accounts of his encounters with nature, they also emphasized and advocated for the protection and preservation of wild places. His work as a citizen and as a Supreme Court Justice greatly influenced the future of the Minam and Hells Canyon, both areas he experienced with Schaeffer. For Hells Canyon, he wrote the majority opinion of the court, *Udall v. Federal Power Commission* (1967), which essentially stopped the construction of the High Mountain Sheep Dam. For the Minam, he strongly advocated against further logging on the river corridor, ultimately leading to the wilderness status of the area many years later.

Working with the legendary Schaeffer, Merel too created a solid name for himself in the outfitting and packing business. In 1957, Merel and an uncle, Don Locke, bought the Lostine River ranch from Schaeffer's son Arnold. Shortly thereafter, Merel's brother and father obtained Locke's interests. The Hawkins family operated from the Lapover locale until Merel partnered with Carol Higgins in 1972, at which time he sold his interest in the Lapover operation.[25]

A few years later Merel and Carol were in need of more capital to keep their business going and decided to sell shares of the Horse Ranch to some acquaintances from Wallowa County. Buying into the ranch were: Don Locke, Mick and Sharon Courtney, Dr. Lowell and Jan Euhus, Bill and Margaret Kirby, and Bud and Margaret Stangel. Locke owned an interest only for a short time before his shares were absorbed. The Stangels in particular were not strangers to the Horse Ranch. In addition to being a rancher, Stangel was a professional backcountry pilot, who had been flying supplies and clientele into the Minam for over a decade. He not only flew for the Horse Ranch and Minam Lodge, but also for the Richards family who owned an in-holding upstream from the Horse Ranch.

Francis Neil "Bud" Stangel – A Career Backcountry Pilot

Oregon native Francis "Bud" Stangel moved to Enterprise with his wife Margaret and four children (one daughter and three sons) from Condon, Oregon, in 1958. A fourth son followed the same year. He and his wife had married ten years earlier. Before that he enlisted in the US navy and served two years on a destroyer escort in the South Pacific. By the end of his service he was an officer.[26]

When he moved to Wallowa County with his family, he had recently acquired two airplanes from a person who owed him money. He figured why not learn how to fly them. After some primary training, he met local Joseph-Enterprise pilot Ted Grote. The two hit it off, and Grote helped him obtain his various ratings. The men became lifelong friends, and are considered two of the more legendary pilots of eastern Oregon and Hells Canyon to this day.[27]

Similar to Grote, Stangel started his own flying business as a sideline to ranching. After opening Stangel Flight Service in 1962, he helped to organize the construction of the modern-day Enterprise airport. Stangel and his constituents negotiated a trade with the Wallowa County Road Department to supply equipment if they provided the diesel fuel. He also donated land to the city of Enterprise in order that it afford enough space for the facility – with the stipulation that it had to remain a maintained airport.[28]

As a pilot, Stangel did just about every type of flying. He became the expert on flying passengers and freight in and out of Hells Canyon and the Eagle

(top) Pilot Bud Stangel in the mid-1960s with a Cessna 206.
(center) Stangel's favorite Cessna 206 at the Horse Ranch.
(bottom) Bud Stangel and Ted Grote in November 2013.

Cap Wilderness, sprayed crops, performed Fish and Game surveys, planted fish in high mountain lakes, hauled firefighters in the summer, and regularly took on student pilots.[29]

For his work in Hells Canyon he preferred to use a Super Cub and always had several in his fleet. Even after he retired from flying he hung on to his favorite, Cub N3675Z, purchased new by Grote in 1960. Stangel flew N3675Z thousands of hours in the backcountry, and his son Dick continues to fly it for fun. It was in this airplane that Stangel made many of the last known takeoffs and landings at some of the Hells Canyon airstrips before they were closed. Beyond the Cubs, Stangel flew dozens of different Cessna models and brought in some of the first Cessna 206s to the area. As with his favorite Super Cub, Stangel hung on to a favorite Cessna 206 (N50958) as well. He bought this 1973 model new and flew it home from the factory. After many years of reliable service, the Forest Service informed him that the aircraft was too old and did not meet its standards. Needing to meet the requirements of the contract, he traded it for a newer model. However, the aircraft age stipulation was later changed and Stangel reacquired the plane, which Dick continues to fly.[30]

The simple day-to-day missions remained as some of his most memorable flights in the backcountry. But the humble Stangel, flew all kinds of interesting missions and people. On several occasions he piloted planes with magazine photographers and Disney film crews collecting aerial footage of Hells Canyon. On a personal level, he regularly flew actor Walter Brennan, who owned a ranch near Joseph. Brennan's studio insurance only authorized him to fly in airplanes with at least two engines. However, the studio made an exception, as long as Stangel was at the controls. For many years Brennan would fly to Pendleton, Oregon, and Stangel transported him the rest of the way to Joseph. Brennan also frequented Red's Horse Ranch.[31]

While Stangel's skills may have attracted glitzy clientele, he did not have the time or the care to stay in tune with modern culture. This became very evident one day at the Enterprise airport when a flashily painted Cessna 210 landed and parked. The relatively new airplane, decorated with eccentric multicolored rainbow swooshes down each side of the beige fuselage, stood out like a sore thumb. Clearly not impressed with the overdone graphics, Stangel greeted the two unfamiliar men as he did any stranger, and asked them if they needed anything, such as fuel. One of the men walked forward, gestured for a handshake, and said, "Hi. Johnny Denver. Nice to meet you." With the same you-ought-to-know-who-I-am tone in his voice, Stangel kindly responded, "Well, hi. I'm Bud Stangel." Stangel returned to work. One of his employees, Al Slinker, inquired about the men. Stangel nonchalantly mumbled, "Oh, some guy named Johnny . . . Johnny Denver." Of course, Slinker, who had a background producing television shows in Hollywood, could not resist. He'd never met Denver, but he walked over to the 210 with jovial salutations, as though they were old friends. The combination of Stangel's "who cares" attitude and Slinker's practical joke has brought laughter many times to the Enterprise airport crowd.[32]

In the early 1990s after 40,000 hours of flight time and no longer able to keep his medical certificate, Stangel decided to retire from flying. He had slowly eased out of Stangel Flight Service several years earlier, handing the reins over to former student Joe Spence. When Stangel hung up his wings, he did not stop working. In his retirement Stangel's sons set him up with his own desk/workbench at Stangel Industries & Machine Shop, where he worked daily on all kinds of projects. He restored nearly a dozen antique and classic cars, specializing in 1920s and 1930s Cords. He also restored a very rare 1931 open cockpit Perth-Amboy Bird biplane that he flew often. Stangel died May 31, 2014 at age eighty-nine.

Joe Spence – Spence Air Service

Spence carries on Stangel's tradition of flying Hells Canyon and the Eagle Cap Wilderness under the name of Spence Air Service. Starting in 1986, Spence slowly took over some of Stangel's flying. As a child he became enamored with aviation after taking his first ride at age five with pilot Ray Dunsmore in a Stinson 108. However, it was not until 1979 that he began taking lessons and obtained his license from his friend and mentor Stangel. To build flight time he bought an Aeronca Champ and flew it all over Oregon, Idaho, and Washington. To overcome the limitations of the low-range tanks in the plane he stowed extra cans of gas in the baggage area. Initially, Spence took up flying with the goal of making it a second income to his regular job of commercial trucking. Once he had all the necessary ratings he figured it was his way out of the long monotonous hours of trucking and it evolved into a full-time business. Stangel helped him first by acquiring a Cessna 206 (N35854) for charter work. Then Stangel covered for him while he built the required flight hours for contracts with the Forest Service and the Oregon Department of Fish and Wildlife.[33]

For many years Spence flew the lone 206 until 2001 when the nose gear failed on landing at Pittsburg on the Snake River, causing the airplane to flip over on its back. He most recently flies another Cessna 206 (N35868) and a Super Cub (N7473D) for all his commercial flying. Spence has become the authority for the Oregon Department of Fish and Wildlife on game counts, telemetry work, and fish planting. For fish planting, Spence Air Service stocks about eight to twelve lakes per year, mainly in the Eagle Cap and the greater Wallowa area. He does occasionally plant lakes as far south as the Strawberry and the Elkhorn mountains in Oregon.[34]

The Henry Years

In the beginning the Stangels, Courtneys, Euhuses, and Kirbys, used the Horse Ranch frequently

Pilot Joe Spence with a Cessna 206 in September 2014.

and alternated management duties along with the Hawkins family. Euhuse was a doctor, and Kirby was a lawyer. Courtney on the other hand owned and operated Courtney Motors and Summit Ford, which were main automobile dealerships in Enterprise from 1956 until 2004. Prior to buying the ranch, Courtney learned to fly in 1964 from Stangel, and owned at different times a Cessna 182 and a 206. The planes were used often to help haul equipment to the property. During these years the owners flew in a new diesel generator, building materials, a deep freezer, and a hay elevator. Ted Grote, using a Bell Jet Ranger helicopter, hauled in items that would not fit in a Cessna 206. At the same time, the group brought in several pieces of equipment to maintain

Cal Henry with his Cessna 182 in the mid-1980s.

the runway, such as a dismantled John Deere crawler equipped to handle backhoe and mower attachments. Euhuse and Kirby also were pilots during their involvement with the Horse Ranch.[35]

With full-time jobs, the group's interest paled and they hired ranch managers. But, similar to other backcountry operations, finding good employees who were willing to stay long-term was difficult. In 1981, Stangel approached friend and outfitter Calvin "Cal" Henry about managing the Horse Ranch. He and Stangel had a history together dating back to the late 1960s. Stangel flew for Henry while he was the manager of the Tryon Creek Ranch on the middle Snake River, as well as for his outfitting business at the same location and at Lord Flat. When the Hells Canyon NRA was established, Henry moved his outfit to the Eagle Cap Wilderness. With Stangel's permission, he used the Horse Ranch airstrip to bring in customers and supply his camp located on the North Fork of the Minam River. Knowing Henry's reputation, Stangel felt he would be a good fit to handle the ranch. Henry countered by proposing

to lease the ranch from the partners. An agreement was made, and Henry utilized the Horse Ranch for the next nine years.[36]

Henry worked with the owners to upgrade and maintain the facilities. With Stangel's piloting skills and access to airplanes he flew in all the material needed for the projects, mainly using a Cessna 206. One of the largest undertakings was replacing all the shingled roofs with aluminum. Henry acted as foreman, and Stangel flew in several of his sons and friends to help.[37]

In an effort to maximize the earnings of his outfitting business, Henry quickly recognized that chartering commercial flights in and out of the lodge was a huge cost. To combat the flying expenses he approached Gary Holmes, a commercial operator from Joseph, about the possibility of obtaining a private pilot license. Holmes flew some for Henry and helped him earn his rating. He then needed an airplane. Dr. Vanderbilt, one of the former owners of the Tryon Creek Ranch, happened to fly to the Horse Ranch with his Cessna 182 (N92143). In a casual conversation, Henry mentioned he was looking for an airplane to link to the ranch. At the time Vanderbilt was struggling to keep his medical certificate and offered to sell him the airplane. The deal was made with a handshake. The next day, Vanderbilt and Henry flew the plane to town. Henry dropped him off and returned to the ranch with the 182.[38]

Streamlining the aviation end of his business even further, Henry began to have customers fly with La Grande and Baker-based operators. During hunting season the weather tended to favor routes from the west, instead from the east. In general, it was also more convenient for out-of-state customers to meet an airplane in La Grande rather than Enterprise or Joseph. Flights were frequently chartered with Vern Draper of La Grande and Mike Trindle or Don Doyle of Baker City.[39]

In the winter airplanes also were necessary, as Henry often kept employees at the Horse Ranch year-round. When needed, the runway was plowed with a small crawler for wheeled airplanes, but at times the snow only allowed ski-equipped aircraft. In these instances Stangel flew in using a Cessna 180. Also Henry occasionally hired Gifford Hulse from Elgin, Oregon, to haul supplies with a ski-equipped

C. HENRY

C. HENRY

(top) Packing the runway with horse-drawn equipment in the winter to facilitate the landing of wheel-equipped aircraft.

(bottom) Gifford Hulse [far right] with a group of guests at the Horse Ranch and his Cessna 180.

(top opposite) Attempting to airlift Trindle's Cessna 180.

(bottom and center opposite) After the helicopter failed to lift the airplane, a John Deere crawler was used to pull the craft over onto the main wheels.

C. HENRY

C. HENRY

C. HENRY

185. On one occasion Trindle attempted to land a Cessna 180 with wheels on the airstrip in mid-January. The snow was a little too deep and the airplane nosed over and came to a stop with the tail straight in the air. The uninjured Trindle hired a helicopter to airlift the airplane out. When the copter tied onto the bird it could not gain any altitude – it was too heavy. Trindle then went back to the drawing board and had the ranch crew use the dozer to tip the plane back on the main wheels. A ferry permit was obtained and the necessary parts were brought in to make field repairs. Within a few weeks, the plane was safely flown back to Baker City.[40]

Trindle's competitor in Baker was Don Doyle, who operated an FBO, Don's Flying Service from 1954 until 1985. Doyle closed his business and moved to Boise where he flew for an air ambulance company until retirement in 1993.[41] Trindle flew until the early 2000s and sold his business to Brian Moody in 1997. Moody was killed in a Cessna 206 (N8529Q) on a charter flight for Idaho Power near Sturgill Mountain, in the area of Cambridge, Idaho, in November 2000. The plane was not found until May the following year.

As in the Higgins era, the Horse Ranch remained popular with the media. During Henry's reign the place was featured in many newspapers and magazines. A few of the major articles appeared in *AOPA Pilot*, *Western Horseman*, and *Sports Afield*.

Henry's last season at the ranch was in 1989. Change was in the wind as most of the owners were moving toward retirement and did not see the Horse Ranch as part of their future plan. While they all loved the place, it was in constant need of attention and time. The group collectively decided to list the property for sale. In the meantime, the owners informed Henry that they were increasing the yearly lease rate to cover growing costs. As a businessman, Henry concluded the hike was not affordable, plus he did not want to deal with the property while it was on the market. The next season Henry moved his outfitting business downstream to Minam Lodge where he remained until 1993. Henry left the Eagle Cap area, taking a job with the Flying B Ranch on the Middle Fork of the Salmon River. He retired as a ranch manager in 2010. Henry continues to fly and explore the backcountry with a modified Cessna 150.[42] One interim leaseholder used the Horse Ranch following Henry, but between the unpaid bills and the lack of backcountry etiquette, the occupant caused more problems than it was worth for the owners.

The Forest Service Years

From the time the group expressed an interest in selling the Horse Ranch the Forest Service strongly chased the purchase. The agency justified the acquisition, believing it helped to accomplish two management goals – eliminate a large private in-holding and eradicate commercial activity within a designated wilderness area. The sale was finalized in 1994.

However, since the procurement of the Horse Ranch, the Forest Service has struggled with what to do with it. As protocol required, the agency followed the Future Act Determination process, and found a majority of the buildings were of historic significance, and therefore eligible for the National Register of Historic Places. In fact, the entire site qualified. The historic eligibility finding trumped some land managers' wishes of simply naturalizing the site. With a limited budget and no clear management plan for the ranch, it has remained in a static state. Trail crews and some administrative field workers utilize the lodge and a few of the smaller cabins during the summer and fall. A large network of volunteers has also evolved at the ranch. Volunteers help to maintain the facility and grounds in exchange for a roof over their heads. The airstrip is occasionally mowed and open for public use.

Under Forest Service ownership a number of volunteers and visitors make an annual pilgrimage to the site, since Red's Horse Ranch holds many fond memories for them as past patrons or as family members of former owners. Jon and Donna

(top) The row of guest cabins along the Minam River at the ranch in 2014.
(bottom) A present-day image of the Horse Ranch.

McDaniel Skovlin volunteered early at the Horse Ranch. Jon, a career Forest Service employee, spent decades roaming the hills of the Wallowas. He and his wife found the history of the area fascinating and published their findings in *Into the Minam: The History of a River and Its People*. Richard Cockle is another frequent visitor to the Horse Ranch and the Minam country. As a journalist and correspondent to *The Oregonian* he has helped keep many reminiscences and current happenings of the region alive through magazine and newspaper articles.

Pilot Joe Spence has several sentimental stories of people hiring him to fly them to the Horse Ranch for a quick visit. Rick and Janet Hall are one example. Hall came to Wallowa County as part of the film crew for Disney's *Homeward Bound* in the summer of 1991. As a child he attended one of Higgins's summer camps and claimed it was a life-changing experience. Thirty years later, Hall still stays in touch with some of the kids he met there. After deplaning at the entrance of the ranch, Hall became overcome with emotion – recounting a wrestling match here and a story-telling session there. Spence added, "It was amazing how much the place meant to him."[43] Another regular client of Spences was Terry Valentine, the grandson of past owner Greene Hudspeth. Valentine returned for many seasons as a volunteer at the ranch and he enjoyed working the same ground as his ancestors.[44]

Hawkins Family

The Hawkins family kept a 65-acre parcel on the Minam River separate from the 1970s shareholder sale of the Horse Ranch. Higgins purchased that acreage, located below the Minam Lodge, in 1956. At the time of acquisition the place had several structures, including two log cabins and a barn. One of these cabins continues to be used and the others are visible ruins. His wife Lois much preferred the solitude of the Minam, rather than the constant entertainment demands required by the dude business. The Higgins' long-term intent was to develop the place as a private second home when they retired. The property was used for activities associated with the Horse Ranch summer camp program.

The first known occupant of the land was Gaius Dutton, who received homestead approval for the parcel in September 1919.[45] Dutton failed to pay property tax and it reverted to the county in 1924. Ten years later, Henry Trippeer acquired the land. The Trippeer family had grazed cattle and sheep in the Minam country since the turn of the twentieth century and likely occupied the site prior to their legal ownership. Trippeer brought in his brother-in-law Robert French as a partner in 1939. French ended up as sole owner in 1946 before it was sold to Higgins.

Merel and Carol used the old Trippeer place several weeks per year, depending on the schedule of guests and the use of the Horse Ranch by the other owners. During the summer the Hawkins raised their three daughters Jenny, Mary, and Nora in the Eagle Cap country. All three of them became well versed in handling stock and working in the outfitting business. They all have packed in the Wallowas and two of the three have practiced the tradition in Alaska. Nora explained, "It was something our parents never taught us, it was just something we all observed and just did. We were riding horses at a young age, so small we would sit on pillows on the front part of the saddles." While all three of the daughters continue to enjoy the family heritage of the Minam, Nora has spearheaded the construction of a new log cabin on their wilderness property. Inspired by do-it-yourself cabins and log building techniques she witnessed in Alaska, she spent a winter perusing how-to books on log construction. Self-taught through reading and trial and error, she along with family and friends started construction in the summer of 2012 on the new residence. The previous fall, Nora and friend Todd Pederson girdled and felled trees to cure. The cabin was completed a little over two years later.

Construction on the latest cabin at the former Dutton homestead in August 2014.

Russell Elmer

Russell Elmer was one of the most prolific pilots of the Minam country, often flying the drainage daily from about 1960 until 2006. Elmer by trade was a farmer and built his own home and airstrip complete with hangar on his family's homestead near Cove, Oregon. After years of hunting, fishing, and grazing cattle as a young man in the Minam, it only seemed natural that he become a pilot. However, it was an enjoyment that he did not start until he was nearly forty years old in the late 1950s. Previously, Elmer considered himself a nervous flier, until one day when his cousin Don Thompson landed in hayfield on the ranch and offered to give him a ride. Thompson was a professional pilot who eventually retired from Fedex. Once in the air Thompson taught him the basics and Elmer felt very comfortable. Right away Elmer bought a Piper Cub and began taking flying lessons. From then on he was hooked.[46]

He and his family became routine visitors via airplane to the Horse Ranch and the Minam Lodge. Depending on the year and the decade, he bounced back and forth between the two locations, setting up semi-permanent camps that he used throughout the year near the airfields. At the Horse Ranch he gained permission from the owners to camp off the southwest end – they even buried a culvert so he could taxi a plane over to his camp. His encampments were fairly complex and he enjoyed bringing in his wife

33

Russell and Norma Jean Elmer at the Horse Ranch with one of his many airplanes.

Norma Jean and any number of their five children along with friends. At one time he even rigged a pair of speakers to the wing struts of an airplane and plugged in a cassette player so he could listen to his adored big band music.[47]

Throughout his flying career he owned dozens of different airplanes and many of them at the same time. Some of the planes in his fleet included Piper Super Cubs, American Champion Scouts, a Cessna 180, a Cessna 182, a Cessna 206, two different Maules, a Cessna Skymaster, and toward the end two helicopters.[48] Commercial pilot Joe Spence often crossed paths with Elmer while working in the Minam. One season it seemed like every time he saw Elmer he was with a different plane. Curious, Spence asked him one day, "Russell, just how many planes do you have?" His humorous response, "Well, Joe I'm not sure, but I know I have four mules."[49]

Elmer became a regular fixture in the country, and was always willing to help the various ranch owners along with their clientele and employees. He flew many missions in and out of the Minam hauling freight and passengers for free. A bout with cancer caused complications with his feet, and therefore he could not handle planes that required forceful rudder inputs. To resolve the problem he switched to tricycle gear aircraft. A second round of cancer put him in a wheelchair and he felt his flying days were over, but then at age eighty he thought he could handle a helicopter, so he bought one. An instructor came to live with Elmer for two weeks and showed him the fundamentals. He then spent hours practicing hovering maneuvers in hayfields until he felt confident. Elmer continued to avidly fly until about six months before his death at age eighty-five in 2006.[50]

Mail Plane Accident

In January 1929, the Horse Ranch became a hub of activity for a search and rescue of the first airplane crash in the area. The Varney Air Lines mail plane (Stearman C-38), piloted by Harold Buckner, age twenty-two, was enroute from Boise to Pasco, Washington. Varney had a contract with the US Postal Service to deliver mail between the remote communities of Pasco, Boise, and Salt Lake, which were also connected to larger cities via railroad.

The challenging triangle course was known as the "sagebrush route." The contract was procured in 1925 and active missions began the next year. Interestingly, the company, founded by Walter Varney, was one of the first scheduled air routes in the nation. United Airlines eventually acquired the company and continues to claim that it is the oldest commercial airline.

Buckner was reported missing on the leg between Boise and Pasco, when his plane failed to show up at the Pasco field on January 17.[51] A search was launched the same evening and eyewitnesses last noted the plane in the area of La Grande trying to outmaneuver bad weather, consisting of snow and fog. Lost, he made his way into the Minam River drainage at treetop level. Late in the afternoon men at the Horse Ranch heard the plane circle and continue upriver. Several miles to the south trappers Jack Hamby and W. L. Brockam were sitting in their cabin and also heard the murmur of the lost plane followed by breaking trees and then silence. The two men immediately set out on a search. Tromping around in the deep snow they surprisingly found the plane, and even more amazing – Buckner still alive. Although conscious, Buckner's physical condition was ghastly. It was later reported that he had a crushed chest, compound leg fractures, and had broken both arms. The rescuers managed to pack him to the warm cabin where they made him as comfortable as possible. In need of more help, Brockam snowshoed eight miles to the Horse Ranch, which took him several hours. At the Horse Ranch he telephoned La Grande requesting assistance.[52]

Nearly twenty-four hours after the crash, a rescue party was organized and left Cove on horseback following the Minam River. The group consisted of Forest Service Ranger Keith McCool, Dr. R. G. McCall, Ralph Puckett, Harold O'Connell, Charles Wrightson, Cecil Richards, and Clarence Richards. The men met Brockam at the Horse Ranch and continued on to retrieve Buckner. When they arrived at the cabin the crew was disappointed to learn that Buckner had died. In spite of the dire situation, the rescuers rallied and began the long journey back to town with the body on an improvised sled.[53]

The young Buckner left behind his wife Ann and two children in Boise. For the era, Buckner was an experienced aviator, having logged more than

2,500 hours of flight time, 700 of which were mail service. His aviation career began when he joined the military during World War I, and resumed in 1921 after he graduated from the College of the Pacific in California.[54]

Forty-some years later, the wreckage caught the attention of Dean Wilson, an aircraft builder, designer, and restorer based in Boise. At the time, Wilson was employed as the head of maintenance and curator for Idaho businessman Joe Terteling's private aircraft collection. As Wilson traveled the United States collecting parts and pieces for rare aircraft, he regularly stopped at newspaper offices in small towns and searched their archives for long-forgotten airplane wrecks. Amazingly, he located and salvaged several wreckages of antique aircraft through this method, including Buckner's Stearman.

Armed with information about the crash from old newspapers, he contacted Red's Horse Ranch and confirmed that parts of the wreckage still existed. Excited, Wilson arranged a visit, flying a Cessna 206 to the ranch, and then rented a horse. Following a pleasant ride up the Minam, he discovered the remains of the Stearman. He was not surprised that all the structural pieces made of wood had rotted or that souvenir hunters had carted away most of the easy to grab items. The only components left were the steel tube fuselage, gas tank, wing hardware, and tail feathers. So it was fairly complete. He did not expect to find the rare nine-cylinder Wright J4 radial or any instruments. Varney had a reputation for salvaging two things from his crash sites – the pilot and the engine. At the time of the wreck, the 215-horsepower Wright J4 was a reliable and powerful engine. In an effort to increase the safety of his operation, Varney replaced stock engines with the Wright J4s. However, these specific radials were not available to the public and required a special loan from the navy, thus he could not afford to lose one of them.[55]

Happy with his find, Wilson returned to the ranch and hired the packer to move the remains back to the Horse Ranch airfield. He then loaded the parts and pieces in his airplane and headed for Boise. There was no plan for what was going to become of the Stearman, but he had also recovered another Varney wreck from King Hill in Southern Idaho. Terteling auctioned off his airplane collection in 1986 and the two Varney airplanes were sold separately.[56]

MINAM LODGE

Early Years

The present day Minam Lodge property.

Harry B. Case received homestead approval for 47.50 acres at this location in March 1925.[57] Bill Ogden, who owned the upstream property that became the Horse Ranch, had some involvement with the place around the same time as Case. James Houx of Cove followed their ownership. Houx served his country in World War I and suffered badly from side effects associated with mustard gas. In poor health during most of his postwar life he died in 1935 at age forty-three. Two years later, his sister Connie Blanche Richards and her husband Clarence, bought the property from his estate. During the same era the Richards were involved with the Horse Ranch property. They ultimately sold their interests in both these holdings upon obtaining acreage upstream from the Horse Ranch. Here the family built a complex of buildings that became known as "Richards Retreat." These log structures can be seen off the southeast end of the Horse Ranch airstrip. Clarence died in 1966 and Blanche in 1968. The Richards family still owns and actively uses the private ground.

Lorees – Minam Lodge

In 1951, Merton and Erma Loree of Cove bought the undeveloped downstream property from Richards. Since 1946, the Lorees had been leasing the upstream Richards Retreat cabins, where they ran an outfitting business. Deciding they wanted something more permanent, they struck a deal. By the following year work began on the Minam Lodge – an all inclusive backcountry guest ranch. Within a few years the main lodge, constructed of vertical logs that were cut and milled on the property, was finished. The Lorees packed in all the other material for the lodge from the end of the road on mules. As the years marched on they added other amenities, such as a laundry room, showers, bathrooms, guest cabins, barn, tack room, and a generator that supplied electricity. In addition to the growing facilities, their family also grew to include three children, John, Sharon, and Charles, who all loved to help at the ranch.[58]

In about 1960, Loree hired an equipment operator from Baker City to build an airstrip in the open meadow below the lodge. The equipment man walked a Caterpillar D8 up the Minam River in late summer. By early fall the north-south airstrip was complete and the cat-skinner moved his D8 back down the river. The first pilots to land here were Eldon Down and Lyle Flick of La Grande.[59] Down served as the La Grande airport manager and operated an FBO – Blue Mountain Air Service. Down eventually left La Grande and took a job flying air tankers for the Forest Service. He retired in 1982. He and his wife Shirley settled in the mountains of Idaho the same year. Downs died in 2004.

A few years after the initial construction of the runway, Loree walked in his own piece of equipment – a John Deere crawler. He followed the unobstructed route of the D8. The little crawler was used for all kinds of chores including the lengthening of the airstrip to its current 2,500'. Quickly the runway became the main avenue of access, allowing transport of a wide assortment of clientele and supplies. Nearly a decade after the project was begun, the Lorees sold the lodge and moved permanently back to Cove. Loree, semi-retired, continued on as a house painter, which was his main occupation before buying the Minam River venture. He and his wife returned several times to the old lodge before his death in February 2010.[60]

37

(top) The lodge originally constructed by the Loree family.
(bottom) Looking down the Minam Lodge runway from the hangar area.
(opposite) Landing upstream at Minam Lodge.

HOLM

HOLM

HOLM

New Ownership

Business partners Ranny Munro and Glen Stevens bought the Minam Lodge from the Lorees. Munro was from Portland and Stevens from Salem. This duo was able to expand the holdings by purchasing another 80 acres of deeded ground between them and the Horse Ranch in 1975. Two years later, a tragic accident caused the Munro and Stevens families to lose interest in the remote ranch. On September 28, 1977, Glen's son Robert (Bob), who was the CEO of the family corporation, Stevens Equipment Company, dropped off a load of hunters and gear. Bob then planned on returning to La Grande by himself in a Cessna 206 (N35904). Bad weather – rain, fog, and mountain obscuration plagued the area, but he thought he could sneak out by following the Minam River corridor. When he was not heard from the following morning, the plane was reported missing. On September 30 the 206 was found in a heavily wooded area after searchers noticed a large stand of broken trees. Stevens's body was recovered from the site a day later.[61]

Soured by the death of their promising forty-year-old son, Stevens sold the ranch to George Peekema of Vancouver, Washington. Under Peekema's ownership it was only used privately a few weeks per year. Marion Michael "Skip" Breshears of Woodburn, Oregon, became involved with the lodge and was instrumental in maintaining it. By the mid-1980s, he and his wife Shirley became part owners, along with Peekema's nephew Tom, and Stacy Peterson. Most of the time this group of owners accessed the ranch by flying with a commercial operator from La Grande. However, Tom, a pilot, also flew in occasionally with his own aircraft.[62]

Cal Henry of High Country Outfitters started leasing the Minam Lodge in 1990. Previously, Henry had been leasing the Horse Ranch, but when negotiations began with the Forest Service he became skeptical of the future of the property and approached Peekema about the use of his lodge. Henry enjoyed his few years at the property and even built the current hangar for his airplane. After the hunting season of 1993, Henry sold his company to outfitter Woody McDowell, who based from a pack station at Wallowa Lake. McDowell used the Minam Lodge for several years before selling his business. The lodge then cycled through several lessees before Shawn and Shelly Steen picked it up. Their company, Steens Wilderness Adventures, used the lodge for many years and was the last tenant during the Peekema era.[63] In 2008, Peekema's wife Joanne died, and two years later Breshears died. Peekema bought out the Breshears interest, before his death in October 2009.[64] However, Peekema also had the property listed on the real estate market for many years at $4.6 million. By 2010, his heirs and remaining partners reduced the asking price to $2.25 million.[65] When that price failed to attract a buyer, the property was slated twice for auction, but both attempts were unsuccessful. Finally in August 2011, Barnes Ellis of Portland obtained the lodge in a sealed bid auction for $605,000.[66] Ellis promptly hired crews to begin upgrading the rustic facility. In more recent years the lodge has become popular with the public as the last fly-in type ranch in eastern Oregon.

MINAM INTERNATIONAL AIRPORT
ELV. 3600 FT.

Cal Henry's Cessna 182 parked in front of the hangar in the early 1990s.

NOTES

1 "Hunter is Killed When Rifle Goes Off Accidently," *Eugene Register-Guard*, 1 October 1935.

2 "Big Minam Horse Ranch (advertisement)," *The Oregonian*, 9 July 1944.

3 "25 Planes Land at Remote Wallowa Resort Accessible Otherwise Only by Pack Trail," *The Oregonian*, 5 August 1947.

4 "Pilots Bound For Mountains: Group to Frolic At Dude Ranch," *The Oregonian*, 2 September 1949.

5 "Red's Horse Ranch," *The Oregonian*, 27 May 1961.

6 "Magic Vacation Carpet," *Northwest Rotogravure Magazine* (published by *The Oregonian*), 29 July 1956.

7 Paul F. Ewing, "Fly Fishing in the Wallowas," *The Oregonian*, 24 August 1947.

8 Ewing.

9 Merel Hawkins, Personal Communication, 29 July 2014.

10 Carol Hawkins, Personal Communication, 6 August 2014.

11 "Local Airman Dies in Crash," *The Oregonian*, 21 August 1955.

12 C. Hawkins, Personal Communication.

13 Dick Cockle, "Ranches Cater to Privacy-Seeking Stars," *The Oregonian*, 12 August 1984.

14 C. Hawkins, Personal Communication.

15 C. Hawkins, Personal Communication.

16 "Oregon Men Say 'Abominable Snowman' Seen In Wallows," *The Lewiston Morning Tribune*, 1 April 1959.

17 John Jobson, *John Jobson Biography*, (Unpublished, date unknown), 1–3. John Jobson Papers, MG 445, Box #4, Special Collections and Archives, University of Idaho Library, Moscow, Idaho.

18 Jobson, 3–4.

19 Jobson, 4–6.

20 John Jobson, *The Complete Book of Practical Camping*, (New York, NY: Winchester Press, 1974), 46.

21 Jobson, 179.

22 John Jobson, Letter/Obituary for Ralph (Red) Higgins, *The Oregonian*, 19 October 1970.

23 M. Hawkins, Personal Communication.

24 William O. Douglas, *Of Men and Mountains*, (New York, NY: Harper & Brothers Publishers, 1950), 232–34.

25 M. Hawkins, Personal Communication.

26 Stangel, Personal Communication.

27 Stangel, Personal Communication.

28 Stangel, Personal Communication.

29 Stangel, Personal Communication.

30 Stangel, Personal Communication.

31 Joe Spence, Personal Communication, 24 March 2014.

32 Spence, Personal Communication.

33 Spence, Personal Communication.

34 Spence, Personal Communication.

35 Mick Courtney, Personal Communication, 31 July 2014.

36 Calvin Henry, Personal Communication, 27 July 2014.

37 Henry, Personal Communication.

38 Henry, Personal Communication.

39 Henry, Personal Communication.

40 Henry, Personal Communication.

41 Don Doyle, Personal Communication, 13 August 2014.

42 Henry, Personal Communication.

43 Joe Spence, Personal Communication, 31 July 2014.

44 Etha Schowalter-Hay, "Big Minam Horse Ranch," *The Observer*, 12 October 2007.

45 Gaius Dutton, BLM General Land Office Records.

46 Norma Jean Elmer, Personal Communication, 13 August 2014.

47 Patti Wise, Personal Communication, 13 August 2014.

48 Wise, Personal Communication.

49 Joe Spence, Personal Communication, 12 August 2014.

50 Wise, Personal Communication.

51 "Air Mail Pilot Missing," *The Oregonian*, 18 January 1929.

52 W. L. Brockham, *Account of Rescue and Death of Harold Elwin Buckner*, (Self-published, date unknown).

53 "Fliers Body Returned," *The Oregonian*, 21 January 1929.

54 "Rescuers Battle Blizzard to Reach San Jose Aviator," *San Jose News*, 19 January 1929.

55 Dean Wilson, Personal Communication, 11 August 2014.

56 Wilson, Personal Communication.

57 Harry B. Case, BLM General Land Office Records.

58 John Loree, Personal Communication, 24 July 2014.

59 Loree, Personal Communication.

60 Loree, Personal Communication.

61 "Salem Man Found Dead," *The Oregonian*, 1 October 1977.

62 Katy Nesbitt, "Minam River Lodge to be Auctioned in Silent Bid," *The Observer*, 15 July 2010.

63 Henry, Personal Communication.

64 Nesbitt.

65 Brain Addison, "Minam River Lodge Up For No-Reserve Auction," *Wallowa County Chieftain*, 3 August 2011.

66 Richard Cockle, "New Owner Visits Minam River Lodge," *The Oregonian*, 12 September 2011.

A Super Cub landing at Salt Creek – date unknown.

Chapter 2

MIDDLE SNAKE RIVER
(HELLS CANYON DAM TO CACHE CREEK)

The color scheme of Nature's handiwork is spectacular because of the invisible blending of shades. Like a beautiful Rembrandt, the chromos weave, intertwine, and melt into a western sunset at dusk. In contrast to the vivid splashes of the Grand Canyon of the Colorado, the blending of Snake River canyon seems to have been wrought with more infinite care as some great hand twisted the color oils from the multiple tubes of Nature . . . Gleaming granite, glowing red porphyry, colored marble, limestone and wooded water courses, all in blended chromos, make for solemn beauty.

–R. J. Wood
"Through Hells Canyon" Idaho Highways and Public Works (1939)

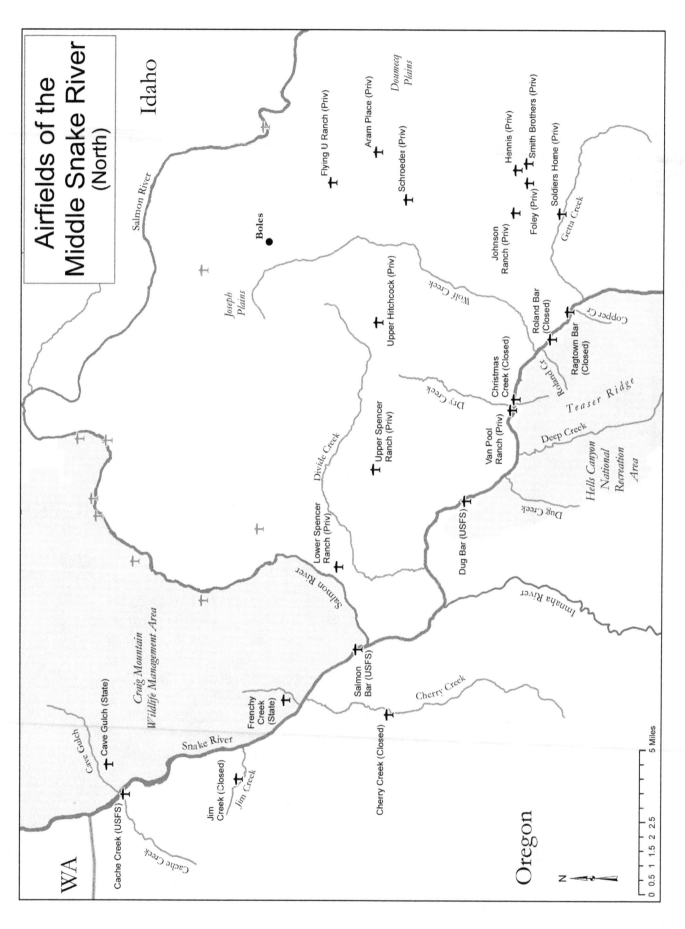

Airfields of the
Middle Snake River
(North)

Idaho

Salmon River

Flying U Ranch (Priv)

Aram Place (Priv)

Doumecq Plains

Schroeder (Priv)

Hennis (Priv)

Smith Brothers (Priv)

Foley (Priv)

Soldiers Home (Priv)

Boles

Getta Creek

Johnson Ranch (Priv)

Joseph Plains

Upper Hitchcock (Priv)

Wolf Creek

Roland Bar (Closed)

Copper Cr

Christmas Creek (Closed)

Ragtown Bar (Closed)

Dry Creek

Upper Spencer Ranch (Priv)

Divide Creek

Van Pool Ranch (Priv)

Roland Cr

Teaser Ridge

Deep Creek

Dug Creek

Hells Canyon National Recreation Area

Lower Spencer Ranch (Priv)

Dug Bar (USFS)

Salmon River

Imnaha River

WA

Cave Gulch (State)

Cave Gulch

Craig Mountain Wildlife Management Area

Salmon Bar (USFS)

Cherry Creek

Frenchy Creek (State)

Snake River

Jim Creek (Closed)

Jim Creek

Cherry Creek (Closed)

Cache Creek (USFS)

Cache Creek

Oregon

N

0 0.5 1 1.5 2 2.5   5 Miles

46

A 1960s Forest Service interpretive sign indicating the significance of Hells Canyon.

The dramatic, vast, steep, and rocky terrain of the middle Snake River is scattered with aviation history, although it is not widely evident or well documented. The remote region between Hells Canyon Dam and Cache Creek has always proved difficult and time-consuming to reach. Despite its toughness, the center portion of the river has lured Native Americans, fur trappers, miners, homesteaders, ranchers, boaters, pilots, scientists, archeologists, geologists, and thrill seekers of all kinds. Aviation is somewhat recent compared to other forms of transportation in the canyon – beginning in the mid-1930s. This chapter covers landing sites from Hells Canyon Dam to Cache Creek – just a small sliver of the 1,056-mile long Snake River that stretches from Wyoming to Washington, creating the distinctive zigzag boundary of Idaho and Oregon.

Within the distinguishable state line is the chasm most commonly known today as "Hells Canyon." Prior to this name many people knew it as Box Canyon, Snake River Canyon, Snake River Gorge, Seven Devils Gorge, Oregon's Grand Canyon, and the Grand Canyon of the Snake. Of all the titles this section of river was most regularly referred to as "Box Canyon." However, by the 1930s, Hells Canyon (or Hell's Canyon) became the most frequently used term. Authors Richard L. Neuberger and Vinton H. Hall popularized the name in numerous magazine and newspaper articles supporting the National Park Service's interest in incorporating the

middle Snake River into the national park system. Neuberger's use of the term even came under fire by an *Oregonian* newspaper reader. Substantiating his use, Neuberger referenced a 1920 US Geologic Survey Report exercising the name. Other sources indicate the name dates as far back as 1895. Even further complicating the derivation, some believe it was merely a confusion associated with the nearby Hells Creek and related Hells Rapid.

The origin of the name is as much debated as the actual location of the "canyon." Some believe it starts a few miles above Hells Canyon Dam and extends to Upper Pittsburg Landing. Others insist

Inland Navigation Company's middle Snake River promotional brochure illustrating the most popular mode of transportation in the canyon.

it begins below the dam, and yet some argue that it reaches as far as the mouth of the Salmon River or even farther to either Lime Point or Heller Bar. The disagreement has sparked many feuds and debates on the river for generations. One of the more famous disagreements was between boatman Dick Rivers and Floyd Harvey. To prove the other one wrong it was believed Harvey painted "Entering Hells Canyon" high on the rocks on the Idaho side of the river downstream from the confluence with the Salmon River. For Rivers, the signage was merely graffiti and did nothing to sway his opinion. Longtime Snake River outfitter Jerry Hughes has his own ideas about where the canyon begins and ends, but added, "I don't really think anyone knows. On the other hand, Congress clearly defined it to be from the Hells Canyon Dam to Cache Creek."[1]

Although Hells Canyon is often boasted as the deepest canyon in the United States and sometimes even in all of North America, it is actually the second deepest on both accords. Most often measured from the peak of He Devil Mountain to the water surface of the river, the relief of the canyon is 7,900', six miles from the river. Topping this depth at an even closer distant to the river by two miles is Spanish Mountain standing 8,240' above the Kings River in the Sierra Nevada.[2] As for North America, Copper Canyon in the Sierra Madre Occidental mountain range in Mexico is the deepest, measuring 12,140' from the top of Mohinara Mountain to the canyon floor.

Regardless of the competition for depth, the sheer vertical drop of the canyon from alpine ecosystems in the upper reaches to the more temperate desert climates along the river makes for some wonderful and unique seasonal cycles. For thousands of years, Native Americans wintered in the lowlands of the canyon with milder temperatures and bountiful game. As spring and summer ensued they migrated with the animals to the cooler parts of the high country. Early homesteaders and later ranchers also followed the seasonal pattern. By the time the homesteading era

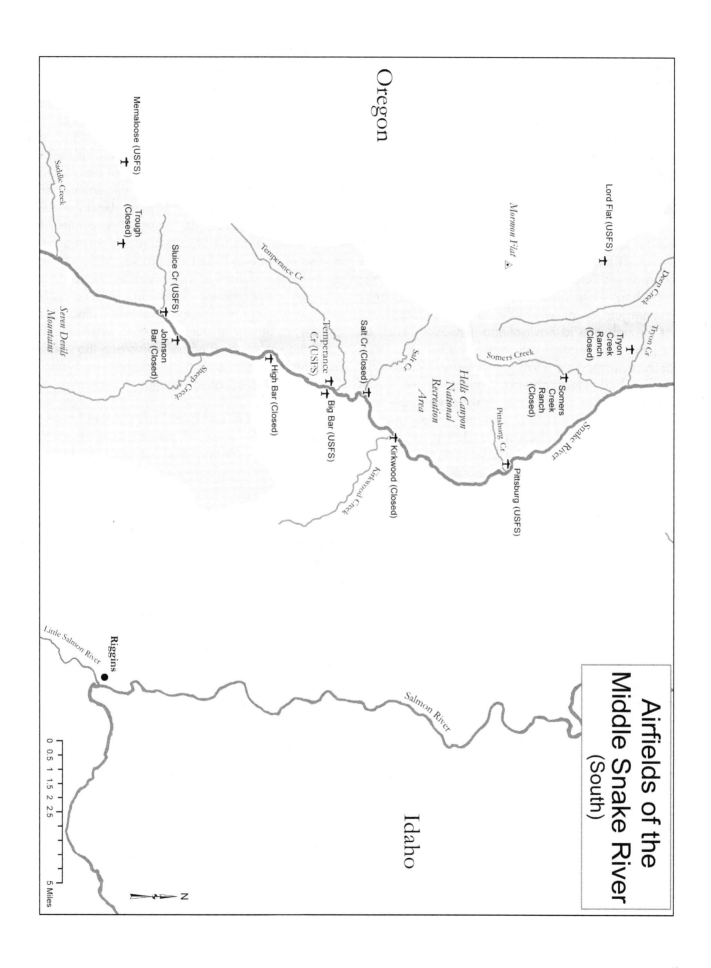

Oregon

Idaho

Saddle Creek

Memaloose (USFS)

Trough (Closed)

Sluice Cr (USFS)

Johnson Bar (Closed)

Seven Devils Mountains

Sheep Creek

High Bar (Closed)

Temperance Cr

Temperance Cr (USFS)

Salt Cr (Closed)

Big Bar (USFS)

Kirkwood (Closed)

Kirkwood Creek

Salt Cr

Hells Canyon National Recreation Area

Mormon Flat

Lord Flat (USFS)

Deep Creek

Tryon Cr

Tryon Creek Ranch (Closed)

Somers Creek

Somers Creek Ranch (Closed)

Pittsburg Cr

Pittsburg (USFS)

Snake River

Little Salmon River

Riggins

Salmon River

0 0.5 1 1.5 2 2.5

5 Miles

N

Airfields of the Middle Snake River (South)

waned and the land became combined by large sheep or cattle operations, the ranches had at least two homes – one on the river for winter and one along the canyon rim for summer. This more modern migratory cycle placed demands on contemporary forms of transportation. The weekly mail boat from Lewiston to Johnson Bar was vital for importing needed supplies throughout the year, but it was also crucial for exporting goods such as wool, from the river to market.

For decades, boats granted the main link to the outside, especially during the winter. Slowly, as the airplane came of age, it too became incorporated into the lives of the canyon residents. In the beginning, airplanes were only used in times of emergencies or when the mail boat could not get through due to navigational limitations such as ice jams. As aviation advanced and became more common in the late 1940s and early 1950s most ranchers had at least an airstrip near the river. These landing patches granted relatively quick entry and exit from the snow-locked canyon. Inhabitants on the Oregon side of the river tended to align with commercial air carriers from Joseph and Enterprise, while those on the Idaho side leaned more toward commercial pilots from Lewiston and Grangeville.

By the end of the 1950s and into the early 1960s many ranchers themselves became pilots and aircraft owners. In contrast to other regions where backcountry aviation lent itself to fire control or recreational purposes, on the middle Snake, aviation was largely utilitarian. Planes were merely another tool of the ranch and commonly treated as pickups. Aircraft hauled supplies, ranch workers, and used to look for lost sheep and cattle. Also occurring during this era was the development of landing sites in the higher elevations to access remote parts of the ranches in the fall and summer.

From the 1940s through the 1970s the middle Snake River became a battleground for debates over conservation, land use, energy, and dozens of other controversial subjects. The area had long been recognized as something very special, unique, and inspiring. The National Park Service looked at designating the high Wallowa Mountains on the Oregon side of the river as a national park in 1929 – but rejected the idea. Ten years later, the National Park Service again launched a study for making Hells Canyon part of the national park system. It too was denied, based on potential mining opportunities. Before another decade slipped by, controversy raged over damming the river for hydroelectric power. While there were many facets to the debate, it mainly became an issue of public versus private power. The Idaho Power Company won with its three dam proposal (Brownlee, Oxbow, and Hells Canyon), which took twelve years to build.

As Idaho Power constructed the dam complex other companies looked to harness the power of the middle Snake River from Hells Canyon Dam downstream to the mouth of the Salmon River. Countless books have been written about the details of this long drawn-out controversy. In a nutshell, it too became an issue of public versus private power to begin with and then an entirely different beast as questions of how to preserve the canyon arose. An ugly confrontation followed, waging private landowners against public interests. Fearful that private landowners were going to subdivide their land into recreational home sites along the river, the government exercised eminent domain and officially created the Hells Canyon National Recreation Area (NRA) in 1975.

Since the formation of the NRA, several thousand more acres of private land have been incorporated. Within the current 652,500-acre NRA, 216,900-acres are designated as wilderness. However, the river is not under wilderness classification. A quarter-mile wide corridor of the river, spanning nearly sixty-eight miles, is designated as part of the Wild and Scenic River System. The upper thirty-one and a half miles from Hells Canyon Dam to Upper Pittsburg Landing is "wild," and the rest is "scenic." On top of these designations, the Hells Canyon NRA is home to the 12,000-acre Hells Canyon Archeological District, a historic district listed on the National Register of Historic Places. The district includes hundreds of contributing sites and many contributing buildings and structures.

Boaters are by far the largest user group in the canyon. Current estimates show about 3,200–5,000 people float the whitewater of Hells Canyon each year, of which 2,000–3,000 are with private groups and 1,200–2,000 are with commercial companies. As the use of jet boats has risen exponentially in the past decades, the largest user groups on the river are now the power boaters. Current estimates show about 29,000–50,000 people jet boat on the middle Snake River each year, of which 12,000–16,000 are with private parties and 17,000–38,000 are with commercial outfitters.

Airplane usage is far lower than the boaters, and aviation issues generally tend to stay on the periphery of the power verses non-power conflicts. Unlike other regions in the West defined as "backcountry aviation," this section of terra firma is sparsely treed, lending itself to small open benches and bars suited for airplane landing patches. Throughout the aviation history of the canyon, fixed-wing aircraft have likely used countless open places. When researching the airstrips for this chapter, a concentrated effort was made to include all sites with a history of regular or continued use – instead of just a one-time event. Many of these more obscure sites are no longer in use and in several cases are located within the Hells Canyon Wilderness Area – making landings illegal. With the establishment of the NRA, some airfields were grandfathered-in and are used for administrative and recreational purposes. In the last twenty years, air traffic has increased in the canyon as pilots have slowly discovered it as one of the best places to fly, hike, camp, and fish during the winter and spring.

Although I have plainly noted this publication is a history and not an instructive flying book, there are several sets of power lines in this section of the river that present a significant flight hazard. All pilots ought to obtain a complete briefing of line locations prior to flight in this area. At a minimum aviators should become familiar with the series of lines near Oxbow and Hells Canyon dams, the line that crosses the river approximately three miles below Dug Bar at Divide Creek, and finally the line that crosses the Snake near Rogersburg and the mouth of the Grande Ronde.

TROUGH (FUNK PLACE)

The Airstrip

A contemporary glance down the Trough landing area.

Ranch owner and pilot Greg Johnson used this 750'-airstrip located above the Funk Place (between Smooth Hollow and Hat Point) regularly to supply sheepherders starting in about 1966. The location earned its name after Johnson found several old troughs nearby. One afternoon Johnson walked around the area and figured he could safely land and takeoff in his Cub, which would equate to about a twelve-minute flight from his Temperance Creek headquarters, instead of a seven-hour horseback ride. After making the decision to land there, he packed a horse-drawn harrow to the site and worked out a smooth area. After some landings with his Cub, he felt comfortable enough with the strip that he decided to check his brother Duane out with Duane's Cessna 180. Landings with this bigger aircraft were only done a few times. Johnson stopped using the Trough landing site in the late 1970s.[3]

History of the Funk Place and the Pete Wilson Family

Below the natural bench where the airstrip is situated are the ruins of the Funk family farmstead. Andrew Funk received homestead approval for 127.57 acres in July 1911.[4] He built several log dwellings along Smooth Hollow Creek but struggled to make a living. Some locals also know the landing location used by Johnson as Reeves Flat, which was associated with another early homesteader John Reeves. Pete and Ethel Wilson bought the Funk land for grazing connected with their Saddle Creek home that was purchased in 1916. The Funk dwellings also provided some relief from the hot temperatures at Saddle Creek and became their primary residence in the summer months. To accommodate the growing family that eventually amounted to eight children, a second log structure was started.[5]

A well-groomed trail was carved out between Saddle Creek and the Funk Place as the Wilsons migrated back and forth. During the summers their massive garden at Saddle Creek required frequent attention. On one of the return trips from garden duty in about 1925, Ethel's horse rolled over on her in the switchback section of the trail. Tragically, the accident caused the miscarriage of her first set of twins.[6]

Pete and Ethel divorced in 1937, and all of their land holdings were sold to Ken Johnson of Temperance Creek. Pete continued his cowboy lifestyle working for ranches across the West and died in 1968. Ethel worked in several Oregon state hospitals and eventually settled in Riggins where she worked for the telephone company. They are both buried in the Riggins Cemetery.[7]

Jim Wilson, the oldest son of the Pete Wilson family, married Murrielle McGaffee in 1935. During their first year of marriage, the Funk property was home. Shortly after moving in, Jim came down with the flu. To keep busy as he recovered, he collected nails from the ashes of a building that had burned on the ranch. He then spent hours straightening the nails so they could be reused. By spring, the couple started the construction of a larger cabin. Like a lot of young folks their plans changed, and they moved on. Jim and Murrielle lived the rest of their lives in Riggins where they raised four boys. However, they spent many summers working in the remote region

(top) Pete Wilson's livestock on the bench above the Funk homestead in the 1930s. Thirty years later this became the Trough landing location.
(bottom) The Funk Place in May 1935. The Wilson's unfinished log cabin is on the right.

A view of the Trough landing area [center] from the Dry Diggins Lookout in 1971.

R. WILSON

for the Forest Service, including five years of service at Hat Point Lookout (1935–39), directly above their Smooth Hollow home. Jim had actually started spending summers at the lookout in 1931.[8] Murrielle chronicled much of their time living, working, and visiting Hells Canyon, in her book *A Hells Canyon Romance: An Idaho Teacher Marries An Oregon Cowboy.*

Violet, one of Pete Wilson's daughters, returned to the Saddle Creek property with her husband Buster Shirley in 1939. The two were haying for Ken Johnson and planned on using the old house for their living quarters. After a long hard hike to the place, they awoke the next morning and built a fire in the kitchen stove. Several hours later while tending to some outdoor chores they looked up to see the house in flames. It was later determined the cause of the fire was a packrat's nest lodged between the roof and the stovepipe. With several days of haying still ahead of them the Shirleys slept in the old blacksmith shop.[9] Over the years, wildland fires have claimed the remaining buildings at Saddle Creek and the Funk Place. The only relics at the sites today are some farming equipment. Violet Shirley returned often to the canyon throughout her life. For many years, she served as a Forest Service volunteer caretaker at Kirkwood.

Don Wilson – Professional Backcountry Pilot

Don Wilson, one of Pete and Ethel's twins, went on to become a professional backcountry pilot. As a young man Don started a trucking business hauling logs for the Salmon River Lumber Company. He soon tired of the job and became interested in flying through cousin Tommy Wilson, who owned his own aviation business in Anacortes, Washington. Wasting no time, Don enrolled in the Ag Aviation Academy located in Minden, Nevada. After earning his ratings, Don stayed with the school as a flight instructor when they relocated to Stead, Nevada. From Stead he hired on with Tommy helping fly passengers, freight, and mail in the San Juan Islands. Tension between the two developed, and he returned to Idaho where he flew for Jim Mitchell's Orofino-based operation that primarily transported customers to the Selway-Bitterroot Wilderness area. Mitchell was killed in a spray plane, and the business dissolved. Wilson worked briefly for Frank England in Kamiah, Idaho, and then for Sherrill Benham in Challis, Idaho.[10]

In Challis, Wilson got a big break in his flying career when he met pilots working for Harrah's Hotel and Casinos of Reno, Nevada. The pilots were flying in and out of Challis daily hauling supplies for the Middle Fork Lodge, located on the Middle Fork of the Salmon River at Thomas Creek. Harrah's extensive remodeling and building at the lodge, along with frequent visits from friends and guests, required a full fleet of aircraft and pilots. Don hired on with them in 1974. He worked for Harrah mostly flying the backcountry in Cessna 206s and Twin Otters. Nearing the end of his career, he upgraded to an early Falcon 20 jet, but he missed the stick and rudder flying in the backcountry and essentially moved back to it in 1982. Don retired from Harrah's in October 1987. He died the following spring of a heart attack, while working for a boat distributer in Oregon City, Oregon.[11]

Throughout most of his career as a pilot, Wilson owned personal airplanes that he used for flight instruction. They included two Cessna 150s and two Piper J-3 Cubs. He frequently flew the Cubs to the Snake River to visit family and friends and to recreate.[12]

MEMALOOSE

Guard Station and CCC History

A cockpit view of landing south at Memaloose.

When the Forest Service took over management of this area in 1907, it was briefly designated as the Imnaha National Forest (NF), then changed a year later to the Wallowa NF. In 1954, the Wallowa NF was combined with the Whitman NF, creating the Wallowa-Whitman NF. The area around Memaloose was used for administrative and fire control purposes by the agency, starting in the 1910s. The 1920s-era Memaloose Guard Station built of log is still in use and located about a mile northwest of the airstrip. The term "memaloose" is derived from the Chinook Indian word "memalust," meaning, to die, to be dead, death, or also used in reference to burials. In the case of this site, memaloose was applied because of a Native American burial site situated to the northeast of the field near Hat Point Lookout. Sadly, a Hat Point Lookout observer looted this gravesite in the 1930s. It was rumored he even used some of the burial goods as cookware at the lookout station.[13]

During the Great Depression, the Civilian Conservation Corps (CCC) was formed to create jobs for young men. The Wallowa-Whitman NF was assigned two permanent CCC camps along with several summer spike camps. One of the permanent camps was first located outside the town of Imnaha, Oregon, along Deer Creek. While the men stationed at this camp accomplished many things, the largest was the construction of the twenty-four mile Grizzly Ridge Road to Memaloose and Hat Point in 1933–34. The Imnaha Camp also built many of the other roads on the Oregon side of the middle Snake River, which enhanced access for fire control, administrative interests, and for public use. In addition to roads, the CCC was instrumental in building administrative facilities.[14]

Airstrip

The Oregon State Board of Aeronautics proposed nine scenic locations for landing fields within national park and forest lands in August 1936.

The final site listed in the proposal was none other than Memaloose. Other locales included: Brookings, Reedsport, Government Camp, Diamond Lake, Lake of the Woods, Summit Prairie, Tollgate, and Warner Valley. The primary purposes for most airstrips built during the 1930s on national forests were for utility, such as fire control and administrative management. Making the nine sites particularly unique is that they were selected first and foremost for scenic beauty, recreation, and tourism, and secondly for the practical aspect. Gerry Weaver, aviation editor for *The Oregonian* newspaper in 1936 commented, "The board believes that establishment of airports in the scenic and recreational areas throughout the state will not only beckon to northwest fliers, but also to pilots all over the country. The plan also has merit in that landing fields at strategic points in the forest areas would be a fire-control aid, not to mention national defense factors."[15] Weaver, who had been on an automobile tour of the Wallowa NF earlier in the summer, was excited about the Memaloose airfield above the others and wrote, "The field would be within an easy hike to the edge of the famous Hell's canyon of the Snake river . . . Grouse and deer inhabit this scenic eastern Oregon upland. On a recent motor trip to the rim of Hell's canyon with Forest Supervisor Rolland Huff, the possibilities were pointed out to the writer, and it was agreed that it would be far more enticing to fly up to Memaloose from Enterprise in a few minutes than to chug up the narrow but excellent auto road cleft in the face of the precipitous mountainside."[16]

Besides Weaver's enthusiasm for the airstrips, he sensed that the aeronautics board wanted to act quickly to take full advantage of funds available through the Works Progress Administration (WPA), which could be obtained by the associated federal agency – in this case the Wallowa NF.[17] Little time was wasted. The Memaloose field was in active use within two years of the proposal.

At about the same time the airstrip was built, the Wallowa NF began its first experimental cargo drops to supply fire crews in July 1937. Fitting for the ranching-based economy of the region, the cargo chutes were made of woolsacks. As summer drew to a close the supply of woolsacks in Wallowa County soon depleted, causing them to be imported from surrounding areas. Two planes were used on the project. A. L. Sohlet piloted one aircraft and Roy Shreck flew the other.[18] Shreck of Spokane was a former business partner of Nick Mamer – who is now known as the "Grandfather of Backcountry Aviation."

Helitack Base, New Building Complex, and Airstrip Improvements

The Memaloose airstrip was modified starting in the early 1960s. The high elevation runway (6,710' AGL) was afforded with better drainage, smoothed, and widened. By 1964, the airstrip had been lengthened to its current 3,500'.

Five years later in 1969, the Forest Service decided to develop a state-of-the-art helitack base at the site. The reason for the construction was to help solve regional dilemmas concerning fire control within the agency. Three different regions: Region 1 (Northern), Region 4 (Intermountain), and Region 6 (Pacific Northwest) of the Forest Service merge in the vicinity of Hells Canyon.[19] Each region was responsible for their own initial attack, rather than the base of operation nearest to the fire. Region 6's solution to the problem was to create an interregional base at Memaloose that would provide initial attack for all three forests. An advanced generator-driven electrical system was installed along with underground utilities for communications. Three concrete helipads were poured on the west side of the strip for a fleet of helicopters. Additionally, a huge 3,000-gallon

Looking north at Memaloose with the airstrip on the left and Hat Point Lookout on the right.

sump was built, from which copters could fill their water buckets. To house crews and provide indoor workspace, bunkhouses and offices were erected on the northeast side of the runway. The Memaloose Helitack Base hit its pinnacle during the early 1970s. Unable to overcome regional politics until decades later, the Memaloose Helitack program slowly declined.[20]

Freezeout Ridge Fire – 1973

Shortly after the Memaloose Helitack Base was completed, the large Freezeout Ridge Fire started on August 15, 1973. Initially crews from Memaloose thought they had it under control, but four days later canyon winds caused the blaze to spot and spread, burning nearly 8,000 acres. By nightfall the fire encroached on the Memaloose airstrip, surrounding it on three sides.[21] Despite the proximity to the crews stationed near the runway, fire bosses felt it was safe because of the high water content of the meadow. A few hours later, the fire swept over the road cutting off access and communication to the main fire camps. As the fire marched through the tinder-dry stands of timber killed by tussock moths, ground and air reinforcements were dispatched to the blaze.[22] Increased air traffic and low visibility conditions caused by the smoke prompted the Federal Aviation Administration (FAA) to set up a temporary air traffic control tower at Memaloose. Two air traffic controllers and equipment were trucked in after the road was reopened and a backfire was set off the northeast corner of the airstrip. The makeshift tower was nothing but a wooden platform and a table supported by sawhorses holding the necessary radio equipment. The control tower was used for four days at twelve-hour intervals.[23] The fire was contained by early September after it had burned roughly 20,000 acres.

Hat Point – A Guardian of Hells Canyon

Within a two-mile walk or drive from the north end of the airstrip stands the historic Hat Point Fire Lookout. The site earned its name after a cowboy lost his hat to a gust of wind that blew it out into Hells Canyon – unable to recover the wide-brimmed cap it was dubbed "Hat Point."[24] With fairly easy road accessibility an estimated 1,000-plus people visit the lookout each year, as it offers some of the best vantages of Hells Canyon, the Wallowas, and the Seven Devils.

First established as an observation point in the 1910s, the lookout has been consistently staffed each season since. The first permanent lookout structure constructed on the 6,982' summit was a 7' X 7' cab atop a 60' pole tower. The person staffing the lookout lived at the nearby Memaloose Guard Station. The early tower was replaced by a similar design in the summers of 1931 and 1932. At about the same time a log cabin was added below the mountaintop to provide more convenient living quarters for the lookout personnel. Ray Rahn Construction erected the current 82' timber treated tower with 7' X 7' observation cab as the final replacement in 1948. Walter Young and crew built the existing framed Hat Point live-in dwelling under the direction of Imnaha-Snake District Ranger Gerald Tucker in 1956–57.[25]

Hat Point Lookout and the Seven Devils.

SLUICE CREEK

Early History - The Winnifords

A downstream vantage of the Sluice Creek airstrip [lower center].

HOLM

The Sluice Creek site is noted as one of the oldest occupied ranching areas in the canyon. It earned its name from early stockmen who found sluices at the location. In the 1880s, the Warnock brothers began using the place as a cow camp and built a small log dugout cabin covered with a sod roof.[26]

The Marks brothers, Clem, Jake, Charlie, and Alfred, followed the Warnocks in the early 1900s and used the drainage for grazing sheep and cattle. Clem officially homesteaded 107.14 acres at the site in February 1913.[27] The brothers constructed two log cabins connected by a breezeway, commonly called a "dogtrot cabin." This architectural style was adopted from the southwestern US.

The Winniford brothers, Walter, William, and John Franklin "Frank," moved to the Sluice Creek area with their families and each established their own homestead. The Winnifords collectively operated their in-holdings together and ran about 900 head of cattle. The first brother to arrive in the canyon was Walter with his wife Mina. The two built a home constructed of cottonwood trees downstream from Sluice Creek at Pony Bar. In the beginning, Walter worked for the Wisenors who ran cattle in the neighboring drainages of Salt and Temperance creeks. Instead of money, he was paid in cattle. Seven years after moving to the bar and battling with insufficient water, Walter dug a ditch that routed water from Rush Creek to Pony Creek. Although Rush Creek dried out in the summer, like Pony, it provided enough irrigation to get two cuttings of

alfalfa from the fields. In addition to the ditch work, Walter built a new large home constructed of pine logs. The interior was finished with milled lumber cut at the Temperance Creek sawmill. Making the building particularly unique was a dumbwaiter in the kitchen that could be run up and down from the main floor to the cellar. Walter later moved this home to Rush Creek near a spring and increased its size with bedrooms and a sleeping porch.[28] He proved up on his place of 64.49 acres in 1919.[29]

C. HENRY

The Marks brothers' cabin on Sluice Creek in 1981.

William and his wife Stella moved to the Snake River in the fall of 1913. After living two or three years at the Hill homestead located above Pony Bar to the north, they bought the Marks Cabin on Sluice Creek. Brother Frank and his wife Gertrude then took over the former Hill homestead and proved up on 117.59 acres in 1921.[30] Prior to this move, Frank worked for the Forest Service as a district ranger on the Oregon side of the river.[31]

At the Sluice Creek home Stella home-schooled six of the Winniford children along with two Wilson boys from neighboring Saddle Creek. To provide shade, Stella gave each of her three daughters black locust seedlings. Part of their daily chores was to water the trees. The small locust grove grew to supply welcome shade to the home. Trunks of the large trees stand to this day. The Sluice Creek house was the best of the three Winniford places, as it had a constant supply of water year-round. William even built a small dam and diverted water to irrigate an orchard.[32]

By 1923, the Winniford's cattle venture was on the brink of bankruptcy. All three families were forced to leave the canyon the following year. The hard times were partially caused by the difficult winter of 1918 when most area residents lost cattle, but even more so by the debt owed on the Sluice Creek parcel. The bank in Joseph was unable to work with them and the only option was to move on.[33] Walt and Mina's daughter Florence published a detailed account of the Winniford's time on the river in her book *Snake River Daze*. The Johnson family, headquartered at Temperance Creek, ultimately acquired the Winniford's in-holdings.

Airstrip

Fred Zimmerly made the first known landing associated with Sluice Creek with a Cessna Airmaster (NC17050) on August 8, 1937. The destination in his logbook actually indicates "Pony Bar."[34] Considering the terrain, available landing space, and the aircraft he was flying, Zimmerly most likely landed between Pony and Sluice creeks at the site of the current airstrip. The Sluice Creek airstrip was used by the Johnsons to resupply ranch hands and sheepherders for over forty years. After Zimmerly made the first landing the Johnsons occasionally filled an old irrigation ditch and smoothed out spots as necessary, but overall the 950'-runway is just a former hayfield with a few runway markers. Johnson's employees commonly used the Sluice Creek cabin, and it made for a convenient access point. In the Johnson years, the upstream room of the twin-cabin served as a shop and storage area, and the downstream room functioned as sleeping quarters. A wildland fire burned the cabin in about 1998.

Early-on an arrow made of rocks was placed on the downstream end of the runway indicating that it was a one-way only airstrip. Several planes have ignored the common rule of thumb and wrecked as a result. When the government condemned the property the airstrip was closed. In fact, Forest Service personnel rearranged the arrow constructed of rocks into an "x" to re-enforce the closure to passing pilots, an action since reversed. Former property owner and pilot Greg Johnson protested the closing, as he was granted permission in the condemnation process to operate as he had in the past, including the use of his airplane to access various parts of the permitted rangeland. While his protest did little to re-open the airstrip, he simply continued to use it until he left the river permanently in 1980.[35] The Forest Service has continued to view the Sluice Creek airstrip as closed, but pilots have generally considered it to be an emergency use airstrip. Confusing the situation further is the fact that there is no "x" on the common approach end of the runway to indicate it is closed, and a windsock has continued to be maintained.

The controversy on this airstrip dates back to the drafting of the early NRA management plans. Many felt this airstrip should be closed since it sits within the designated "wild" section of the river, which extends from Upper Pittsburg Landing to the Hells Canyon Dam. The same camp strongly believed Salmon Bar should also be closed. The opposition voiced concern about providing public air access in the upper section of the canyon – pointing out Sluice Creek was the most viable option. In an attempt to please both parties, the Forest Service decided to "close" Sluice Creek and keep Salmon Bar open.

(top) Looking upriver at Sluice Creek — notice the unusual arrow on the approach end of the runway.
(bottom) The 950' Sluice Creek runway.

Blackberry Picking

The Snake River has a profusion of blackberry bushes. While the fruit bearing shrubs are found all over the area, two Council, Idaho, women thought the berries found near the Sluice Creek airstrip tasted the best. So, if Council pilot Clint Yates was going to get his annual summer blackberry pies he had to fly his wife Phyllis and her sister to Hells Canyon for berry picking. While it made for a great Sunday outing, Yates loved every minute of it – pies and flying.[36]

The pleasure trips to the canyon were a great interruption for the busy Yates. Yates moved his family to Council in 1978 and retired from a department head position with an Arizona power company. The Yateses previously had explored Idaho on summer vacations via private airplanes with family friends. One of their close flying companions purchased a place near Cuprum, Idaho, where they all loved to bird hunt in the fall. An opportunity arose when the town of Council and the state of Idaho obtained a federal grant to pave the runway. Looking for a career change, Yates saw the prospect of running an air taxi service from the newly upgraded airport facility. He and his wife opened Council Air Service the same year. The company's aircraft fleet included a Maule, two Citabrias, and a Mooney.[37]

Yates was known to have some of the cleanest and best maintained airplanes in the Idaho charter business. Several outfitters, private hunters, and river rafters quickly became customers. He also picked up a fire patrol contract with the Southern Idaho Timber Protective Association. Yates operated the company year-round until his wife became tired of the mountain winters in 1995. The Yateses then spent winters back in Arizona where he enjoyed instructing in gliders. His efforts to bring commercial aviation to Council and the surrounding area were recognized after his death in 1997 when the town named the airport – "Clint Yates Field." The Yates's son Mark and his family also continue to take pleasure in the outdoors through their tour company – Hells Canyon Adventures.[38]

Johnson Bar

History and the Barton Family

Looking upriver at Johnson Bar. The landing site was in the lower left of the photograph.

Not to be confused with the Johnson family that owned Temperance Creek, the name of this bar was most likely derived from Johnny Johnston. Although the spelling of his last name has become distorted, Johnston placer mined here in the early 1900s. When rumors spread about the Union Pacific Railroad surveying this section of the Snake River, investors sought ownership of the bar, since it was one of the largest flats between the Red Ledge Mine and Pittsburg Landing. Mining entrepreneur, Frank Johnesse took note of the valuable real estate and filed on it in October 1911. Three years later with no action from the railroad, Johnesse sold the entry right to Snake River homesteader Ralph Barton.[39]

Barton first came to the Snake River at the suggestion of friend Martin Hibbs in 1905. He and his brother Guy bought squatter rights to a place at the mouth of Battle Creek. In the canyon he did a little of everything from cattle ranching to mining. Barton married Lenora Hibbs in 1911, and before Ralph's death in 1934 they had three children Ace, Hazel, and Ruth. The family only lived one year at Johnson Bar before selling it to Lenora's brother Glenn, who ultimately proved up on the property. He sold out to Glenn's father Martin in the 1920s. Nearby neighbors Ralph and Mary Stickney then acquired the property in 1935 and left the country in the fall of 1940. In a twist of fate, Lenora and son Ace repurchased Johnson Bar in 1942. In the interim they ranched on the Imnaha River and traded the latter ranch to the McGaffee brothers for their property on Bernard and Sheep creeks. Lenora remarried around 1938 to Pete Wilson. The couple along with Ace lived at Sheep Creek. The Johnson Bar acquisition gained more wintering ground for livestock. The Wilson/Barton in-holdings were sold in 1952 to Bud Wilson who incorporated the land, including Johnson Bar, into his downstream Kirkwood ranch. The Forest Service now owns the land.[40]

While many of Ace Barton's relatives, came and went from the country, he became a legend in the region. He left the central area of Idaho only during World War II. After the war, he worked his way through several seasonal jobs with the Forest Service and took a permanent position with the agency in 1951. During his career he became a fire control expert and community leader in Riggins. While he loved collecting military memorabilia, he also became one of the foremost authorities on Hells Canyon history and co-authored the book *Snake River of Hells Canyon* with Johnny Carrey and Cort Conley. Additionally, the Bartonberry, a low growing shrub with white flowers that is endemic only to Hells Canyon, was named in the family's honor after Ace's mother brought it to the attention of botanists in the 1930s. Ace died of natural causes at his home in Riggins at age eighty-eight in August 2013.[41]

Transportation

Johnson Bar has some interesting history tied to the canyon transportation activities besides being just a critical site for railroad construction. The bar marks the farthest point mail is delivered by boat from Lewiston. It serves as the stopping point for the Army Corps of Engineer's navigation markers from the ocean. Lastly, it has a history of airplane landings starting in the late 1930s. Zimmerly pilots frequented Johnson Bar through the World War II era and after, flying various Piper Cubs. The small landing site void of rocks is still visible on the lower downstream end of the bar and parallel to the river.[42]

HIGH BAR (WILLOW CREEK)

Floyd Harvey and an Airstrip

Looking south at High Bar. The dogleg landing area was situated on the upper end of the bar.

A small approximately 800'-landing area on High Bar that paralleled the river was used in connection with Floyd Harvey's Willow Creek Resort. His main lodge and buildings were situated upstream at the mouth of Willow Creek. Harvey used the strip, like others in the canyon, for emergency situations and for some supply services. Harvey more commonly had pilots use the runway across the river at Temperance Creek. The closer airstrip was only used for light loads and smaller airplanes. By trade, Harvey was an insurance agent from Lewiston who leisurely began jet boating for fun and as a way to entertain clients in about 1958.

Soon after he began boating, Harvey became a commercial jet boat operator. His love affair with the Snake River and Hells Canyon grew to an infatuation. Along with the commercial license, he became a partner in a jet boat business after loaning money to an acquaintance. Six months into the venture, the fellow left town and Harvey found himself to be the sole owner. The company, Hells Canyon Excursions, hauled tourists up the river to a camp at Willow Creek offering overnight fishing excursions.[43] Eventually Harvey acquired a special use permit from the Forest Service to utilize the property.

While Harvey was known to push the limitations of his special use permit, he was unquestionably one of the biggest advocates of preserving Hells Canyon and the middle Snake, especially from the construction of dams.[44] For over a decade, the dam controversy on the Snake

consumed him. In regards to Harvey's activism on the subject author William Ashworth stated in the book *Hells Canyon: The Deepest Gorge on Earth*, "[I]f one man deserves the credit, finally, for keeping dams out of Hells Canyon, Floyd Harvey is undoubtedly that man."[45]

Harvey and the Hells Canyon Preservation Council

Harvey at first spoke out alone in opposition to the power companies at various local and town hall meetings. People thought he was foolish, and in his own words he was dubbed an "idiot." He then rallied others with his opinion.[46] Some of the key players he engaged were Russ Mager, Boyd Norton, Jerry Jane, Al McGlinsky, Paul Fritz, Cyril

(top) The Willow Creek camp in the 1960s.
(bottom) Harvey's company brochure from the 1960s.

WHITEWATER ADVENTURE!

THE ONLY RIVER TRANSPORTATION INTO HELLS CANYON

Captain Floyd Harvey invites you to —

YOUR MOST MEMORABLE VACATION WITH

HELLS
CANYON
EXCURSIONS

I N C O R P O R A T E D

Complete Radio and Radio-Telephone Contact At All Times
From Our Willow Creek Camp
Phone 208-743-7701 — Box 368 — Lewiston, Idaho

E. HEIMGARTNER

HOLM COLLECTION

Slansky, and Jack Barry. This group formed the Hells Canyon Preservation Council in 1965. After successfully helping to create the NRA, the council was disbanded, but was reactivated in 1982.[47] The organization more recently focuses on stewardship efforts, such as trail maintenance. When the council was first getting on its feet, Harvey invited the group to stay with him at Willow Creek. It was at this meeting that the group solidified their goals.[48] In reference to these early efforts, noted environmental attorney Brock Evans who was also involved with the Preservation Council, commented, "It is a classic story of ordinary people standing up for a place they love.[49]

Harvey and the Council Host Radio Personality Arthur Godfrey

From the beginning, Harvey and the leaders of the Hells Canyon Preservation Council had lofty ambitions – most were met. In hope of gaining public support many letters were written to conservationists and environmentalists with public notoriety throughout the nation asking for help. People on the list included: Dave Brower of the Sierra Club, Cliff Merritt of the Wilderness Society, Supreme Court Justice William O. Douglas, US Senator Robert Kennedy, and Arthur Godfrey, an NBC radio personality. While many of the well-known people offered their support, Godfrey was the only one to accept an invitation to visit the canyon for an overnight stay at Harvey's lodge.[50]

Godfrey was not only an advocate of trying to save Hells Canyon from further dam construction, he was an ardent promoter of aviation. Godfrey started flying in 1929 and from there forward it became one of his greatest hobbies, when not in the spotlight of radio or television. He held an Airline Transport Rating (ATP) and logged over 17,000 hours in the air during his fifty years of flying. Through Godfrey's ability to promote aviation safety he became close friends with many flying celebrities such as Curtis LeMay and Eddie Rickenbacker. While it may have been for show, Godfrey was commissioned as a

commander in the Navy Reserve and later accepted a retired commission from the Air Force Reserve. At one time in the 1950s he had flown every type of airplane in the US armed forces. Supplemental to Godfrey's military activity, Rickenbacker, who was president of Eastern Airlines, arranged for him to be an honorary captain for the airline, where he was type-rated in the Lockheed Super Constellation. With the intent of promoting airline safety, he worked with Eastern in 1953 to produce a promotional film entitled, *Flying with Arthur Godfrey*. In the picture, Godfrey captains a Constellation and walks the audience through a typical flight, pointing out all the safety features of modern commercial flying. The film even takes a short break by showing viewers Godfrey's private grass airfield where he operated his own DC-3 and Navion.

In the course of visiting Idaho for the tour of Hells Canyon in July 1969, Godfrey flew his Learjet from New York to Lewiston. For Harvey to pull the trip together he relied heavily on his friends to volunteer their time and equipment. Actually, Harvey leaned on friends throughout the entire tourist season to help with clientele. The group was mostly comprised of Lewiston-Clarkston businessmen who just enjoyed recreating on the river. A few names involved were Ernie Heimgartner, Mack Blakely, Chuck Grubin, and Bob Williams. Heimgartner owned the Red Shield Restaurant and Armor Room in Clarkston, which was a combination bowling alley, restaurant, and lounge. In the mid-1960s, he had purchased a new inboard-powered jet boat and used it to help Harvey move customers, sometimes as much as three times per week. It was Harvey, Heimgartner, and the others that boated Godfrey up Hells Canyon from Lewiston to Willow Creek.[51]

Along the route Harvey and his men showed Godfrey the sights of the canyon. The following day Bob Williams, an expert Snake River fisherman, took Godfrey fishing at his favorite holes near camp. Godfrey landed three sturgeons, all over seven feet long, and one steelhead. He also caught a dozen trout – many of which were packaged and taken back home with him.[52]

On the last day Russ Mager, president of the Hells Canyon Preservation Council, met Godfrey at

Harvey [far left] and his crew for Arthur Godfrey's 1969 Hells Canyon visit. Pictured with Harvey are Ernie Heimgartner [second from left] and Bob Williams [far right].

Arthur Godfrey, Burl Ives, and Walter Hickel at Willow Creek in May 1970.

Willow Creek. The two men hit it off. They both agreed on the importance of preserving the canyon. Perhaps another reason for their mutual respect was Mager was an Air Force pilot serving on active duty before, during, and after World War II. In his retirement he also joined the Air Force Reserves. After a pleasant discussion on the banks of the Snake River, the two were flown by helicopter from High Bar back to Lewiston.[53] Piloting the Hiller 12E copter was Jim Pope Sr. of Clarkston – owner of Valley Helicopter Service. Similar to the others in the group, Pope donated his time and equipment for the trip in an effort to help save the middle Snake River from being dammed. On the return trip to Lewiston, Pope gave Godfrey and Mager a tour of the Hells Canyon country.[54]

Godfrey later raved about the Hells Canyon trip on several of his radio programs. He mentioned more than once that a major highlight of the trip was Pope's aerial tour through the Seven Devils. Listeners also had the sense that Godfrey was completely amazed by the remoteness and beauty of the area. In combination with a long list of adjectives, he made statements such as, "Greatest piece [Hells Canyon] of paradise you will ever see in your life." As a small thank you and as an avenue to help stop dam construction on the river, Godfrey flew Harvey to New York for a guest appearance on one of his many shows.[55]

Godfrey Returns with Friends – May 1970

Astounded with the splendor of Hells Canyon, Godfrey returned the following year in May and invited a group of friends to join him. His entourage included two marine biologists, singer Burl Ives, songwriter/actor Lyle Moraine, and US Secretary of the Interior Walter Hickel.[56] As with the previous trip, Godfrey flew many of his crew to Lewiston with his Gulfstream jet.[57] Pope again volunteered his services along with a helicopter, which proved key for Hickel's attendance. As secretary of the interior, Hickel had to be available at all times in case of a national emergency. Therefore, Pope remained at Willow

Creek during the entire event with a helicopter.[58]

Unlike the visit the previous year, the 1970 trip was far more political. The idea was to get Hickel, the man with political clout, to endorse saving Hells Canyon. Summarizing the attitudes of the high-profile figures on the trip, Heimgartner commented, "Hickel was calculating and all politician. Godfrey was noticeably reserved compared to the year before. Now Ives, he was just great, talking all the time about something. He didn't seem to have a worry."[59] Of course it was not until Hickel returned to his DC office that he gave his endorsement of saving the canyon. Hickel later wrote in the book, *Who Owns America?*, "There are places to put dams and places not to, and this is a place not to."[60]

Harvey caused quite a stir with the pro-dam advocates who demanded he carve out time for them to meet with Hickel and perhaps join the trip. Harvey, once the underdog on the issue, just laughed.[61] However, some of these folks did get to meet Godfrey and Hickel at the airport and received some attention from the press.[62]

The 1970 trip was clearly a success. Several of Harvey's friends boated in and offered assistance. A few of them even flew in – one pilot in a Cessna 172 landed at the High Bar airstrip and another landed a Cessna 185 on floats right in front of the camp.[63] The friend with the floatplane gave Hickel a tour of the middle Snake from the Brownlee Dam to the mouth of the Salmon River.[64]

The Demise of Willow Creek Resort and Harvey

In 1973, with the success of the first two trips, Harvey began to plan a third outing with Godfrey for the following summer. For this excursion Godfrey and Harvey were making an effort to assemble influential people to support the establishment of the Hells Canyon NRA.[65] However, his support for the NRA was ironic. A year before, the Forest Service found him in violation of all but two of over a dozen required criteria for his permit. The reason for the oversight was the Salmon River Ranger District of the Nez Perce NF did little to monitor Harvey's compliance requirements. In 1972, the district was consolidated with the Slate Creek District and Assistant Ranger Art Seamans took over the management of the permits. When Seamans first observed Harvey's Willow Creek Resort, most violations were blatantly obvious. He was only allowed to have temporary buildings due to the fluctuating water levels of the river, but there stood several structures on concrete foundations. He had illegally put in a sewer system, generator, and was pulling water out of Willow Creek. Seamans tried to work with Harvey but found him uncooperative. With Harvey's stonewall tactics of avoiding any solutions to fixing the violations, the Forest Service intended to pull the permit. Also, the future NRA would not have allowed Willow Creek Resort to exist as Harvey had built it.[66]

In the end, none of the special use permit violations or the planning for the next Godfrey trip mattered, as Harvey's life dramatically changed on January 31, 1974. On this cold January night, people boated up to Willow Creek Resort and stole hundreds of dollars of equipment. Once the loot was stowed in the boat, the people vandalized the property by pouring acid over metal fixtures and equipment and then destroyed the power plant with an ax. Then the drunken offenders placed burning bags of charcoal briquettes in each of the seven buildings – destroying the main lodge and one other structure. The crime put Harvey out of business.[67]

In the beginning, Harvey was looking for answers and started fishing for the culprits. Rumors quickly spread throughout the river community. One version suggested Harvey's liberal political stance was at fault. His anti-dam and pro-NRA support threatened the livelihoods of local businesses. Those in opposition to his viewpoints shut him down. Another version pointed the finger at the Forest Service since Harvey had vocally told people about his recent run-ins concerning his special use permit. Harvey even went so far as verbally accusing Seamans at the Slate Creek Ranger Station of committing the crime. All trivia and rumors aside, the real motive rested with Bruce Oakes.

Oakes and Harvey had an ongoing dispute over a boat and money. Harvey hired Oakes to build a custom jet boat, but had many stipulations to the design. He also insisted the watercraft be powered with a diesel engine, which was uncommon for the era. Oakes agreed to build the boat per Harvey's request, but Oakes warned him of potential design flaws. From the start the boat had problems. The diesel engine did not turn enough RPMs (revolutions per minute) to drive the jet pump, and consequently, Oakes had to install a heavy transmission. The extra weight compounded problems already associated with the hull design of the boat. Harvey was unhappy with the product and refused payment to Oakes.

In retaliation it is alleged Oakes and friends Keith Flugstad and David Gilkey took revenge on Harvey by burning and vandalizing his property. While Oakes and his constituents were not criminally convicted, several civil lawsuits ensued. Harvey filed a $3.5 million civil damages suit. Harvey was granted a $1.75 million default judgment, but that amount was set aside and the case was ordered to trial.[68] As the lawsuits dragged on and appeals were heard, Oakes was charged with perjury in 1978 for lying to a grand jury during the arson investigation.[69] This separate case went to trial, and he was acquitted of the charge.[70] In the end, a jury tried the original civil case and found in favor of Harvey in the amount of $219,200, and judgment was entered in favor of Harvey and jointly and severally against Oakes and Flugstad in that amount plus costs and attorney fees.[71] The long drawn out civil suits finally ended in 1989. Harvey died in August 2010 at age eighty-four.

Modern Willow Creek

The beautiful sand bar once associated with Willow Creek Resort is now gone. Since the construction of the Hells Canyon Dam this beach and others on the river have slowly diminished. The complex of dams blocks the natural depositing of sediments and the fluctuating water levels increase bank erosion. Gone with the sandy beaches of Willow Creek are the remains of Harvey's camp. His Hells Canyon Excursions company dissolved, as did the Forest Service's issuance of the special use permit.

HOLM

The High Bar landing area is visible in the upper corner of the photograph. The sandy beach at Willow Creek once extended from the right bank to the large rock (Sturgeon Rock), in the lower center of the river.

TEMPERANCE CREEK (JOHNSON RANCH)

Early Settlers

Looking north at Temperance Creek

Miners Bob and Alex Warnock arrived at this site in the early 1880s. When the Warnocks packed in the supplies for their first winter camp, the horse that carried their liquor supply rolled off a steep section of trail, smashing all the contents. One of the miners commented that their camp was going to be temperate. Word spread about the dry camp, and it became known as "Temperance Creek."[72]

Three more brothers joined Bob and Alex by the end of the century. All five entered the cattle business. Several years passed and the brothers spread out, claiming various land parcels in the canyon. As competition stiffened for rangeland, the Warnocks sold their Temperance Creek holdings to Frank "Bow" Wyatt in 1904. Wyatt's nickname was derived from his bow and arrow cattle brand based at Deer Creek on the lower Salmon River.[73] Wyatt's holdings ranged far and wide and when he

The grave of Louis Shields. This site is located between the sheering and lambing sheds on a small knoll overlooking the river. Shields worked at Temperance Creek for the Warnock brothers and shot himself near the bunkhouse circa 1895. It is unknown whether his death was self-inflicted or accidental.

sold his Oregon operation to Walter Brockman in 1908, Temperance went along with the transaction. Brockman proved up on 91.19 acres at the mouth of the creek in June 1914.[74] Two years later, Brockman was killed in a horse accident as he returned to the ranch from Imnaha on the Zigzag Trail.

After Brockman's death, neighbor Jack Titus from Pittsburg Creek oversaw the land to help satisfy the bank until it was sold to Dr. Herman Trappier. Trappier owned the ranch for a number of years before selling it to Leonard and Kenneth Johnson.[75]

The Kenneth Johnson Family

Leonard Johnson and son Ken acquired Temperance Creek as part of their sheep operation in the early 1930s. Leonard began his career as a herder and slowly accumulated sheep as payment for his work. His operation grew and he found himself roaming the Oregon side of Hells Canyon with a headquarters located at Dug Bar.[76]

Ken ultimately bought the Kirkwood place three miles downriver from Temperance Creek, where he made many improvements. Ken and his wife Hazel then relocated to Temperance Creek in 1935. While at Temperance Creek they raised two sons, Duane and Greg, who helped immensely with the family business (Temperance Creek Livestock Company). The family migrated with the sheep, living at the ranch from the middle of October to the middle of June. They lived in Enterprise the remainder of the year. At the height of their business they owned eighteen homesteads that varied in size from 100 to 400 acres, all within about a fifty-mile stretch of the Snake River from Battle Creek to Dug Bar.[77]

When the Johnsons first moved to Temperance Creek, many of the old homestead buildings were present. However, Ken promptly built a new three-story log home on the north side of Temperance Creek. Over the years, they gradually added structures and modified some of the originals, such as the interior of the shearing plant. One of the most unique buildings added to the site was a structure the Johnsons relocated from the Iva Miller Jarrett homestead located between Quartz and Temperance creeks. The well-constructed log cabin

built circa 1917 was positioned near the Johnson's main dwelling and was enlisted as a bunkhouse. The quaint building was one of the Johnsons' favorites as it retained all the original elements constructed by the homesteaders, right down to the windows and the hardwood floors.[78]

As Ken and Hazel grew older, a transition was made with their sons to take over more of the general operations. Both boys attended Washington State University, and ultimately Greg took over the ranch in 1966. However, the Vietnam War did not make this easy, and Duane and Greg joined the National Guard. Duane's guard unit activated. As a result, Greg received a hardship deferment to manage the ranch. While his parents rarely visited Hells Canyon, mainly due to Ken's struggles with emphysema, they were generous in sharing their lifetime of knowledge and experiences, which greatly aided Greg. Seven years after Greg took over, Ken died. Hazel died nearly thirty years later in 2000.[79]

When Greg finally began to settle into the rhythm of the ranch as an adult and sole owner of the operation, he, like other landowners in Hells Canyon, were forced to deal with the government's threat of eminent domain. He made multiple proactive efforts to combat losing his family's heritage in the canyon, but no middle ground could be made. He felt the best compromise for landowners was to sell restrictive scenic easements to the government. However, his efforts were stymied. After a battle over the actual appraised value of the land, he reluctantly gave in. He then operated from the ranch for a few more years on a permit, but he grew tired of the government red tape. Johnson officially left his beloved Temperance Creek home in 1980 and bought a ranch near Enterprise.[80]

The Post Johnson Years

After Johnson left the river, the Forest Service continued to lease the Temperance Creek buildings along with some permitted grazing land. One of the first lessees accidentally burned down the Ken Johnson-built home. The cause of the fire was later determined to be a faulty water heater. When Greg

HOLM

(top) An aerial view of the current building complex at the mouth of Temperance Creek.
(opposite) Looking south at the modern Temperance Creek runway.

left the ranch, he warned them of the hot water heater issue, but nothing was done to repair the problem. The Forest Service replaced the historic Johnson home with the current living quarters south of Temperance Creek. To build this functional but bland structure, the agency tore down the shop Greg constructed in the 1970s and used its foundation. The only identifiable part of the Johnson's 1930s house is part of a retaining wall associated with the front lawn. Greg Johnson's treasured bunkhouse was also torn down, piled into a heap near the shearing shed, and burned.

Johnson's grazing permit was picked up by at least three different individuals after his departure. Outfitters Butch and Karen Brown obtained the lease for the Temperance Creek headquarters in 1995. The Browns ran their business, Hells Canyon Packers, from the ranch for fifteen years before retiring to Medical Springs, Oregon. In addition to running his own business, Butch worked several years for Hells Canyon Adventures as a jet boat pilot.[81] He had an excellent reputation for his skill as a boatman. Veteran middle Snake River outfitter Jerry Hughes remarked, "Butch was probably one of the best commercial jet boat drivers to ever run a boat on the river [Snake River]."[82] When the Browns left the river they sold out to Brice Barnes. Barnes, the owner of Lewiston-based Custom Weld Boats, continues to offer hunting and fishing trips from the ranch.

Multiple Landing Areas

Around the time Ken Johnson moved the family sheep operation to Temperance Creek, he used a horse-drawn harrow to level the upper hayfield above the house on the south side of Temperance Creek. This airstrip evolved into a well-groomed 1,500'-runway used by airplanes as big as Zimmerly Air Transport's Travel Air 6000s. At the time the runway was considered by pilots to be the best airfield in Wallowa County.

Possibly out of mere convenience a second airstrip was developed parallel to the river and became known as the "Short Strip." This field generally required an approach from the north. With this approach option it became crucial not to land short, as the area off the end was steep and

soft. Several pilots who did land short suffered the consequences of having a stuck airplane. Greg erected a well-built hangar near this landing area in 1972. The large lambing shed, built post-1980, located on the south side of Temperance Creek absorbed a portion of his hangar and now covers most of this runway.

Greg developed a third informal landing area around 1966 in the hayfield closest to the house between the upper field and Temperance Creek. He favored this location because of its proximity to the house and used it the most during his ownership. This field is no longer used.

The Forest Service developed the current 2,300' north-south airstrip in the mid-1980s. It was later lengthened to its present dimensions with the removal of a fence. Since Forest Service ownership, the airstrip has been used for administrative purposes and open only to the current permit holder of the Temperance Creek facility or their patrons. All other public air traffic cannot legally use the runway.

Pilots and Airplanes

Growing up at the remote ranch, both Duane and Greg loved being around airplanes. Duane started taking flying lessons from Bud Stangel in the mid-1960s. Greg also wanted to learn to fly, and in 1965 joined the Chief Joseph Flyers, a local flying club. Stangel gave him dual instruction and helped him with his initial license. Greg soon became checked out at the ranch and made frequent trips with the club's Comanche 140 and a Cessna 172. Needing air access to various sheep camps along the canyon, Greg purchased his own Piper Super Cub (N3374Z). Greg viewed the Cub similar to a truck and flew it for various utility purposes. To improve his backcountry flying skills, he flew and rode along as often as he could with Stangel and Ted Grote.

Duane bought a Cessna 180 and eventually became a career aviator, retiring to the Seattle area as a corporate pilot. The two Johnson brothers' uncle, Raymond, also flew to the ranch frequently in the 1950s and 1960s. He was a rancher in the Wallowa Valley and occasionally used an Ercoupe owned by the Chief Joseph Flyers to visit Temperance Creek. However, he more commonly flew the club's Cessna 182.

Mail boat pilot Dick Rivers loading a wrecked Piper aircraft onto his boat at Temperance Creek in 1961.

BIG BAR

Early History – Brownlee Murder, a Hanging, and a Tunnel

Looking north at the Big Bar airstrip.

Mac Myers occupied a small rock cabin on the south end of Big Bar starting some time around 1900. During the same period, the C. J. Hall cattle outfit used Big Bar for grazing. Hall and Myers did not get along – often arguing over water rights and livestock trespass issues. The problem came to a crossroads in May 1904 when some of Hall's ranch hands allowed cattle to graze through Myers's garden and orchard. Upset, Myers tracked the men down near the present day Brownlee Saddle and confronted them with a gun, killing Hall employee George Brownlee. Several more shots were fired at Brownlee's partner Wallace Jarrett, but he escaped with minor injuries. Soon after the confrontation, Myers was apprehended and hung from a cottonwood tree at Charles Bentz's ranch at White Bird, Idaho. Bentz was not home at the time. When he learned of the happenings from his wife he was appalled. Apparently the authorities did not even have the common decency to remove Myers's body from the tree. Upset by the lack of respect, Bentz ordered the men to fetch the hanging corpse, and he later felled and burned the tree.[83]

With Myers out of the picture, the Halls proved up on 199.88 acres at Big Bar in May 1914.[84] Ken Johnson, Len Jordan, and Bud Wilson succeeded the Halls and used the acreage as part of their larger ranching operations. When Jordan owned the property, he hired Ace Duncan to blast, drill, and dig a tunnel through the ridge that separates Myers Creek from Big Bar. After two years of construction and working alone eight hours per day, Duncan completed the excavation. An irrigation line was then laid through the tunnel, allowing water from Myers Creek to be piped to Big Bar for irrigation. Portions of the pipeline and excavation work are still intact and are so distinct that they can be seen from the air.

The Wilsons reportedly spent $34,000 building up Big Bar. By the mid-1950s, the ground was covered by several large corrals and huge lambing sheds. After the Forest Service acquired the land, the fences and sheds were torn down.

Airplanes may have landed at Big Bar prior to the removal of the sheds, but it is unlikely. However, in the late 1960s small aircraft used the upper bench running parallel and slightly more downstream from the current airstrip.

Airplane Usage

Once the sheds were removed circa 1974–75 aircraft commonly began to land at Big Bar. It slowly became the only airstrip open to the public on the Idaho side of the middle Snake River. When first opened, the airstrip measured about 900' and was plagued by several hazards. One of the worst dangers was large rocks protruding through the runway surface. For bigger wheeled aircraft it was not too much of a concern, but airplanes with small tires were commonly reported with substantial

C. CONLEY

HOLM

(top) *Bud Wilson's Big Bar sheep operation circa 1952.*
(bottom) *A few pieces of equipment still linger at Big Bar as a reminder of the former land use.*

wheel and landing gear damage. Another problem was punctured tires. When the buildings were demolished, no attention was paid to collecting debris – especially nails. The nail dilemma has since been solved.

Airstrip Improvements

On a routine recreational flight in about 1987, pilots Gene Nelson and Gene Lombardo stopped at Big Bar in their own respective airplanes. On landing, Nelson hit a rock on the runway causing his airplane to flip over on its back. The plane had to be disassembled and taken out by boat. The accident prompted Lombardo and pilot friend Rusty Bentz to volunteer with the Forest Service to help improve the airstrip. The two returned the following year with a gas-powered jackhammer to drill and blast a few of the more problematic rocks. The Forest Service gladly approved the project. In fact, Fire Management officer Dave Lukens and Cliff Nevouxe chartered Joe Spence with a Cessna 206 to fly them in and watch the process.

Over ten years later in spring 1999, Bentz and Idaho Aviation Association (IAA) President Boyd Miller worked in cooperation with the Forest Service to extensively repair the airstrip. In April, a large group consisting of: Johnny Stewart, a commercial pilot who flew with the Clearwater-Potlatch Timber Protective Association, Mike Miller, a former Grangeville Air Service pilot, Ed Redke, Gene Lombardo, and several other IAA members participated in the work. Lombardo's brother Roy, who was a river ranger, used a Forest Service boat to haul in sand and gravel for mixing cement. The cement was used to create a base for a windsock and four tie-downs. At the same time, the runway was mowed and the upstream end extended 200' using hand tools and wheelbarrows to its current length of

1,100'. After the major work was completed, Bentz, Redke, and Boyd Miller returned in May with friends Jack and Kenny Morrison to blast a few final rocks and hang the windsock.

Boyd Miller Backcountry Aviation Advocate

Miller's work at Big Bar was just one of many examples of his dedication to keep backcountry airstrips open to the public. In the 1980s, a fight with cancer forced him to resign from his job as the North Carolina commissioner of motor vehicles. To help boost his spirits a friend suggested they take a flying and camping trip to Alaska. Miller loved flying. He had flown countless hours as a young boy with his father on business trips to Cuba and Mexico. At age fourteen his father offered to buy him either a car or an airplane. Miller chose a J-3 Cub. On the trip to Alaska, he discovered many wonderful things, but he was particularly taken by the brief stops in Idaho. Each year thereafter, Miller returned, flying his Cessna 185 (N185BM). By 1986, Miller left Salsbury, North Carolina, moving permanently to McCall. In Idaho he joined the IAA, of which he ultimately served as the president of for six years. When not camping at places such as the Chamberlain Guard Station for weeks on end, he was working behind the scenes to ensure the public could continue to enjoy and visit Idaho wilderness areas by air. He traveled to Washington DC to weigh-in on meetings and hearings concerning airstrip closures and constantly wrangled with Forest Service policies that threatened backcountry aviation. His wife Kathy Poston supported his aviation efforts, and she too became a licensed pilot and very involved with the IAA. When Miller died of cancer in November 2000, she filled the remainder of his term as the president of the association.[85]

Miller's enthusiasm for the backcountry spread to many pilots and other IAA members who continue to campaign for the same causes. John McKenna of Bozeman, Montana, is one of the many examples of people influenced by Miller. McKenna, now one of the largest advocates of recreational backcountry aviation, helped to start the Recreational Aviation Foundation (RAF). The RAF strives to preserve, maintain, and create public access to backcountry airstrips nationwide. Reminiscing about Miller's sway, McKenna commented, "It was the summer of 1988 after meeting Boyd that got me into understanding that if folks didn't stand up for the aviation activity they enjoyed, they likely would be left on the sidelines. It was Boyd Miller and his infectious attitude about the subject that got myself and countless others involved. I just happened to stick with it and formed the RAF in 2003 along with some others. Most of all of those early founders of the RAF had a Boyd Miller encounter somewhere along the way."[86]

George Hauptman – River Outfitter and Pilot

George Hauptman started river guiding in the summer of 1977 while attending the University of Oregon. He obtained a Hells Canyon permit in 1980 with a friend and then became the sole owner of Canyon Outfitters two years later. He ceased working on other Oregon rivers and in 1989 moved from Salem to Halfway, Oregon, where he focused solely on the middle Snake. In the early years of running his outfitting business, Hauptman chartered with pilot Jim Zanelli of Canyon Navigation Company, located in Oxbow, Oregon, for flying customers on back hauls. Interestingly, Hauptman had obtained his license in 1967 but never exercised it. Thirty-

three years later this changed when he decided to buy a Luscombe to fly for fun. He and his wife Lynette then bought the Halfway airport in 1999. During sale negotiations Lynette kept reminding George that just because he owned an airplane did not mean he needed to own an airport. The Hauptman's acquired the runway from the Ellington Lumber Company of Baker. The company had owned it for about forty years after buying it from the Jones family who built it in 1952. The Joneses owned a lumber mill and the runway was used for business, primarily with Piper Cubs.[87]

Since Hauptman owned an airport he erected a hangar and upgraded to a Cessna 170 that he imported from Australia. This interestingly-appointed 170, which he later found out had been fused together with the rear fuselage of a 172, was sold for a more original 170B (N8365A) in 2010. The latter plane was acquired from Gene Lombardo of Lewiston. When time and weather permit he uses the 170 to meet his rafting parties at Big Bar. It is an easy way for him to help his guides with the evening camp and haul in extra supplies if needed. Hauptman also allows his competitors to use the Halfway runway for commercial charter flights related to Hells Canyon float trips.[88]

Bud Stangel's Crazy Field Repair

In August 1979, Bud Stangel landed at Big Bar with a Cessna 180 to pick up a few clients and gear. On takeoff the plane veered too far left of center and hit a big rock, damaging the left main gear and tire. With a quick correction he somehow saved the plane from nosing over and prevented a prop strike. Stuck with the broken airplane and his pride hurt, he was then lucky enough to get the attention of friend Greg Johnson across the river at Temperance Creek. Johnson jumped in his Cub and flew across the river

STANGEL

STANGEL

Pilot Bud Stangel's creative field repair after hitting a rock at Big Bar in August 1979.

to see what had happened. Stangel grabbed a ride from Johnson to Enterprise where he retrieved a Cessna 206 and mechanic to repair the crippled airplane and fetch the waiting passengers. After the mechanic assessed the damage, Stangel was apprehensive about leaving it on the bar with the concern rafters might vandalize it or another airplane might run into it. To avoid further problems, Stangel and his mechanic decided to make an innovative field repair and forgo obtaining the required ferry permit from the FAA.[89]

The field repair safely worked. Two days later the FAA showed up at the Enterprise airport and walked into Stangel Flight Service. Stangel opted to tell them about the airplane incident. As he opened the hangar door where the 180 sat, he started to justify why he did not obtained the ferry permit. The two officials, who were shocked by the creative field repair, quickly interrupted him. They were amazed by Stangel's genius engineering feat – twine, rope, wire, and blocks of wood all in perfect harmony. One of the them chuckling turned to his partner and said, "Take a couple pictures of this . . . We have to send this to Cessna to show them how their planes are fixed here in the West!" The men ogled the repair for what seemed like hours to Stangel. In the end, they never did ask him anything more about the ferry permit or issue a violation![90]

Domestic Sheep Trouble at Big Bar

Beginning in the late 1970s, the canyon saw a rise in problems with domestic sheep. The worst die-off occurred in the winter of 1983–84. Vic Coggins, a biologist with the Oregon Department of Fish and Wildlife, discovered the major issue when he spotted hundreds of dead domestic sheep on North Temperance Creek, while on a routine aerial survey on March 24, 1984. The same problem occurred on the opposite side of the river in the range allotment associated with Big Bar. To clean the Idaho allotment up, the sheep were gathered and piled at the Big Bar airstrip, then burned to dispose of the carcasses.[91]

The cause for the sheep deaths was linked to the rapid turnover of permit holders in the canyon, after the knowledgeable ranchers left due the establishment of the NRA. The newcomers who lasted on average only two years, were inexperienced and lacked understanding in raising sheep in the tough terrain and harsh climate. Previously, all the replacement ewes for the bands were raised in the canyon. The new operators mistakenly brought sheep in from foreign environments that were not adapted to the conditions. On top of this issue, the old-timers would have brought the ewes and the sick sheep down closer to the river for feeding. However, the new permit holders just left them out.[92]

During the same era, the reintroduction of the native Rocky Mountain bighorn sheep began in Hells Canyon. Once the most abundant big game animal in the area, the bighorn had completely disappeared in Idaho by the early 1950s and in northeastern Oregon by the late 1930s. The first reintroduction efforts failed on the Oregon side of Hells Canyon in 1971. They were repeated in the 1980s with some success. The Idaho reintroductions have also had difficulties. To help prevent the poor management decisions of the permit holders in the early 1980s from reoccurring, the range allotment associated with Big Bar was closed and reissued farther to the south on the Cecil Andrus Wildlife Area and on an adjacent allotment within the Payette NF.[93]

SALT CREEK

The First Airstrip

The Salt Creek cabin build by Arnold Hiltsley as it appeared in the mid-1960s.

Lem Wilson used two small landing areas in the Salt Creek drainage. The first landing spot had a unique small two-room cabin likely built by early settler Arnold Hiltsley. Jim and Stella Wisenor ultimately proved up on the property and sold it in 1916 to Jack Titus, who headquartered his sheep operation at Pittsburg Creek. At about the same time Titus acquired the property he married Celia, one of the Wisenor daughters.[94] Jack and Celia sold their entire business to Lem and Doris Wilson in 1951.

The Grangeville Crowd

Beginning in the early 1960s, Wilson allowed several of his friends from Grangeville to use the small 650'-airstrip and the Hiltsley Cabin for recreation. The group included: Travis Wadley, Burris Russell, Bob Zehner, Gib Eimers, Carroll Adkison, and Jay Shinkle.[95]

Besides all being a part of the Elks Club with Wilson, four of the six men in the group were pilots and belonged to the Solar Club. The Solar Club was a Grangeville flying organization that owned several fixed-wing aircraft and a hangar. For a small buy-in

and a per-hour fee it offered an extremely affordable way to fly. Its members informally met at the hangar on weekends and ventured about the surrounding country, often with the destination of Salt Creek in mind.[96]

Travis Wadley, originally from Oklahoma, moved to Grangeville in the 1930s. For decades he owned The Squires Shop, a men's clothing store in downtown Grangeville. He took up flying by joining the Solar Club and received instruction from George Foster. After earning his various ratings, Wadley began to fly commercially for Frank Hill, who had purchased Grangeville Air Service from Foster. Wadley mainly flew fire patrol and charters in the summer.[97]

Bob Zehner also belonged to the Solar Club. Zehner was killed in one of the club's Piper Cubs in July 1964. Zehner had been visiting his father and relatives Walt and Mary Reemer in Lewiston. Zehner and Reemer shared an interest in aviation, as he owned the Concord airstrip located near the present-day Gospel Hump Wilderness area. Upon leaving, Reemer, who worked at the local pea factory, gave Zehner a box of peas. On his return to Grangeville, Zehner buzzed his brother-in-law's house near Cottonwood, Idaho.[98] As he pulled the stick toward himself to gain elevation, the box of peas, which he had placed near the backseat, jammed the rear

Looking upstream at the Salt Creek airstrip.

(top) Pilot Travis Wadley relaxing at Lem Wilson's Pittsburg ranch.
(bottom) The Wadley-Hanson accident at Salt Creek in September 1967.

control stick, causing the plane to stall. The crash killed him. In spite of the loss, his son Bob Jr. took up flying at a young age, likely under the influence of Greg Hill, a close childhood friend. Greg's father Frank took the young Zehner in as one of his own and helped him with his various pilot ratings. Zehner even purchased one of the Hill's old Piper Cubs to build time. Zehner eventually became an ag pilot. While on a contract as a crop duster in Hawaii in the mid-1980s, he was killed when the wing fell off his airplane.

Eimers and Burris were also avid pilots. Eimers worked as a Farmers Insurance agent, and Burris was an employee of the Rural Electrical Association (now Idaho County Light and Power). As a result of the group's aviation enthusiasm, it only made sense to further improve the Salt Creek airstrip. This was done by clearing more brush and placing white markers at the foot of the runway before it broke off toward the river.[99]

Within a year or two of getting the airstrip ship-shape, they decided to spruce up the interior of the cabin with tongue-and-groove cedar siding. Much thought was put into how the supplies should be hauled in. The men had improved the trail to the river and made a nice tie-up area for their boats, which is how they often reached the remote property. Boating the wood in was ruled out when Grangeville pilot Sid Hinkle agreed to help by flying the supplies in with his Cessna 185. Several pilots in the Grangeville aviation community thought Hinkle was crazy to attempt both the takeoff and the landing at Salt Creek with the bigger airplane (relative to a Cub). Hinkle, who retired at a fairly young age from his trucking and petroleum business in Redding, California, ran the Elkhorn Motel in Grangeville. He and his wife Mae also ran commercial outfitting trips from their beautiful property on the Selway River known as the "Selway Lodge." Hinkle felt an airplane was the key to accessing the backcountry. He built a runway at his lodge and was involved with developing airstrips at Mallard Creek and the town of Dixie, both in the Clearwater Mountains of Idaho. For Hinkle, flying in a load of six foot pieces of lumber was nothing to worry about – simply another

flight to the backcountry.[100]

When Hinkle's young friend, Bob Black (also a pilot and eventually a son-in-law) heard about the flight, he offered to go along to help load and unload the wood. By the time the plane was loaded, the only seat available was the pilots', and there was no room for Black. However, the two mulled it over and Black opted to lie on his stomach on top of the lumber. Thinking back about the trip, Black recalled it was actually pretty comfortable; he even documented the event by taking along his 8mm movie camera.[101]

The only major mishap at the airstrip among the group of pilots occurred a few days before Labor Day 1967. Wadley and another friend from the flying club, Clyde Hanson, flew to Salt Creek to inventory needed supplies for the big upcoming weekend. After circling the airstrip several times, and with no indication of wind, Wadley decided to land. Moments before committing himself to the landing, Wadley explained to Hanson that it was a no go-around airstrip. Once you turn final, you have to land – the terrain will out-climb the airplane. As Wadley made the turn for final, the Super Cub's (N7533K) tail received a gust of wind. Finding himself high and too fast he attempted a go-around. Just the reaction he mentally told himself not to do! Looking out the cockpit the topography quickly rose. There was an instant where Wadley thought he was going to clear the upper end of the strip and be able to make a turn back toward the river, but the front end of the plane impacted some trees and the tailwheel snagged an old hay rake.[102]

After the crash the two men assessed the situation. Other than a few scrapes and bruises, they concluded they were lucky. Earlier, while circling over the runway they noticed a group of men fishing downstream from Salt Creek and decided to hike toward them for help. After miles of walking, Wadley and Hanson reached the party. The fisherman boated the two downed fliers to Pittsburg Landing and loaned them an automobile to return to Grangeville. Eight days later, members of the Solar Club boated from Pittsburg to Salt Creek to retrieve the airplane. The Super Cub was disassembled and packed down to the river and boated out in pieces to

Pittsburg. Hanson flew over the party in a Cessna 172 (N7339T) to check on their progress. The ground crew of course enjoyed Hanson's buzz job.[103]

When the NRA was established, the Forest Service obtained the land and closed the airstrip. The old cabin has since burned in a wildland fire. The Grangeville families who enjoyed it for so many years still fondly remember Salt Creek. When Travis Wadley died in 1995, his daughter Teri and pilot Frank Hill scattered his ashes over the site from an airplane. During the large flood of late December 1996 and early January 1997, a portion of the downstream end of the airstrip was washed out.

An Additional Strip – The Grotes

Ted Grote used another landing patch above the old Hiltsley place. It sat along the current Forest Service trail #1785 where a small cabin stood. This structure has since burned in a wildland fire. Grote and his wife Okal purchased the cabin and an adjoining 160 acres from Lem Wilson. Grote and Wilson had become good friends

GROTE FAMILY

Ted Grote – 1962.

through their mutual work on ranching and aviation in the canyon. The Grotes loved their remote getaway and used it only for recreational purposes – fishing, hiking, hunting, and relaxation.

Ted Grote's Flying Career

Ted Grote grew up in southeastern Washington. He started his career as a wheat farmer in Hooper, Washington. While in Hooper, he took flying lessons with Zimmerly Air Transport pilot Miles Rugenberg. Arrangements were made for Rugenberg to fly an Aeronca Model K Scout to the neighboring town of LaCrosse where he would land on the road behind the grain hall. From this road Grote learned to fly – soloing in March 1936.[104]

Wanting to earn some side money, Grote obtained a 220-horsepower Stearman biplane (NC3670) equipped for spraying and began a small aerial application business. He eventually married and had two daughters. Growing tired of the constant eastern Washington wind and looking for new opportunities, he moved his family to Wallowa County outside of Enterprise. Grote purchased a large acreage for farming and ranching and continued his small spray operation on the side. Within a few years, he divorced his first wife. In 1962, he married Okal Kiser with whom he remained for over forty years until her death in 2010. She became an essential part of his life in his various businesses and at home, where they raised seven children together.[105]

Around the same time as the move to Wallowa County, he acquired a new V-tail Beech Bonanza (NC5053B). Seeing an opportunity for local charter and spray jobs, he officially opened Grote Aviation. His principal base of operation was from a small unpaved strip on Verner Hill situated between Enterprise and Lostine. While at this locale

Ted Grote and a Bell 47 in the Wallowa Mountains on a survey in the 1960s.

he hired Bill Bailey, his first pilot. Bailey mainly flew a Piper Cub outfitted with a small tank and spray bars. The plane was a good setup, but was considered dangerous in the event of an accident, since the tank was located toward the back and could easily explode on impact. Bailey affectionately called Grote, "Dad" and was looking to learn. Not too long after Bailey started with the company, Grote sold him the Cub. Bailey died in the plane when he stalled it in a tight turn between spray runs.[106]

Mourning the loss, Grote continued his aviation career. With a growing clientele, he relocated Grote Aviation to the Joseph airport. Starting in 1950, Grote began exploring Hells Canyon and saw potential in providing aviation services there. His first client in the canyon was friend and rancher Ken Johnson. For the short field work he chiefly used Piper Cubs. Over the course of his career, he owned a half-dozen of them. However, these small craft were paired with planes more capable of hauling oversized items and heavy loads. The first of these larger aircraft was an early model Cessna 180. Through the years, his fixed-wing department grew to include Cessna 206s and a Rockwell Aero Commander 560 (N9505). In fact, the Aero Commander occasionally flew missions in Hells Canyon carrying loads in and out of Temperance and Cache creeks. Looking back, Grote remembered the Commander as one of his favorite pieces of equipment to fly. He specifically purchased the plane with an aluminum finish – no unnecessary paint. The unpainted surfaces not only prevented ice build up in IFR conditions, but also increased the useful load by nearly 200 pounds.[107]

In 1964, Grote added another dimension to his aviation company by learning to fly helicopters. His instructor was Bud Darling of Chehalis, Washington. The first helicopter Grote acquired was a Bell 47. A few years later he transitioned to a Bell Jet Ranger, and by 1970 it was solely a rotorcraft operation. With an emphasis placed on helicopters, he built a hangar at his ranch and ran his business from there. Even with the changes he continued his work in the canyon with the versatile pieces of equipment – he strung power lines, hauled government trappers, and moved outfitters. He even occasionally flew celebrities living in the local area such as Lloyd "Tommy" Doss of the Sons of the Pioneers singing group. At age seventy Grote retired from aviation in 1990, after logging more than 30,000 hours. However, his passion for Hells Canyon, the Wallowa Mountains, and aviation continues.[108]

The Grote's Canyon Property

Grote found himself in a difficult situation with the Hells Canyon dam battles and the government's threat of eminent domain. From a business perspective, he relied on contracts with many of the parties involved. As an individual and a landowner, he detested many of the people and organizations. He took an active role in opposing the High Mountain Sheep Dam and the formation of the NRA. In truth, he was one of the last private landowners in the canyon to hold out. His opposition to the NRA was not just personal, but philosophical. Grote believed that taking land that had been logged, ranched, grazed, and generally "improved" was not eligible for such designations as an NRA.[109]

When Congress officially established the Hells Canyon NRA a ceremony was held for top government brass at the Hat Point Lookout in July 1976. The lookout was a fitting location for the reception with its wide panoramas of Hells Canyon in the background. Grote, who held the fire and transportation contract with the Forest Service, was called to haul people to the event. That year, along with several previous, he had two Jet Ranger helicopters stationed for the season at the nearby Memaloose airstrip. Quick shuttles were made back and forth.[110]

When the ceremony was over, Grote returned with the helicopter to move people back to their vehicles parked at the airstrip. On the last trip he landed and began to load his passengers. Grote promptly recognized one fellow as Senator Bob Packwood. Packwood was a major influence on crafting the Hells Canyon NRA, and Grote despised him. In a calm manner Grote pulled a Forest Service official aside, commenting that there was not enough money in the world for Packwood to ride on his helicopter. The statement surprised the official. Having a good rapport with Grote, he pleaded with him. Grote stood his ground – absolutely not.[111]

Still displeased about the establishment of the NRA, Grote smiles today about his refusal to carry Packwood, "It was a matter of principle . . . but I can also be a cantankerous SOB." Grote chuckles remembering the scene of Packwood standing there as he took off. "Well, it was no surprise I did not get the Forest Service contract the next year . . . why it didn't matter, I just went and secured another one with the BLM [Bureau of Land Management]."[112]

KIRKWOOD

Early History

A current view of Kirkwood. The meadow in the lower left of the photograph was used as an airfield for decades.

Dr. Jay Kirkwood and his wife, along with their child, are the first known Euro-Americans to follow the Indians to this bar, arriving in 1885. The Kirkwoods frequented the location, traveling between the river and Grangeville, likely as miners. The family salvaged lumber from a nearby Chinese mining claim and used the material to construct two cabins.

Between Kirkwood's departure and 1901, several men squatted on the bar, either mining or running cattle. George Brownlee settled on the place in 1901 and earned homestead approval for 138.6 acres in October 1909. His brother Tom, who also lived on the river, inherited the acreage after he was killed. The property then became used by several cattle operations before Leonard Johnson and his son Kenneth purchased it in the 1920s. One of their most noteworthy additions to the place was the construction of the white-framed house that is still in use. Ken spent the remainder of his life ranching in the canyon. In the beginning, he attended classes at Washington State College (now Washington State University) during the fall term and then worked on

the ranch the remainder of the year. The Johnsons moved their sheep ranching headquarters upriver to Temperance Creek and sold Kirkwood to Dick Maxwell and Len Jordan in 1932. Maxwell's sister Anna had been a cook with the Johnsons prior to the sale and stayed on at Kirkwood to help the Jordans adjust to ranch life. Once they settled in, she relocated to Temperance Creek, taking over as the main cook.

The Jordans

The Jordans bought Maxwell out after a brief time and continued to live at Kirkwood for about ten years. The family ran roughly 3,000 head of sheep on approximately 17,000 acres of land. Grace homeschooled the three children: Patsy, Stephen, and Joe. The Jordans made several notable changes to the ranch house by incorporating a sleeping porch on the front, installing indoor plumbing, and hand digging a root cellar and basement. Len also disassembled and rebuilt a small cabin that Carl Hanna had constructed on Kirkwood Creek near the present ruins of the Carter Mansion. Carter's unique five-room structure was listed on the National Register of Historic Places in 1984. That same year, the Kirkwood buildings were also listed on the register separately.

The main Kirkwood dwelling built by Kenneth Johnson.

HOLM

J. JORDAN

(top) The Carter Mansion — 2014.
(bottom) The Jordan family at Kirkwood in the 1930s.

While Len had a background in sheep ranching (he had worked for Jay Dobbin seasonally as a teen), the economic struggles of the Great Depression made their life in the remote setting challenging. However, the experience became one of their family's fondest memories. When daughter Patsy came of high school age they left the ranch and moved to Grangeville where she and her siblings attended public school. Len obtained a Ford dealership and founded Jordan Motors, selling Ford, Mercury, and Lincoln automobiles. He also carried a line of Ford tractors and Caterpillar farm equipment. For a time, he also owned an insurance and real estate business.[113]

In 1946, Len was elected to the state senate and four years later became the twenty-third governor of Idaho. He did not run for re-election, but was appointed by Governor Robert Smylie to the US Senate in 1962 to fill the seat of Henry Dworshak who had recently died. Jordan went on to serve in the US Senate through 1972 and was succeeded by Jim McClure. As a senator he was involved with the Hells Canyon Dam and other Snake River dam controversies and helped establish the Sawtooth NRA. On June 30, 1983, Jordan died in Boise at age eighty-four.[114]

The family moved to Boise for Len's governorship, and Grace started working on a book about the family's Hells Canyon experiences. To refresh her memory, she used her childrens' diaries. At Kirkwood she required her children to keep a daily diary as part of their homeschooling curriculum. Each morning they started school by writing about the previous day. These dairies widely became the basis of her book. The final outcome - *Home Below Hell's Canyon* was published in 1954. The title became very popular among a wide variety of readers and remains the standard about life in Hells Canyon. Joe remembered kidding his mother about the depiction of Hells Canyon on the front cover of the book. He told Grace that artists Larry Hoffman's rendering looked nothing like the actual canyon. When Grace finished her next book, *Canyon Boy* (1960), she insisted Joe create the artwork for the dust jacket. The book is a fictionalized account of a

young boy growing up in Hells Canyon. Pieces of the story were based on her childrens' lives at Kirkwood. Joe was flattered by the opportunity and designed a very realistic color image of the river canyon. Grace published a total of seven books between 1954 and 1984, but of all her writing efforts she was most proud of *Home Below Hell's Canyon*. The book has been through ten printings and translated into six different languages. Grace died in September 1985.[115]

Len and Grace never returned to Kirkwood, but their three kids, especially Joe, returned several times. In Joe's later years, he and his family purchased a second home three miles north of Bear, Idaho, not far from the top of Hells Canyon. During his retirement he enjoyed Bear several months per year, and he often ventured about the canyon. Joe was asked if his father ever had sentimental thoughts about his time living on the middle Snake River and if this part of his life bore any weight in his decisions as a US senator about Snake River dam moratoria. Joe's quick response was, "No. My dad did not really have a sentimental bone toward the place – it was a political view and that was that. But I, on the other hand, have many fond memories there. I enjoyed re-visiting it. It always amazed me how nothing really ever changed at our old home. Really amazing that time passed it by. Of course the government has put a lot of money into preserving it."[116]

The Bud Wilson Family

Bud and Helen Wilson of Nyssa, Oregon, bought the place in 1943. The Wilsons moved in the same fall arriving by horseback with their two daughters Donna, age nine and Lois, age seven. Also on the trip was their six-month-old son Mike, who rode buttoned in Bud's jacket on the front of the saddle. The family settled into the well-constructed white-framed house, which Bud christened as "headquarters."[117]

Remarkably, between raising her children and helping with the ranch, Helen managed to find the time to pursue her artistic passion of drawing and

Helen and Bud Wilson at Kirkwood in the 1950s.

G. MATSCKHE

painting. From 1941 through 1956, she worked for Caxton Printers of Caldwell, Idaho, as an illustrator, complementing nine books for various authors. These completed works well exhibited her ability to use an assortment of artistic media from pen and ink drawings to watercolors. Helen's background in the industry stemmed from a scholarship to the Chicago Art Institute that she was awarded after attending two years of school at the University of Idaho. She then married Bud in 1933, a year after successfully finishing her scholarship.[118]

Nine years after buying Kirkwood, the Wilsons bought out Lenora (Barton) Wilson (not related) and her son Ace Barton's in-holdings from Sheep Creek to Granite Creek for grazing. One of the most significant changes the Bud Wilson family made to the ranch was the building of a road from Cow Creek Saddle to Kirkwood. Equipment operator Dale Garrison was hired for the job and completed the work in 1946–47. In addition to this access, Bud also leveled the hayfield parallel to the river and north of the building complex for a landing strip.[119] Bud's brother Lem, who owned a Super Cub, used the field occasionally, as did Ted Grote. Grote was the first to land on the ranch circa 1952. The field, kept mowed, measured nearly 950' long.[120] While the landing area was used throughout the year it was primarily utilized when airplanes were needed to look for lost cattle or when other access options were impassible.[121]

Along with modifying the hayfield, the Wilsons, with the help of their employee Dick Sterling, built a beautifully-crafted log bunkhouse. The Forest Service currently houses a museum in this structure. Dick's wife Bonnie wrote the book *The Sterling Years*, a biography of their lives in the backcountry with several stories related to Kirkwood.

From Kirkwood, the Bud Wilson family ran the ranch for thirty-five years, until 1973, when the government forced them out. During their ownership of Kirkwood the Wilsons also maintained homes in Nyssa and in Burley, Idaho. In Nyssa the three kids attended school and the Burley residence allowed Bud to better manage a feedlot operation that he owned. Bud and Helen continued to use these dwellings after leaving Kirkwood. Helen died in 1990, and Bud died six years later. Before their deaths, the couple, and their daughter Donna revisited the former Kirkwood home in the late 1980s at the invitation of the Forest Service. The Wilsons enjoyed the trip and donated many photographs of their time on the middle Snake River. The images are now on display in the museum.[122]

A view of the airfield during the Wilson ownership.

PITTSBURG

Early Years

Looking downstream at the mouth of Pittsburg Creek and the airstrips (lower center).

Both sides of the Snake River at this location have been a hub of activities dating back thousands of years. The large flat bars were major wintering grounds for Native Americans. By the 1880s, Mike Thomason occupied the Oregon side of the river across from the present day recreation and boat launch area. Thomason established a ferry across the river in 1891.[123] Twenty-six years later he received official homestead approval for 151.44 acres at the site.[124] Everett Marion "Jack" Titus was one of the men he hired to assist him in the ferry operation. He eventually acquired the Pittsburg Creek property.

Titus – Early Aviation

In 1916, Titus bought out Jim and Stella Wisenor's upstream holdings in the vicinity of Salt Creek and combined them into one ranch. The same year Titus married Celia, one of the Wisenor's daughters. The Tituses had one son named Robert. Celia's brother Rufe and wife Carol ended up living in Grangeville and toward the end of his life worked for Lem Wilson, the future owner of their ranch. The Tituses built a nice two-story framed house, barn, tack shed, and some other outbuildings. By the mid-1930s, they designated the bench about a half-mile above the house to the northwest as a landing field. The 1,000'-runway with an eleven percent grade was used into the 1950s. Fred or Bert Zimmerly was probably the first person to land at the ranch. The hayfield along the river near the building complex where the airfields are currently located was not used because it was considered too valuable for crops. Other early landings were made on the opposite side of the river in several different locations on the Circle C Ranch hayfields, owned by the Campbell family of New Meadows.

From the beginning, the Pittsburg airfield proved its worth. Several rescue missions were flown to and from the Titus Ranch to aid people in trouble deep in Hells Canyon. One of the first missions was to help Titus himself, when he had a stroke. Although Titus fully recovered, initially the stroke was considered very serious. With no easy way for him to reach medical attention, Bert Zimmerly Sr. flew a Travel Air 6000 to transport Titus to the Lewiston hospital. Flying with Zimmerly was Dr. John E. Carssow and *Lewiston Morning Tribune* reporter J. Clarence Moore. Moore wrote an adventurous version of the occasion for the paper. A few years later, parts of the article were transcribed along with other accounts of Zimmerly's heroic aerial feats in Robert G. Bailey's colorful book *Hell's Canyon: Seeing Idaho Through A Scrap Book.*

Zimmerly and other early canyon pilots must have made an immense impression on the young Bob Titus growing up at the remote ranch, as he too became a pilot. In January 1942, as a junior at the University of Idaho he and a friend decided to fly from Moscow to the ranch. The friend, who was flying the single engine Luscombe Model 8A (NC23091), attempted to land in about a foot of

(top) *The Titus ranch house in 1948.*
(center) *Celia and Robert Titus at Pittsburg Creek in 1925.*
(bottom) *Boatman Kyle McGrady hauling the wrecked Luscombe from Pittsburg on his boat the Idaho.*
(top opposite) *A current view of the Pittsburg airfields. The original landing area is situated perpendicular to the river [to the right and above the building complex] in the center of the photograph.*
(bottom opposite) *A close-up of the original upper bench airfield.*

snow in the upper field. On landing, the wheels of the plane caught and flipped the aircraft over. Neither boy was injured, but they had to travel by horse to White Bird and catch a ride back to school. The wings were removed from the damaged airplane and loaded onto the front of Kyle McGrady's boat the *Idaho*. The fuselage was then hoisted onto the bow of the vessel, stood on its nose, and taken to Lewiston.[125] It is interesting to note that the same day Titus wrecked, nineteen Army Air Force airplanes were involved in accidents in the United States alone, the same week one other civilian airplane from Spokane wrecked on landing in Grangeville. Newspaper and radio headlines were consumed by the crash of TWA Flight 3, a DC-3 (NC1946) that killed actress Carole Lombard just three days before the Titus accident.

Explorer Amos Burg

Famous Explorer Amos Burg – Partial Party Rescued by Air

Amos Burg pulled together his third assault by boat down the rugged center section of the middle Snake River in September 1944. Burg was the first person to conquer the entire river from source to mouth with a canoe in 1925 – a feat he tackled solo, with the exception of John Mullins, whom he hired to guide him through the upper section of Hells Canyon. Burg, a well-educated journalist, successfully funded his excursions by selling photographs to major railroad companies, lecturing about his travels, working for the National Geographic Society, and producing educational films for companies such as Encyclopaedia Britannica. He made many first descent-type trips down other noteworthy western rivers – the Green, the Colorado, and the Columbia. Later in his life, he traveled the world while completing various assignments. Burg retired to Alaska where he died in 1986. His incredible life has been the subject of many articles and Vince Welch's book *The Last Voyageur: Amos Burg and the Rivers of the West.*

On Burg's third trip down Hells Canyon in 1944, he brought with him three men of equally impressive status. The first was Dr. Russell "Doc"

Frazier who had served as the physician for Admiral Richard Byrd on the third Antarctic expedition to Little America in 1939–41, for which he received a congressional medal in 1947. At the time, the adventuresome river-loving Frazier was the chief physician and surgeon for the Utah Copper Company (mining) in Bingham Canyon, Utah. The second was Charles Wheeler, a wealthy man from San Francisco with a long list of honorary memberships and involvement with organizations dealing with big industry and international shipping. At the time of the river trip, he was the executive vice-president of Pope and Talbot, Inc., a large lumber company with divisions in land and steamships. The third was A. W. Patterson of Seattle, whom Burg knew through Puget Sound boating connections, and who allowed Burg to moor his personally owned ocean-going sailboat the *Endeavour* at his private residence.[126] Although not an aviator, when Burg refurbished the 1909 *Endeavour* in 1946 he utilized a Boeing B-17

Plexiglas nose piece to cover the cockpit of the boat, protecting him from rain and spray. The prominent dome extending from the deck was noticeable in several pictures appearing in Burg's 1947 *National Geographic* article, "Endeavour Sails the Inside Passage."

To run Hells Canyon the group launched at Huntington, Oregon, and planned to exit the river at Lewiston. Each of the men had their own boats, all in the twelve-foot range and constructed with wood and canvas, with the exception of Patterson who rowed a scant six-foot rubber raft. The group promptly ran into delays caused by problems with the boats. Frazier's boat was quickly damaged. Field repairs were made, but inadequate. The vessel was replaced with a fourteen-foot boat bought from a ferryman near Homestead. The rubber boat also had issues navigating through the large rapids. Compounding issues occurred again with Frazier's second boat. In spite of the problems, the group had a marvelous time. Burg much enjoyed reconnecting with river dwellers he had met from the previous two trips. With the boat issues and their leisurely pace, they began to run several days behind their estimated arrival in Lewiston. When the prominent men failed to show on the expected date, Wheeler's family and business associates informed the Army Air Force.[127] This was likely done because Wheeler was heavily involved in wartime manufacturing.

Responding to the Wheeler family's concerns, the Army Air Force notified Zimmerly Air Transport in Clarkston who had a contract with the military for operating a Civilian Pilot Training Program (CPTP). The Zimmerly's dispatched pilot Ivan Gustin for the task. On September 28, Gustin took off in a Fairchild M62B (PT23) (NC37172) trainer, powered with a rare Warner radial engine, and flew upriver. After about forty minutes into the flight Gustin spotted the stragglers between Sluice Rapid and the Titus Ranch.[128] According to Burg's account of the event, Gustin swooped down so low that he could see him waving from the cockpit. In reply, Burg gave him a smile and a thumbs-up.[129] Through the Tituses, arrangements were made for Zimmerly to fly in and pick up Wheeler and Patterson. It took the group seven days to boat from Homestead to the Titus Ranch. The next morning two Zimmerly Piper Cubs

were sent to fly the men out to Clarkston. Gustin flew one of the Cubs (NC23276). From Clarkston, Wheeler and Patterson flew on to Portland in a large chartered airplane.[130] Several days later, Burg and Frazier arrived safely in Lewiston.

More Boaters Rescued

Dr. Willis B. Merriam, a geology professor from Washington State College, arranged a multiday raft trip for students in August 1947. The purpose of the outing was to study geological features and obtain photographs for educational purposes. The group, comprised of Merriam and three students, launched at Homestead and made it four days before the loss of one boat forced them off the river at Pittsburg Landing. The quartet was divided into two rubber rafts. When one boat was overturned in a rapid everything but the cameras and a broom, vanished. The broom was being used as a makeshift rudder. Without sufficient rations, a call was made to Grangeville for help. Grangeville Air Service pilot and owner George Foster flew in and rescued the group. Regarding Foster's efforts, Dr. Merriam stated in the *Spokane Daily Chronicle* that it was, "The greatest piloting I have ever seen." Even with the upset the trip was considered to be a success as sixty-five "color slides" were obtained "showing the geographically important Snake river area."[131]

The Lem and Doris Wilson Family

Lem and Doris Wilson bought the Titus ranch in 1951 for $150,000 plus the Wilson's Nyssa home and land. The sale included the ranch at Pittsburg, one band of sheep, and 150 Herefords. The Tituses lived for a time at the Wilson's former house. Jack died of heart problems in 1953. In the end, Celia moved to Durkee, Oregon, where she lived the remainder of her life with the assistance of her son Bob. Celia died in October 1966.

Over time the Wilsons acquired more land; twenty-three old homesteads that covered 4,318 acres, all on the Oregon side. The Wilsons and their two sons, Ray, age eight, and Gary, age two, moved to the old Titus residence in March 1951. Celia assured Doris, who had never seen the place, that it was a tidy well-kept house and yard. However, Doris and Celias' ideas of good housekeeping were apparently far apart. Undiscouraged, Doris and Lem took it with a grain of salt and improved the place greatly over the next several years.[132]

Once the Wilsons became comfortable at Pittsburg, they bought a second home in Grangeville so Ray and Gary could attend school. Five years later, son Gerald Mickey was born. From time to time people were hired to watch the main ranch house while the Wilsons were attending to other parts of the operation or were in town. In their absence, a caretaker accidently built too large a fire and burned the house down in 1961. Construction on a new home began right away. The Forest Service presently uses this modern house. The same year the new home went up Ray graduated from Grangeville High School. He married Donna Fine and officially became a business partner with his father. The operation became Lem Wilson & Son. Several years later, brother Gary and his wife Ellen also joined the business, making it Lem Wilson & Sons. By the time the youngest son Mick finished college the controversy over developing the NRA had begun.[133]

Lem and Doris led the charge, fighting alongside canyon neighbors to keep their land. The Wilsons became very vocal advocates against federal condemnation and were often the subject of

The Wilson's home built in 1961.

regional newspaper headlines and feature articles. While the parties tried to determine what the land was actually worth, another controversy arose. The government only wanted to pay appraised value for rangeland. The landowners' argument was that it was worth far more and needed to be appraised as recreation land. The government balked, claiming the value was actually very little. The simple question from landowners was - why then do you want our land for its recreational values?

While the Wilsons worked on building a strong case that argued for recreation-based appraisal values, Lem decided to really kick a hornet's nest. He arranged to subdivide parcels of land near his Salt Creek in-holdings. The pro-NRA conservation groups were outraged. The Wilsons received aggressive calls and letters about the proposed land divisions. Doris noted in her memoir, "News traveled quickly, and we were soon being threatened by various environmental groups telling us what scoundrels we were to let anyone build cabins along the Snake River. On one such occasion we received a call from southern Idaho telling what dire things were going to happen to us if we didn't stop. Lem told them he would meet them at the Wallowa County Courthouse the following Monday as he had two more sales to record. However, they didn't show up."[134] Lem voiced privately the only reason he was creating the subdivisions was to prove the ground was worth far more than the government was willing to pay, and it would serve as a comparative sale, boosting the assessed value.[135] Whatever the reasoning, the conservation organizations persuaded Congress that the commercialization of the middle Snake should be prevented. To ensure that no further development could occur, Congress appropriated four million dollars to buy the privately owned lands.

When condemnation became imminent, each individual owner had to battle out the final price in local courts with local juries – a situation that really tended to favor the landowners. The Wilson's attorneys did their best. The lawyers even convinced Ted Trueblood, a well-known Idaho author and outdoor authority, to testify about the scenic values of Hells Canyon and the remote river corridor. The Wilsons hired independent land appraisers and a professional photographer who were flown by Ted Grote in a helicopter all over their Hells Canyon holdings. After a week in court and two hours of jury deliberations, the Wilsons were awarded far more than the original offer.[136]

Post-trial, the Wilsons moved out of their adored Snake River home on Pittsburg Creek to Ontario, Oregon. Settling into their retired life they were surprised one day when the Forest Service served them with a notice requiring all farm machinery be removed from the ranch. Lem explained he would only do so with proper compensation. The agency agreed and paid him $35,000. It was no easy task considering their former land contained over twenty homesteads with active use of over seventy years accumulation of equipment. With boats, horses, and trucks, Lem and his sons moved it all out of the canyon.[137] Lem died at age eighty-seven in January 2006. Doris lived three more years dying at age eighty-eight in April 2009. Prior to her death, she published an autobiography of their lives at the ranch entitled *Life in Hells Canyon: A Private View*. They are both buried in the Grangeville Prairie View Cemetery.

The Wilson sons also stayed in Oregon.

Mick established himself in La Grande. Ray bought a ranch in Pine Valley and operated it until 1980. He continued to outfit some in Hells Canyon, but mainly moved in to the Eagle Cap Wilderness area. By 1981, Ray had relocated to Baker City. He eventually worked his way to Wallowa County and was employed on various ranches. One of his life's hobbies has been leathercraft – working and tooling leather. Following his passion, he started Wilson's Saddlery in 2003.[138] Working in Joseph, Ray custom builds incredible saddles, bridles, chaps, halters, and everything in between.

Pilot Lem Wilson

Unquestionably, Lem Wilson became one of the most distinguished pilots of Hells Canyon. Although most people remember him as a larger-than-life man wearing a big cowboy hat, his enormously tall physique seemed to fit perfectly into the cockpit of a Super Cub. And the Super Cub seemed to fit him – durable, tough, and rugged. Wilson landed his

R. WILSON

Lem Wilson and his brother Bud with a Super Cub.

The result of high winds at Mormon Flat. The wind was so severe the concrete tie-downs were pulled out of the ground.

Cubs in probably more places in the middle Snake River country than any other pilot and without major mishaps. Wilson started flying in the mid-1950s and retired his wings in 1980 after logging more than 7,000 hours in the canyon alone.[139]

When Wilson decided he wanted to learn to fly, he joined the local Grangeville flying organization called the "Solar Club." Travis Wadley, who worked part-time at Grangeville Air Service, gave him instruction in an Aeronca Champion. Wilson wanted his license to help ease the commute from town to the ranch and to help look for lost sheep and cattle. At the ranch headquarters, Wilson did not use the Titus's upper bench landing area, but instead took off directly from the main house across the hayfield (a taxi area today).[140]

The more he flew, the more and more he realized what a valuable tool the airplane was to the ranch. Not to mention, he loved every minute of flying. With success, but little experience, Wilson started pushing the boundaries of his flying skills and began landing in difficult places. He became enamored with what the airplane could do. Other members of the flying club questioned what he was doing after he wiped the gear off one of the

organization's airplanes. He understood their concerns, but nothing was going to stop him – so he bought his own Champion. No one could tell him what he could or could not do with his own plane.[141]

The Aeronca Champ was a fine airplane, but when he came in contact with his first Super Cub he knew he had found the machine for his needs. After flying one, he bought a brand new model with large tires and the biggest motor available. The Super Cub became a fixture of the ranch and when the motor timed out, requiring a rebuild, he traded it in for a new one. In due time he ran out three motors, equaling three new Cubs.[142]

In the summer the airplane was used habitually to supply summer sheep camps along the upper rim of the canyon. To supply one particular band of sheep the Wilsons used the Horse Creek Cabin, which was located on Forest Service land. They kept a Jeep at Memaloose, to reach the spot. When the agency removed the cabin, the Wilsons built a replacement on private ground near Schaffer Spring.[143]

Several years into his flying career, Wilson found a whole new purpose for his airplanes. He and his sons started an outfitting business, the T-Bar Ranch, named in honor of their brand. Multiple camps were set up across the ranch and adjoining Forest Service land. Wilson landed all over the place, including: Teaser Ridge, Coffee Pot Springs, Mormon Flat, and Palace. The last two locations were the only places Wilson had significant issues with an airplane, other than losing a number of tailwheels. At Mormon Flat, one of his Cubs was flipped over on its back while it was parked in sixty-plus mile an hour winds – even though he had roped it to concrete tie-downs. Wilson nosed an airplane over in a draw along Deep Creek near the Palace or "Palisades" (named because of the circle shaped landscape). This was probably the trickiest spot he ever landed. On the particular occasion of the accident, Ray had requested Lem to fly in his hounds to help track a problem cougar that was killing sheep. Lem managed to squeeze the airplane into the tight steep drainage where he then unloaded the dogs and gear. To position the plane for a takeoff required a steep uphill taxi. As the power was added to get up the mountain, the main wheels of the Cub hit a hole causing the craft to tip over on the engine. Surprisingly, the mud was so thick and soft where the propeller spun in, no damage occurred. After wrestling the plane out of the mud hole, Lem took off.[144]

In addition to hauling meat, supplies, employees, and customers to and from hunting camps, the airplanes were also used to scout hunting grounds and big game. Often in the months leading up to the opening of hunting season, Lem and his sons would scout out the best deer and elk herds. Years later after Lem retired from flying, Ray hired a pilot to do some reconnaissance and was disappointed. The reason for his dissatisfaction was the pilot would not fly low enough to see anything. He had never thought about it until that moment, but his father would literally, "Just crawl up a drainage, right above the trees, and then make a tight turn at the top and work his way back down, over and over."[145]

Tragedy

Misfortune struck the Wilson family in June 1972. Gary and Ray departed from the main ranch in a boat headed downstream for Christmas Creek. Shortly after leaving, the motor quit. Lem had helped push them off and watched the event unfold. Before the motor could be restarted the boat turned in an unfavorable direction into a rapid, swamped, bobbed to the surface, and then capsized. Lem, knowing he could not accomplish anything from the shore, ran to his airplane and took off with the hope of being able to land downstream and retrieve his two sons. Meantime, Floyd Harvey and Earl Pea came by in a boat and found Ray clinging to a gas can. Gary could not be found. Friends and family organized a search with boats and airplanes. The high muddy water hindered their attempts. In desperation to find his son, Lem hired a man to camp at the mouth of Somers Creek and keep watch. About three weeks later, Gary's body surfaced.[146]

The untimely death of the Wilson's twenty-three year old son paralleled the tragedy that boatman Kyle McGrady endured after losing his son on the river nearly twenty-five years earlier. McGrady ran the weekly Snake River mail service from 1938 through 1950. He was adored by his customers and became quite well known regionally by reputation and through magazine and newspaper articles. During a nice Sunday cruise with passengers aboard the *Florence*, the river was high with spring runoff and the usual debris. Trying to power through Wild Goose Rapids, the boat operator hit a submerged log, damaging both propellers. McGrady's eighteen-year-old son Kenneth and deckhand Bill DeVault jumped off the boat with a rope in an attempt to tie it around a hackberry tree. The effort was foiled. Fighting the fast flowing current, DeVault hung on to the line and was helped back to the boat. Kenneth could not make it, but did manage to stay on the island. The current swept the crippled boat downriver, and McGrady yelled to his son to stay put.[147]

As in the Wilson accident, an air search was started. McGrady hired Bert Zimmerly Sr. to fly him to the island in a floatplane. Zimmerly and McGrady landed the Cessna 140 (NC2517N) and taxied up to the island and searched. With no luck they continued flying up and down the river. After nearly seven hours of flying and fighting darkness, they returned to Lewiston.[148] It is believed Kenneth tried to swim to the distant shore and walk out. Days of aerial and ground searches followed. His body was found weeks later at White Salmon on the Columbia River. After the heartbreaking event, McGrady gave up. He left the river and Lewiston in 1950 and moved to Pasco.[149]

Doris Wilson voiced similar discontent in her

autobiography. For her it was doubly difficult. Faced with the loss of a child and the loss of their home in the government condemnation process she noted, "In one way it was a relief to carry on as naturally as we could at Pittsburg. We could still be 'at home' in our house. We had all contributed in making it a home . . . We still had our horses and mules and Lem and Ray could schedule hunting tips for deer and elk hunters. But our hearts had been broken by the loss of Gary . . ."[150]

Current Pittsburg Airfields

When the Forest Service took over the Wilson's land and main ranch headquarters at Pittsburg, they wanted to continue air access. Although Wilson had used the lower field as a landing site since he bought the place, nothing formally indicated where to land. In an attempt to make the field available for public use, the Forest Service decided it needed to be better defined and properly marked. The agency consulted with Bud Stangel, one of their primary contract pilots, to help layout the first airstrip. However, Stangel, always the optimist, suggested the best place for a runway was on the Idaho side of the river where the current parking and launch site are located.

The fairly well marked 850'-runway, plus the unusable taxiing stretch to the house, remained the lone option until two accidents occurred in the late 1980s that caused pilots to rethink the configuration. The first accident occurred in February. A husband and wife flying a Super Cub attempted an upstream approach and badly bounced it on landing. Determining they did not have enough room, full power was added for a go-around. The right wing of the plane stalled, dipped, and amazingly held together as the plane fell out of the sky back to the runway. The right wing tip dug into the ground creating a pivot point that swung the plane in an arc before coming to a complete stop. With a damaged wing and bent tail the Cub was disassembled and boated across the river. It was then placed on a trailer and hauled to Lewiston. The second accident occurred within two years of the first. The pilot flying a Stinson Station Wagon tried to land downriver to the north and came in too fast. Instead of trying a go-around, he forced it on the ground about halfway down the runway, locked the brakes, and flipped.

Reassessing the problem at Pittsburg – beyond the common deduction of pilot error – several aviators discussed aligning a cross runway more to the southwest-northeast. Local pilot Rusty Bentz acted on the idea and simply mowed the grass to make it happen. Later, the Forest Service made it more pronounced. Although shorter, this 800'-runway tends to work better for stopping and taking off with heavy loads, since it has a nice upslope on the south end. The alignment also favors the most common wind pattern, where the air generally flows down the small draw above the open field.

WILSON

104

R. BENTZ

(top and center) Two of the accidents occurring in the 1980s that helped catalyze a change in the airfield facility.
(bottom) An upstream view of the cross runways at Pittsburg.
(opposite) An example of the many accidents at Pittsburg creatively hauled out of the canyon.

R. BENTZ

HOLM

SOMERS CREEK RANCH

R. WILSON

Lem Wilson landing at Somers Creek

Frank Somers began using this site in the 1880s, mainly eking out a living here through various mining ventures.[151] He earned homestead approval for 160 acres in February 1906.[152] Somers sold the property six years later to Elbert B. "Dad" Wilson.[153] Wilson and his wife raised seven children on the creek. Frank (Wilson), one of three boys, took over the ranch. Apparently his father fell on hard times and could not keep up with the bank payments. Frank married Minnie Kelly who grew up on the Idaho side of the river along Wolf Creek. The two lived here several years and raised daughters Darlene and Shirley. Son-in-law Jim Renshaw recalled, "Frank lost his left leg as a young man in a horse accident. This caused him to always mount a horse from the wrong side and it tended to work. Minnie was not only his left leg, but his right arm as well. She was very supportive." The grazing ground was expanded in 1943 when the family acquired the Christmas Creek Ranch. Not long thereafter, Frank and Minnie sold the Somers Creek property to Jess and Alice Earl and worked for them for a short time before moving to Clarkston.[154]

In Clarkston, the couple bought and managed an apartment complex. While the low-elevation town was a great place to spend the winter, the Wilsons loved the mountains and found seasonal work on the Clearwater NF. Frank ran a pack string and Minnie and Shirley stood watch for two seasons at End Butte Lookout, beginning in 1947. After a few summers working for the government, the Wilsons started their own outfitting business in the Selway-Bitterroot Primitive Area where their base of operations varied among Moose Creek Ranger Station, Moose Creek Ranches, Selway Lodge, or Fish Lake. They sold the outfitting business to son-in-law Jim Renshaw and daughter Darlene who built it up as one of the more reputable operations in the Idaho backcountry. Relieved of their business, the Wilsons worked for the Renshaws and for their other son-in-law Gerald Ritchie, who outfitted on the upper Selway from Paradise. Frank and Minnie lived the remainder of their years in Clarkston. Frank died at age seventy-seven.[155]

Lem and Doris Wilson (unrelated) acquired the property in the 1950s and joined it with their Pittsburg headquarters. The Forest Service obtained the land during the creation of the NRA, and the original Somers structures burned in a wildland fire.

When the Lem Wilson family first incorporated this area into their grazing operations they used the Somers homestead buildings regularly in the spring and winter. Ray Wilson noted, "The Somers Creek Place was one of the most elaborate homesteads in the country. It had a separate kitchen, living area, and a couple of bedrooms. For the first few years we were there we even hayed the fields and put it up."[156] Lem generally accessed the property by airplane, landing in the small meadow on the north side of the creek near the house. He even installed a set of tie-downs on the upper end. The largest plane to land here was a Cessna 206 piloted by Bud Stangel. Apparently Lem hired Stangel to fly in a full load of fence posts figuring it was more cost efficient than several small loads in one of his Super Cubs.[157]

Looking down Somers Creek at the landing area. An aft view of Lem Wilson's Super Cub is visible in the center of the photograph.

R. WILSON

A Word on the Piper Cub

By Dick Williams

Former safety editor of the Super Cub Pilots Association

When talking about backcountry planes, several classics come to mind: DeHavilland Beavers and Otters, Ford Tri-Motors, Travel Air 6000s, Cessna 185s and 206s, and maybe a Britten-Norman Islander. But perhaps the most classic of all in the Hells Canyon country of Oregon and Idaho, if not the most venerable, is the trusty Piper Cub. First designed in the 1930s with the J-series, it had a light frame covered with fabric, a two-seat tandem configuration, and engines ranging from forty-five to eighty-five horsepower. They were relatively cheap and utile, with slow stall speeds that allowed pasture and other short-field operations.

After World War II the Js were followed by the PA-series. The marquee of this model was introduced in 1949 and designated as the Super Cub. It was essentially a grown-up J-3, a little beefier all around, with of course more power (135 hp motor). The Super Cub has had an integral history with any bush or backcountry operation, but they became the principal pair of wings commercial operators and ranchers used on the short rocky landing patches of the middle Snake River region. The Super Cub was indeed the backbone of aviation in that area, for often the airstrips were never improved beyond the potential of a Super Cub. Their short-field capabilities were unmatched, making them the first choice of pilots everywhere when a new field was to be tested, whether it was on a steep mountainside or a river gravel bar. Every early backcountry pilot has flown a Cub at some time or another.

However, these early Cubs were vastly different than the highly modified versions seen winging their way through the canyon today. A portion of the stock Cub's success can be attributed to the pilot's skills and abilities. The Cubs of the middle Snake River pioneer flying days generally sported stock tires, brakes, power plants, propellers, wings, etc. But perhaps, the very essence of the plane is that it lends itself to extensive modifications, which makes it unique. Comparatively, other classic backcountry machines have seen very few modifications, except for larger engines and turbo-chargers. The Cub, on the other hand, has been "de-Piperized" to the extreme. The engines now often develop 180 to over 200 horsepower. They throw large "Borer" type propellers (Roger Borer was the holder of an STC that swapped the wimpy Sensenich stock propeller to a longer, beefier McCauley model). One popular mod even changes the thrust angle of the motor by changing the firewall attachment! The landing gear can be beefed up, with safety cables to help hold it in place if the landing area is so unimproved things break. Oversized low pressure "tundra" or "bush" tires enable the little plane to roll over holes or rocks of a substantial size that would break standard size tires and wheels. The puny diaphragm style brakes can even be replaced with high-pressure disc brakes. The original configuration of the joystick located on the right, throttle on the left, and challenging heel brakes has mostly stayed true. Conversions to toe brakes are often considered "bad form" by Cub purists.

Safety alterations, such as wing strut reinforcements, cross braces over the pilot's head, header-less fuel systems, and inertial reel shoulder harnesses, are also popular.

And of course, the interior of the aircraft has been modified to carry more gear, and sometimes allow even some creature comforts! A few hard-core Cub owners strip them down like a racing car, with virtually no interior, electrical, or starting equipment. They might weigh less than a thousand pounds empty, with a minimum of 180 horsepower. The result is an impressive power to weight ratio! The revered Cub wing, however, has actually seen little improvement with the exception of vortex generators. The wing has been played with a lot including extensions, longer flaps, longer ailerons, cuffed leading edges, and wingtips. But many pilots, when all is said and done, prefer little to no mods to the wings.

Make no mistake. These highly modified Super Cubs of today are nothing like the Super Cubs involved in the aviation history of Hells Canyon. What the pioneers did with their little stock machines is remarkable.

Bud Stangel with his favorite Super Cub on a middle Snake River airstrip.

LORD FLAT

General History and Airstrip

Looking down the 2,100' Lord Flat runway.

The Lord Flat area has a long history as a federal grazing allotment and outfitter camp permitted by the Forest Service. From the 1930s through the early 1970s, the various owners of the Tryon Ranch held both the Lord Flat outfitter and grazing permits. In 1927, cattleman Jim Dorrance bought the ranch. Dorrance, the youngest of eight kids, grew up on Cow Creek near Joseph. He and his brothers had a reputation as excellent horsemen, particularly brother Tom who has been the subject of several books. Dorrance lived in the vicinity of Lord Flat during the summers. For living quarters he had a cabin built in 1933, two miles to the south, now known as "Dorrance Cow Camp." Dorrance left the Snake River country in the fall of 1943 and eventually moved to Nevada. Accomplished in his career as a rancher in Nevada and California, he moved to Enterprise and lived his last years with daughter Phyllis. He died at age ninety in 1990.

Dorrence's friend Frank Wilson of Somers Creek ran cattle on the Lord Flat range for a few years during World War II. The Blankenship brothers followed Wilson and, like him, used the high range in the summer. They also established a commercial outfitting camp at the site in the fall. Clientele were housed at the Cow Camp Cabin and people were occasionally flown in via the airstrip.

Approximately four to five years after Dorrance's move to Nevada, the Forest Service began developing plans for the Lord Flat airstrip.[158] Roads constructed in to the area during the 1930s lacked improvement, making for time-consuming travel. Also none of the roads were directly connected to Lord Flat. Still today, with a capable modern vehicle, it is roughly a two-and-half-hour drive from Memaloose to the site. The agency's rationale for the remote airfield was to allow prompt access to the area for administrative and fire control needs.

Tom Willett and Joe Conner contracted with the Forest Service to build the current 2,100' north-south airstrip at 5,300' MSL. Willett owned and operated Cedar Hill Farm, a Grade-A dairy, in Wallowa, Oregon. Soon after acquiring the dairy in 1941, he hired friend and grocery store owner Joe Conner for extra help. The two also farmed together on the side. In need of a tractor with implements, Willett bought

a new International TD-18 crawler equipped with a hydraulic Isaacson blade. Separate from use on the farm, the machine was in demand with the Forest Service, as many of the heavy pieces of equipment in Wallowa County during the post-World War II era were dedicated to logging activities. Willett noticed the need and became a regular freelancer with the agency, taking on tasks such as the construction of the right-of-way up the Lostine River.[159]

For the airstrip project the Forest Service assigned packer Alvie Keeler to assist Willett and Conners on walking the machine out to Lord Flat. Keeler rode ahead on a horse picking the best route. The TD-18 pulled a five-yard carryall attached to the back with a draw-pin. The carryall was packed with cans of extra diesel and all their camp equipment. Conners sat amongst these items for most of the trip. On one steep incline, the draw-pin came loose sending the carryall and Conners plunging down a mountainside. It was a wild ride, but Conners escaped unscathed. The runaway piece of equipment was winched up and reattached.[160]

Once a good portion of the field was cleared, arrangements were made with pilot Ray Dunsmore to fly in and re-supply the crew with diesel fuel. Over the course of the undertaking, Dunsmore flew several loads of fuel in. But the first takeoff on the short incomplete runway was interesting. In order to keep enough flying speed he had to pitch the plane down off the end of the strip into the drainage of Deep Creek.[161]

Double O Bar Years

The Tryon Ranch and associated range permits at Lord Flat were acquired by a group of Oregon businessmen under the name Double O Bar, circa 1966. Cal Henry ran the operation for the majority of the corporation's ownership starting in 1968. In the beginning, Henry used the Dorrance Cow Camp Cabin on a year-to-year permit basis with the Forest Service. After a few years, the Forest Service wanted the cabin for administrative purposes, forcing Henry to establish a camp on the east side of the airfield.[162]

Some of the best hunters Henry had in his camp were Jim Teeny and his relatives and friends. Teeny, the founder of Teeny Nymph Company (now

C. HENRY

The cabin at the Dorrance Cow Camp in the mid-1970s. Outfitter Cal Henry's kids (Tammie and Jason) are standing below the entrance they helped their father build from a massive burl packed in on a mule.

Jim Teeny Inc.) created and patented several popular flies for fishing – the most known is the "Teeny Nymph Fly." Generally, a group of ten would come in and they were such good hunters Henry just ran a pack string for them. Regarding that era and quality of hunting at Lord Flat Henry reminisced, "The Teeny's really put a dent in the trophy population. But still the deer herds were thick . . . on the first day of hunting for each party I could show clients twenty to twenty-five nice bucks, it was just a matter of taking your pick."[163]

The area around the Lord Flat airstrip was a focal point not only for Henry and his patrons, but also for private hunters. In the late 1960s and early 1970s, the herds were enormous and full of excellent animals. Naturally everyone wanted to hunt there, but hunters became frustrated easily because of the number of people attracted to the spot and moved elsewhere the next year. Illustrating the fluctuation, Henry counted twenty-seven private airplanes parked at Lord Flat on opening day one year – the next year only about five or six airplanes showed up. The uneven surface of the airfield also may have deterred a few pilots from returning. One fall, Henry made a trip to town and returned several days later only to find three wrecked airplanes. Nobody was around, but he surmised two crashed on takeoff and the third collapsed a gear on landing. All three were later disassembled and trucked out.[164]

An Easy Hunt – With a Hard Exit

Pilot Bud Stangel exclusively flew for Henry at the ranch and for the outfitting business. Over the years, the two became close friends. Generally toward the end of each hunting season, Stangel flew in with his sons for a short hunt. Henry commonly had a few nice elk picked out for them. After the Stangels filled their tags, Henry packed the meat to the airstrip and sent the party out.[165]

On one of the annual hunts the winter snow came unexpectedly early. Since Henry and his guides still had to drive a pickup and trail the stock out, they offered to lighten the load in Stangel's Cessna 206 and pack the meat of three elk back to Enterprise. Some discussion ensued, and Stangel liked the idea of having less weight in the airplane for a wheel takeoff in the snowy conditions. Not thinking much about it, Henry rode out with Stangel and the next day drove to the Hat Point area where he planned to meet his crew. Along the way, Henry encountered deep snow and realized his employees were likely not going to be able to drive out of Lord Flat, so he returned back to town. His intuition turned out to be correct. When he did not hear from the crew, he and Stangel scouted the road with a Piper Cub and spotted the pickup mired down. His hired hands had accidently slid the pickup off the road and walked back to camp. Henry hired Ted Grote with a

Bud Stangel preparing for takeoff at Lord Flat in a Cessna 180.

Landing uphill at Lord Flat.

helicopter to fly in and haul out his men and the meat stowed in the bed of the pickup. Henry returned a few days later on horseback with a mule packed with come-alongs, chains, and a handyman jack. After many hours of backbreaking work, he inched the vehicle up to the road and decided to park it at the Lord Flat airstrip for the winter.[166]

When the snow retreated from the mountaintops the next year, Stangel flew Henry to Lord Flat to recover the pickup. At first site the truck appeared to be fine, but one glance in the cab revealed animals had destroyed the entire interior. Trying to stay positive, Henry decided he could still drive it back to town. However, the darn thing would not start. In fact, it did not even make a sound when he turned the key in the ignition switch. As the two began to troubleshoot the problem, they discovered that critters had eaten and removed every ounce of wire in the vehicle! Stangel, a mechanical and electrical master, later returned with the necessary tools and parts and re-wired the minimum components of the truck to get it running for the trip to town.[167]

Recent History

The airstrip became the main avenue of access to the Lord Flat area as the Forest Service closed all but one rough road to motor vehicles in 1985.[168] Although a single road remained open to motorized use, it was restricted to non-motorized use during big game hunting season. This controversial road was primarily constructed by the agency to fight the Pony Bar Fire on the east side of Summit Ridge in 1960. The Forest Service decided to leave it in place and open it to motorized vehicles to provide better access to the Lord Flat airstrip. However, the agency gradually began to refer to it, not as a road, but as the "Lord Flat Trail." Three years after the Hells Canyon NRA was created, a large wilderness area was designated within it. Even though the airstrip and camp were not inside the wilderness, one and a half miles of the motorized road dipped into it. In an effort to please both motorized user groups and wilderness advocates the Forest Service realigned the road. However, the Hells Canyon Preservation Council filed a lawsuit against the agency claiming it failed to recognize the proper wilderness boundary, and therefore was in violation of the Wilderness Act. Following a decade of court proceedings, the Forest Service thumped the lawsuit, and thus the road remains open.[169]

Similar to the road, the airstrip surface is arduous. Even though the strip is plenty long and has an easygoing open approach and departure, the surface is anything but smooth – mainly appears as an unimproved field that is vaguely defined along the sides by large white painted boulders. The runway ends are not well marked. In recent years, the Wallowa County Pilots Association and the IAA have worked with the Forest Service to provide as much voluntary maintenance as possible. In the early 2010s, the runway was disked, leveled, and reseeded twice. At the same time a new windsock was installed. At present, the field is still best suited for conventional gear airplanes.

Aero Commander Wreckage

A few pieces of a crashed Aero Commander 500-B (N5080) remain visible about six air miles northwest of the airstrip on a leeward ridge toward the Snake River. The plane actually crashed about a half mile from this location, but several parts were accidently dropped here by the helicopter pilot in charge of the salvage operation. The Aero Commander, owned by Combs Airways of Billings, Montana, was lost from radar on the night of December 18, 1968 and deemed missing for months.

The plane, piloted by forty-three year old Eugene Whittlesey of Spokane was on a routine charter flight from Boise to Spokane carrying mail for the US Postal Service. Before radio contact was lost, Whittlesey reported a loss of engine power caused by icing conditions. A several week search ensued for the lost plane, but it was not found before winter set in.[170] In a strange set of circumstances Combs Airways lost another pilot in an Aero Commander (N6281X) the same night. The pilot of this aircraft knowingly attempted a takeoff on a snowy runway with an inoperative left magneto on the left engine. Banking on the health of the right engine for takeoff turned out to be disastrous, as one of the cylinder exhaust valves on the right engine fell apart just prior to rotation causing it to lose all power. Reacting to the partial power loss the pilot aborted the takeoff, but the plane went down an embankment and killed the pilot on impact.

Whittlesey and his Aero Commander were spotted the following spring by a passing airplane when the snow melted. Ted Grote was hired to recover the body and landed at the accident site on March 22, 1969 with a helicopter. After a thorough examination of the wreckage, Grote found a loose fuel cap hanging by the catch chain. He also observed that no fuel was present in the tanks of the plane. The FAA later released several other facts that reaffirmed the accident was caused by fuel exhaustion. The pilot voiced concern to Air Traffic Control (ATC) early in the flight that he was consuming fuel at an alarming rate. Secondly, it was confirmed Whittlesey had fueled the aircraft himself before departing from Boise.[171]

Following the discovery of the accident, the Lewiston postmaster chartered Grote to fly him to the scene of the accident to retrieve the mail. The postal employees were boated to Dug Bar and Grote airlifted them to the wreckage that had impacted a forty-degree sloping mountainside. The *Spokane Daily Chronicle* wrote that the plane had large volumes of Christmas mail aboard, most of it bound for Lewiston.[172] One remarkable oddity of the crash involved Ralph Longfellow, a former Snake River rancher who owned land miles from the accident site. He had sent several Holiday greeting cards via mail days before the crash. His mail ended up on Whittlesey's plane. Longfellow's relatives in Lewiston finally received the cards in March after they were salvaged from the wreckage and delivered. Even adding another twist to the Longfellow connection is that part of a wing can still be spotted from the opposite side of the Snake River from his old ranch. It is easiest to see when the sun is shining from the east and thus illuminating the Oregon side of the river. Part of a wing is fairly visible in this light, looking northwest about two-thirds of the way up the ridge above Dug Bar.

TRYON CREEK RANCH

Early Years

C. HENRY

The Tryon Creek ranch house in 1969.

Prior to 1906 James Tryon and brother Nate settled a mile and a half up the creek that now bears their name. When the land was first surveyed the drainage was known as "Cottonwood Creek."[174] The brothers built a small two-story cabin as a base for their sheep business.[175] Charles Crader obtained the Tryon's homestead and proved up on another 120 acres adjoining the ranch in December 1917.[176] The ranch exchanged hands a few times later and for many years was owned by J. Ray Johnson.

Blankenship Brothers

Dick and Jim Blankenship bought the Tryon property after World War II. At the same time they also procured extensive stretches of land on Roland and Cat creeks (see Roland Bar). The brothers came from a family of four boys and were raised in Asotin County, Washington. Jim served in the Merchant Marines during the war and was stationed at various places between Seattle and Alaska. His older brother Dick spent his war years as an officer in England. After being honorably discharged, they wanted to get back to their ranching roots. While running the sheep operation they also partnered in several other business ventures in Joseph. Their financial partnership dissolved in the early 1960s. Dick ended up with Tryon and the associated property and Jim with the Cat Creek Ranch. Before Dick's death in 1969 he sold his ranching interests.[177]

Grote and Stangel Arrive with Planes

Similar to Roland Bar the Blankenships consulted with Ted Grote about a suitable landing spot for flying in supplies. A site was selected in a hayfield south of the old ranch house approximately two miles up the drainage from the river. Grote was the first to land an airplane at the locale in the mid-1950s.[178] Later Bud Stangel experimented with landing in several different directions on the hayfield based on wind conditions.[179]

Cal Henry – Cattle and Outfitting

In about 1966, Dick Blankenship sold the Tryon Ranch with a little less than 2,000 acres to a group of investors (all doctors or lawyers) from Portland and La Grande. Three of the men included Ed Walsh (Portland), Dr. Richard Hall, and Dr. Vanderbilt (both of La Grande). The group incorporated under the name Double O Bar and ran about 150 head of cattle and hired a manager to oversee the operation. Cal Henry of Joseph was hired for the job in 1968. Henry became acquainted with Dr. Hall and his family while guiding for Bob Blank, an Eagle Cap Wilderness outfitter, headquartered at the Boulder Park Trailhead. The Halls annually hired Blank for summer fishing trips to high mountain lakes. Henry, just out of high school, had a good rapport with Hall and worked for the group for six years at Tryon. In the summers the investors often sent their teenaged

115

Looking north-northwest at the Tryon Creek Ranch [main house center]. Pilots landed various directions in the open field in the foreground of the photograph.

children in to work on the ranch.[180]

Henry wintered at Tryon living in the old two-story house and then summered on top at Lord Flat. For the first few years the only way in and out of Tryon was via airplane with Stangel, who flew a Super Cub or Cessna 180. Later Henry acquired a small, fifteen-foot aluminum Crestliner boat with a thirty-five horsepower Evinrude motor from the Blankenships, which he kept at Dug Bar. This arrangement allowed him to drive to and from Dug Bar and boat the stretch of water upstream to Tryon Creek. He used a small International 340 tractor crawler to go back and forth between the river and the house on a rough road. Some repeat clients took pity on him having to use the slow rough running vehicle for transportation and gave him a Coot – an early articulating ATV. The clients even strapped it to their boat at Pittsburg and helped him deliver it to the ranch. "I was just a kid when I started there . . . green as a gourd,

but I slowly learned. Neighbor Lem Wilson would occasionally fly in and check on me. He even gave me a backcountry radio for communications, which was very helpful."[181]

On top of caring for the ranch Henry also ran a commercial hunting business from Tryon and Lord Flat. He kept the hunting permits a few years after the Forest Service forced the investors out due to the establishment of the NRA. Henry worked the country a few more years with hunting clients and kept a main camp at Tryon, but he was no longer able to use the cabins under Forest Service ownership. Also at this time landings at the location were made illegal. By the end of the 1970s Henry bought out outfitter Orin McRae and moved his business to the Eagle Cap Wilderness (see Red's Horse Ranch). The Forest Service continues to maintain the old Tryon homestead and uses it for administrative purposes.[182]

(top) The Tryon Creek Ranch in the 1970s.
(bottom) Cal Henry's first boat tied up below the mouth of Tryon Creek. Note the small tent frame used to house equipment that was later replaced by a permanent building.

GETTA CREEK (SMITH BROTHERS)

Smiths

Mike Foley's airstrip with the Getta Creek drainage in the background.

The Smith brothers ran a large ranch on the south end of Joseph Plains starting in the 1930s. The two brothers Justin and Roscoe "Hoot" were raised on the Palouse along with one other brother and three sisters. As young men the two ran sheep with their father Burrell "Bush." In the beginning, they grazed their sheep in the Craig Mountain area and then later along the Magruder Corridor in the summer. Hoot and Justin bought Bush's shares of the company, settled full-time on Joseph Plains, and converted to cattle by the 1940s. Justin, the oldest, managed more the business end of the operation and first married a French woman named Maxine. He later divorced and remarried Jessie Nail. Hoot married his wife Anita at an older age after he left the ranch and moved to Grangeville in 1982. Hoot died in August 2004 at age ninety-two. Justin also moved to Grangeville and then to Boise where he died in a retirement home several years before Hoot.

On a rare occasion the Smiths hired a pilot to look for cattle or haul freight. No formal landing place was developed, but pilots used a rough field just below the main house. This site was used through the 1980s.

Airstrips of Twin River Ranches Subdivision

Gerald Lindsey of LT&L, a development company, acquired the former Smith brothers' land in the early 1980s and then sold it to owners of Twin Rivers Ranch, who subdivided it. Four airstrips have been built on the part once owned by the Smiths.

Mike and Kate Foley constructed the first airstrip in November 1999 after buying the lot two years earlier. Gary Cook of Lucile, Idaho, was hired as the excavator for the 2,300'-runway. The

Foleys first came to the Idaho backcountry in the mid-1980s. They enjoyed escaping the Tri-City area of Washington on weekends to fly, camp, and recreate. Looking for more solitude, they bought land on Joseph Plains and turned it into their full-time residence. In the beginning, they used a Cessna 185 at the strip and later a Cessna 206. The latter was actually owned at one time by former neighbor Dr. Ned Schroeder.

Northeast of Foley's airstrip is the Bradley's property. Bert Bradley of Eagle, Idaho, owns the Smiths' old home and has also built an airstrip, or rather modified a road that is situated northeast-southwest to the southwest of the building complex. A small corral located on the upper end of the strip is used to keep airplanes safe from cattle.

Northwest of the former Smith Ranch headquarters is Jess Hennis's airstrip. Hennis of Nampa, flies a Cessna 180 to and from this 1,400'-airstrip. Construction began on a second airstrip that parallels the first in the summer of 2013

GETTA CREEK (JOHNSON RANCH)

The Arams

The Getta Creek drainage from the Snake River. The Slim Johnson family's former Getta Creek Ranch can be seen in the center of the photograph.

At the turn of the twentieth century the Getta Creek drainage and its tributaries were littered with dozens of families trying to prove up on land. For those that succeeded in obtaining the patent, economic conditions generally forced them out. In several cases the James Aram family picked up the parcels for next to nothing in an effort to expand their cattle operation.

James and his wife Phebe moved to a newly built home at Getta Creek in 1911, the same year they were married. This ranch, located approximately two miles above the Snake River at the mouth of White Bird Creek became their headquarters. Later, they developed a summer ranch on Joseph Plains near the headwaters of Fall Creek that they called the "Joseph Ranch" (mainly identified by others as the Aram Place). The Arams raised four children in the remote country: John, Rosamond, James Jr. (Jim), and Narcie.[186]

The Great Depression put a stop to the Aram's dreams, as they were caught in a case of bad timing while trying to expand. The bank foreclosed on the property in 1930 after the family struggled with bank payments.[187] The ranch was acquired by A. S. Hardy and then sold to V. D. (Slim) and Mary Johnson in 1939.

While the Arams lost the Getta Creek property, son James Jr. pulled together finances, and with his father's help reestablished their cattle business. Principally operating from the Joseph Ranch the Aram's gradually acquired more and more land that others like them had lost to the bank. By 1942, they decided to sell out completely to the Johnsons. In an in-depth biography of the Arams entitled, *The Arams of Idaho: Pioneers of Camas Prairie and*

Joseph Plains, author Kristi M. Youngdahl praises the family's achievement, "Neither Jim nor James felt they had lost the battle to reclaim their ranch, for they had well over 2,000 acres of land owned free and clear. In addition, they held leases on another 1,000 acres of Canfield land and over 600 acres of School Section land . . . Not only did they have the land, but they had rebuilt their cattle herd – over 300 head . . . The Arams were free of debt for the first time in their lives and they had money to invest. Their departure from Joseph was difficult, but it was in no way a failure."[188]

The Johnsons

Similar to the Arams the Johnsons enjoyed living at the Getta Creek Ranch. Slim and Mary raised four children while ranching in the country: Pete, Polly, Tom, and Peg. Peg simply described their years on the family place as, "Perfect and wonderful."[189]

The Johnsons acquired adjacent land as it became available. They bought the Aram's Joseph Ranch in 1942 followed, then Bob and Margaret Dobbins's property in 1948. These both became

The Slim Johnson family — (left to right) Pete, Peg, Tom, Polly, Mary, and Slim.

the summer homes. Other parcels were picked up along the way: Oscar "Bog" Thompson's Rice Creek ranch, the Doumecq property, and then Ray Swank's place on Doumecq. As Slim's ranch hit its zenith he was killed in a haying accident on July 21, 1961. Mary retained a large portion of the ranch, living at the winter and summer places on Getta Creek until her death in December 1984. Starting in 1968, daughter Polly and her husband Lew Hollandsworth managed the Getta Creek operation for fifteen years. During this time Mary worked as hard as ever and enjoyed helping raise her grandchildren, which often required spending some time in Cottonwood as they attended school.[190]

Trying to keep a sense of community as the old-timers of Joseph Plains began to fade, Pete, Polly, and Ellen Lyda started the annual Joseph Picnic in 1986. The event, held on the last Sunday of June at the local schoolhouse, was modestly attended the first year, but has since become a summer event regularly attended by neighbors.

The four kids inherited the land. Pieces were then divided or bought amongst each other. Pete ultimately ended up with Rice Creek and its associated properties. He married Hilda Suhr in 1960 and raised three sons at the place calling it the 1Y1 Ranch. He lived at the ranch until his death in March 2013.[191]

Tom also loved ranching and settled on a portion of land with his wife Sharon near Cottonwood where he continues to work. Polly and Lew worked at the Getta Creek Ranch until it was sold in the 1980s and moved to a spread on Joseph Plains. Their ranching efforts and lifestyle were well illustrated in the December–January 1981 issue of *Farm and Ranch Living* magazine under the title "Idaho Diary . . . 'On Our High Ranch, the Clouds Become Close Friends.'" Bob Stole bought part of the Getta Creek property that contained the house and buildings, along with the portions once owned by the Dobbins. Peg and her husband Jack held on to a segment of the ranch until the early 1990s before selling it to

Dr. Ned Schroeder. Peg, now widowed, continues to ranch with her children near Slate Creek on the Salmon River.

Johnsons and Aviation

While aviation was not a primary tool for the Johnson ranching operation, the occasional airplane did land on their property. Landings were made on a bench north of the Bob Dobbins Place. George Foster of Grangeville was the first person to land there. The Zimmerlys also landed on the bench. One emergency landing was made on an Easter weekend in the 1940s when a Zimmerly pilot flew one of the Dobbins's grandkids that suffered from a broken bone to Lewiston. Landings were also made at Ragtown Bar, Soldiers Home, and in fields owned by them on Doumecq.

Soldiers Home – Emergency Landing

Foster was not only the first person to land an airplane on the Johnson's upper ranch, but also on a lower portion of their in-holdings. The location was a small hayfield in the Getta Creek Canyon at the mouth of Soldiers Home Creek. The site is named after the idea that General O. O. Howard, involved with the fight against the Nez Perce, supposedly stayed here.

William Graham first homesteaded the land in 1920. Dobbins acquired the land from Aaron Wilson and used it for winter pasture ground. The Wilson Place was considered very extravagant for its time; the large two-story main house built of log contained an indoor bathtub, running water in the kitchen, a double-sided china hutch, a mechanical doorbell, and hand-painted wallpaper. The Wilsons created a massive garden and a large orchard. The Dobbins regularly used the living quarters and continued to maintain a large garden. Just before the Johnsons bought the property, Dobbins was still working out of the cabin and became immobile due to appendicitis. Word reached Slim Johnson and he arranged for Foster to land in a small 500' up-

(top) The standing ruins of Aaron Wilson's homestead cabin located near the mouth of Soldiers Home Creek.
(center) The Chevron advertisement depicting George Foster's rescue of Bob Dobbins.
(bottom) Looking down the Getta Creek drainage at the field Foster used to rescue Dobbins.

P. HOLLANDSWORTH

P. MAREK

(top) The wreckage of Ted Grote's Bell 47 at Getta Creek Ranch in June 1968.
(bottom) Salvaging Grote's helicopter in March 1969.

sloping hayfield downstream from the cabin.[192]

Foster's landing was a big occasion in the family, especially for Pete, the oldest of the four children. His sister Polly remembered, "When the decision was made for George to fly in, Pete just sat down there waiting to see the plane land . . . and afterwards he had a real big head about it. It was a very exciting event."[193]

Years later, Foster's daring rescue at Soldiers Home was depicted in a black and white drawing used in a 1956 Chevron ad campaign – promoting the durability of their aviation products. Before moving to Grangeville, Foster worked as a salesman for a major oil company in California, which may explain his connection to the advertisement. Under the ad headline of "Flying rescues – one mile down in Hell's Canyon," Foster is quoted, "The land is all straight up and down, inside the canyon rim. Flying between thousand-foot cliffs calls for plenty of attention, and for lots of power when I need it, too. But I always get the extra power I have to have, with Chevron Aviation Gasoline 80/87 in my Super Cub. Chevron 80/87 never fouls spark plugs for me: delivers smooth, dependable performance. I can lean it down for economy in level flight, too. Because nearly all of my flying is over wilderness, I can't risk any engine trouble. However, I've had such complete success with RPM Aviation Oil that I don't even need top overhauls between majors. Rings and valves stay in perfect condition right up to the last hour in the air. I'll never use any oil but 'RPM' in any plane I own."[194]

Ted Grote and the Search for a Missing Bonanza

Another interesting aviation happening occurred at the Getta Creek Ranch on June 27, 1968. Ted Grote of Grote Aviation based in Enterprise was hired by the Pacific Northwest Power Company to search for a missing airplane. The power company had chartered the plane five days earlier to carry former vice-president Armor B. Martin and his wife Jean to a concrete-pouring ceremony being held during the construction of the Dworshak Dam.

Grote worked with the power company and other searchers to map plausible routes Western

Aircraft pilot Larry Peck might have taken in an effort to avoid bad weather. Logically Grote thought Peck might have flown south from Spokane and then tried to work his way in to the Snake River drainage back toward his destination of Orofino.[195] With this in mind Grote and Clement Stearns, a public relations director from the power company, searched side drainages of Hells Canyon. After several stops, Grote landed his Bell 47 helicopter (N73284) at the Getta Creek Ranch to ask the Johnsons if they might have any information. No one was at the ranch, so they decided to move on. As Grote lifted off from the upper hayfield near the mouth of White Bird Creek, the rear tail rotor hit an old telephone line, tearing it to pieces. Grote lost control of the machine and it smashed to the ground. The two men scrambled out of the cockpit as quickly as they could. Moments later, most of the helicopter burned. Stranded, Stearns walked nearly two miles down Getta Creek to look for help, while Grote stayed with the charred remains of his aircraft. It was later discovered Stearns broke his back. In spite of the pain he made contact with Darrell Greenough, a worker at Dick Rivers's Copper Camp.[196] Stearns and Grote were later taken to a hospital.

With a good bill of health Grote continued the search, but nothing turned up before winter snows arrived. The following April two University of Idaho professors, Dr. James Cooley and Dr. Keith Buck, discovered the wreckage of the missing Beechcraft Bonanza (N4497D) while searching for mushrooms. Cooley and Buck found the plane about eleven miles north of Potlatch, Idaho, roughly fifty feet from a logging road. Searchers concluded the site was overlooked because logging debris masked the wreckage.[197] The cause of the accident was determined to be pilot error. The accident report stated, "Continued VFR flight into adverse weather conditions." The report also noted physical fatigue may have been a factor since Peck was over-extended on the maximum allowed duty time prior to the flight.

About a month before the plane was found, Grote decided he better move the charred remains of his helicopter. Grote landed a helicopter at Getta Creek and arranged to have most of the scraps hauled out by truck. However, one large section would not fit, so Lew Hollandsworth transported it to the river landing and Dick Rivers boated it to Lewiston.

RAGTOWN BAR (COPPER CREEK)

Early History

Looking downstream at Ragtown Bar.

The Henderson family settled at this location in the early 1900s. The family occupied four tents while building a permanent house. The tents were arranged in a square making a courtyard in the middle, and each tent had a specific function: kitchen, dining room, and two bedrooms. As with most places used by the early riverboats the bar needed a name for reference, so legend has it that one mail crew named it "Ragtown," because of the tents.[198] The Hendersons worked hard at the bar and grew a substantial garden that was fed by a three-mile long, hand-dug ditch from Getta Creek.[199] The clay packed ditch could only effectively carry water at night; otherwise it evaporated in the heat of the canyon before reaching the fields.

Tenants of the land after the Hendersons abandoned the ditch and let the bar return to its arid aesthetic, but it remained useful for grazing.[200] This parcel became part of the large Aram family in-holdings. The Arams lost the land to the bank in 1930. A. S. Hardy, a Grangeville attorney and businessman then took ownership. When Hardy's estate settled, Slim and Mary Johnson bought the land as part of the Getta Creek Ranch in 1939. From this start the Johnsons expanded their ranch to include land on Joseph Plains, Doumecq, and Rice Creek.

Slim Johnson's four kids collectively inherited the land and divided various parcels amongst themselves. The property containing the Ragtown Bar airstrip was ultimately sold to LT&L, a development company, circa 1990. Company owner, Gerald Lindsey, planned a major subdivision in the area called "Twin Rivers Subdivision," but it never really materialized. Some six and ten acre parcels were auctioned off. The land containing the airstrip was picked up by a conservation group and then sold to the Forest Service.

Dick Rivers – Copper Creek Camp

Dick Rivers began to use the parcel of land upriver from Ragtown, on the Oregon side at Copper Creek, as a camp for his riverboat business, Rivers Navigation Company. Many of the old-timers on the river called the location "Copper Mountain Bar," but the Rivers family called it "Copper Creek Camp" or simply, "Camp." He and his wife Lois worked hard to convert the one-building mining claim into an oasis with guest cabins, dining hall, and modern amenities such as hot running water. His five sons, Richard "Swede," Bill, Joe, Dennis, and Tim all helped with the family business at some point while growing up. The Rivers family also hired caretakers, cooks, and other boat pilots through their tenure on the river. Elmer Earl was one of the more notable boat captains to work for the outfit.[201] Earl recorded many of his memories in the book, *Hells Canyon A River Trip*. While the camp served as a good overnight spot for the mail route, it was also used during the tourist season to house guests on sightseeing, fishing, and hunting trips.

Rivers, originally of Asotin, Washington, grew up in the presence of the mighty Snake River, but as a boy his first real boat trip up the river was with legendary operator Ed MacFarlane. When MacFarlane retired he also rode with mail boat successors such as friend Kyle McGrady and Oliver McNabb. He also briefly worked as a deckhand on the steamboat, the *Lewiston*. Little did Rivers know that he would become the longest freight and mail boat captain on this stretch of river, serving nearly twenty-five years before selling his business to Wally

(top) Dick and Lois Rivers on the middle Snake River with the Idaho Queen II in the mid-1960s.
(bottom) The Rivers's Copper Camp in 1965. The two prefabricated buildings on the far right were relocated from Salmon Bar.

Beamer in 1983. Rivers died in 1998 and is buried in the Lewiston Normal Hill Cemetery.[202]

As a young man he began logging and founded his own company. He landed a major logging job in the Craig Mountain area located on the Idaho side of the river near Corral Creek. His competition saw it as a difficult locale to log, as road construction in to the area was considered cost prohibitive. However, Rivers's solution was simple – move the logs to the Snake River, tie them together, and haul them behind a boat to Lewiston.[203]

No matter what venture Rivers found himself in, a boat and the Snake River tended to merge. An opportunity arose to earn a living by combining both these facets in 1958 when Inland Navigation Company decided not to bid on the Snake River mail contract. After McGrady left the river in 1950, Inland Navigation boatman Oliver McNabb had made the run.[204]

Over the years, Rivers ran four different boats all named the *Idaho Queen* (I–IV). The first two boats were steel-hulled inboard powered vessels driven with the standard strut, shaft, and propeller setup. The last two boats were aluminum-hulled crafts driven by jet pumps. While he preferred the first two boats steered with rudders, he began to go through too many props and struts as the boats often ran aground due to the accelerated changes in the river and the fluctuating water levels associated with the construction of the three upriver dams, Brownlee (1959), Oxbow (1961), and Hells Canyon (1967–68). Rivers was in constant battles with Idaho Power regarding the irregular flow schedule of the river.[205] His solution was converting to pump-driven boats that drafted less water. Rivers also kept other boats and barges in his fleet. Due to his wide array of equipment the United States Geological Survey, various utility companies, and the Army Corps of Engineers often hired him. Working with the latter he occasionally helped them widen or maintain the navigation channel on the river.[206]

Even with the transition to the large jet boats, one thing that did not change on his weekly mail run was the need for an overnight stop. Rivers left the Lewiston port each Wednesday at 6:30 a.m. for his ninety-two mile route where he delivered the mail as far as Johnson Bar. He then worked his way back downriver. A naturally good stopping place for the night was Billy Rankin's place at Copper Creek. From his Copper Creek Camp he normally arrived back in Lewiston by Thursday evening.[207]

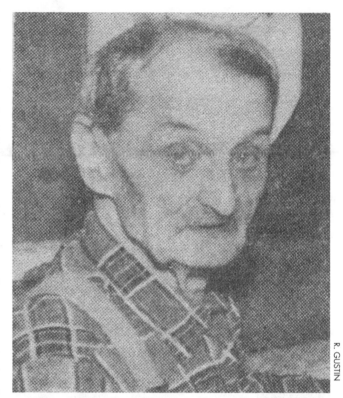

R. GUSTIN

T. RIVERS

(top) Billy Rankin – Copper Creek miner.
(bottom) Rivers was often hired by the Army Corps of Engineers to help maintain the navigation channel of the middle Snake. Here they are dynamiting an obstruction.

Rivers began using Copper Creek at the invitation of Rankin, who had built a framed cabin at the mouth of the creek and a stone cabin farther up the drainage. Rankin migrated to the Oregon area by wagon train with his adopted parents and was raised in Joseph. As a young man he attended an academy in Enterprise where he earned an education that helped him become a schoolteacher. When not teaching, he ran sheep for his relatives, prospected, and did other odd jobs. It was herding sheep that brought him to Copper Creek around 1900. While there he staked claims on Copper Mountain, believing large deposits of the metal were present. Rankin's dream of the claims making him rich never came to fruition as he and his partners could not overcome the challenge of transporting the ore out of the canyon cost-effectively. Rankin occupied Copper Creek during various parts of the year throughout his life. Rankin died in a Grangeville nursing home in 1967.[208]

One of Rankin's last big adventures on the river occurred in July 1959 when he brought potential investors William Brisco and Marion White to his Copper Mountain holdings. Rankin felt he had located a large deposit of copper in the Deep Creek area and wanted financial-backing to extract it. Dick Rivers hauled the men from Lewiston to the mouth of Deep Creek with rendezvous plans. The following week as Rivers passed the confluence of the creek the two men flagged his boat down.[209] As he pulled up to the bank, Rivers's son Joe, who was helping that day on the boat, remembered, "It was strange. There they were and no Billy . . . they kept yelling, 'Billy's lost, Billy's lost.'" Naturally they pulled over in a safe place and loaded them aboard. According to the two men Billy was able to walk up to the claim, but his feebleness prevented him from walking downhill, and he was stuck toward the top of Deep Creek.[210]

Rivers knew help was needed to get Rankin out of the steep canyon and boated up to the Van Pool Ranch at Dry Creek where he called friend Ivan Gustin in Lewiston to conduct an aerial search. Gustin met the Riverses at the Van Pool Ranch with a Super Cub. A plan was quickly devised. Gustin removed the side door for added visibility. Dick then hopped in the back of the plane to provide an extra pair of eyes, and Joe stayed with the boat. Not long after takeoff, the men spotted Rankin hobbling around on two walking sticks. A discussion followed about how to retrieve the old boy. Options were weighed and Gustin decided he could land the Cub on a small flat spot in the area of Teaser Ridge – and that is what they did.[211]

With great finesse Gustin landed uphill. Once on the ground, it required a downhill taxi to fetch and load Rankin. Worried the plane might nose over while taxiing, he instructed Rivers to walk/sit on the horizontal stabilizer to hold the tail down. It was touch-and-go much of the way down the incline. After what must have been an interesting conversation, Rankin was seated in the back of the

plane. Again, Gustin felt it necessary for Rivers to hold the tail down as he taxied to the top of the hill for takeoff. As Gustin navigated the Super Cub through the 180-degree turn at the top of the landing spot, he added power for takeoff, and Rivers ran alongside the airplane. Sprinting as fast as he could he then dove-in on top of Rankin. It was a quick descent to the river where Gustin returned Rivers to his boat before flying Rankin out to Grangeville or Lewiston.[212]

Ragtown Bar Airstrip, Rivers, and Pilots

As in the instance of rescuing Billy Rankin, Rivers occasionally needed speedy access to the outside for help. A landing area at Copper Creek Camp was walked out and some rocks were even painted to mark it, but it was determined to be unsuitable for fixed-wing aircraft. However, helicopters landed at the site many times. Undeterred, Rivers gained permission from Ragtown Bar (downstream on the Idaho side) owner Slim Johnson to use the hayfield that was conveniently clear of rocks from the days when it was used for agriculture.[213] For decades, the strip was outlined with fifty-five gallon oil drums cut in half and painted orange. Pilots generally landed downriver and took off upriver due to the terrain and slight uphill grade of the 800' long field. This aerial access point became a mainstay for Rivers's operation.

The airfield proved its worth many times in just keeping the mail on schedule. It was not uncommon in the days of running prop-driven boats to damage a shaft, strut, or propeller to the point where the boat could no longer safely navigate the river. In these situations Rivers hired friend Jac Garlinghouse, who was a trained navy diver, and ran a side business called "Green Frog Diving Company" in Lewiston. Garlinghouse would dive under the boat with special equipment to make the necessary repairs. Often this required him to be flown to Ragtown Bar or another strip nearest the disabled boat.[214]

On another occasion Garlinghouse was flown to Ragtown Bar by Gustin to search for one of Rivers's employees who drowned while tying up the boat at Copper Creek Camp. After the accident occurred, Rivers and his crew could not locate the

127

(left) Looking upstream at Ragtown bar.
(right) Rivers unloading Ken Johnson's wool from the Idaho Queen II at Lewiston Grain
Growers in 1966.

body, but Garlinghouse was able to recover it in a nearby eddy.[215]

On a lighter note, the airstrip, Rivers, and Hillcrest Aviation were publicized in the television series *High and Wild* in 1964. Don Hobart, the producer and host of the show, grew up near the Snake River in Asotin County. It seemed only fitting to highlight a region he was familiar with. Beyond the flying shots, viewers were introduced to fishing, hunting, wildlife, river residents, and a quick look at Copper Creek Camp. *High and Wild* was one of the first programs to promote extreme outdoor activities. It first appeared on a local Portland station before airing nationwide. A few years prior to the Hobart trip, Rivers was featured in another television program called *Expedition Northwest* hosted by Don McCune.

The Beamers

The Beamers had already been on the Snake River operating Heller Bar Excursions ten years before officially taking over Rivers's mail route in January 1983. Wally Beamer, once a professional baseball pitcher for the New York Giants in the early 1950s, had always longed to own his own boat business, even though he had never operated anything but a fishing boat. Wally and his wife Myrna were on vacation from their Roseburg, Oregon, home when the two discovered a potential business for sale owned by Hollis Oakes at Heller Bar. The Beamers threw out an offer for the company in 1973 and by the following year they were in business.[216]

Over the years, they expanded the operation to include thirteen new boats and improved the facilities at Heller Bar by constructing a new restaurant, guest quarters, and home. After buying out Rivers they did the same to Copper Creek Camp, rebuilding many of the facilities from the ground up. By the early 1990s, the Beamers could house one hundred overnight guests at what they named "Copper Creek Lodge." At the peak of their operation the Beamers hauled 16,000 guests in one season up the Snake River. During their time at Copper Creek they never used the Ragtown Bar airstrip or any fixed-wing aircraft. However, on several occasions helicopters were used in emergency situations on the river in which they provided assistance. The Beamers sold the business in 1993 to Jim and Jill Koch who call it Beamers Hells Canyon Tours. Wally and Myrna left the river and enjoyed traveling the West with their motor home, but eventually settled near the Oregon Coast, and then moved permanently to Sutherlin, Oregon. Wally, an avid fisherman, has returned a few times to the Snake River for steelhead season.[217]

ROLAND BAR (BLANKENSHIP RANCH)

Occupants

Dick and Jim Blankenship field dressing a deer in the 1950s.

The location of the former landing area located parallel to the river between Roland and Cat creeks was initially two separate homesteads. Guy Russell homesteaded 160 acres on Roland Creek in September 1920.[218] Elben Dotson proved up on 154.59 acres on Cat Creek in June 1911.[219] Leonard Johnson's (of Kirkwood and Temperance Creek) brother J. Ray acquired these homesteads along with other adjacent lands. One of Leonard's business associates, Roland Reel, drowned while attempting to swim the river. Reel's body was recovered and buried here, thus the name.[220] Nevertheless, this landmark is often mistakenly called "Rolling Bar."

Johnson sold his land interests here to Jim Dorrance. Several brief owners followed Dorrance - among them were Tex O'Keefe and brothers Duke and Shorty Lathrop. Jim and Dick Blankenship acquired the place after World War II. The Blankenship brothers also owned the Tryon Creek Ranch and bought out Barney Donahue's land on Cat Creek.[221] The combination of the Roland and Cat creek properties became known collectively as the "Cat Creek Ranch." As mentioned with the history of the Tryon Creek Ranch, the Blankenship's business partnership dissolved in the early 1960s. Jim took over the ownership of the Cat Creek Ranch and transformed it from sheep to cattle. Jim and his wife Lois often spent winters at the ranch and summered on top at Lord Flat. With slack time in the fall the two ran an outfitting and guiding service for big game hunts based near Lord Flat.[222] Jim's cousin Gary Bledsoe often came in and helped as the camp cook. Several of their customers would return year after year and fly themselves in. Two groups in particular were the Grew family from Klamath Falls, Oregon, and Albert Skiles of Boise. Skiles, a former World War II flight instructor, generally flew a new Cessna 182 in for the season. He enjoyed helping, as well as hunting, and often flew clientele meat out to Joseph where it was refrigerated at the Blankenship's Gateway Market, a grocery store co-owned and managed by friend Louie Landreth.[223]

Jim and Lois sold the Cat Creek Ranch to river neighbor and friend Lem Wilson. The couple moved to Enterprise where they bought several smaller farms. For many years Jim worked part-time for the US Postal Service, delivering mail on an overnight route down the Imnaha River. Jim died in 1995.[224] Wilson lost the Cat Creek and Roland Bar properties to the government in the condemnation process.

The Airstrip

During the Blankenship's tenure at Roland Bar, the hayfield downriver and across the creek from the main house was designated as a landing area in the late 1940s.[225] A small amount of leveling was done, creating a good 1,200'-runway. It was most common to land upstream and takeoff downstream; however, pilots have used it in both directions.[226]

The Blankenships mainly flew with pilot Ted Grote. One of Grotes most distinct memories of Roland Bar occurred on a cold winter day in the 1950s. He landed to deliver supplies to Blankenship's caretaker, Mr. Smithwick, commonly known as "Cherokee Slim." As Grote taxied to the end of the strip, Smithwick who was not wearing a jacket, greeted him. Grote could not believe he was braving the freezing temperatures without the appropriate attire and asked him about the whereabouts of a coat. He shrugged his shoulders and admitted that he did not own one. Astonished at the man's response Grote finished his other stops in the canyon and flew directly to Joseph to buy Smithwick a jacket. By the end of the day Grote returned to Roland Bar with the gift.[227]

Grote and Jim Blankenship appeared together in the July 1, 1967 edition of the *Saturday Evening Post.* The article, "Farewell to Hells Canyon" written by John Skow, explored the geographic features, history, and the way of life that stood to be lost with the construction of the High Mountain Sheep Dam. Skow lamented, "When the seething Snake River is tamed by a new dam, the stark beauty of Hells Canyon will be buried forever under tons of water – and a part of America's wild heritage will die with it." Other canyon residents and co-workers of Grote and Blankenship were also essential to the article as Skow traversed the terrain by foot, horseback, boat, and airplane to better understand the region. Skow incorporated viewpoints about the future of the middle Snake from the Ken Johnson family, Dick Rivers, the Slim Johnson family, and many others.[228]

Lois, many months pregnant with their daughter Mary Ann, chartered a plane with Joseph pilot Sid Windsler to meet her husband with several horses at Lord Flat. Brother-in-law Dick was also aboard the plane. On landing, the aircraft hit a huge hole causing one of the main wheels to rip off. The plane then nosed over, flipped, and caught on fire. Fortunately all three occupants escaped unharmed. When Lois reminisced about the accident years later she remembered most vividly somehow landing on a watermelon after the plane came to a stop.[229]

Lem Wilson also used the strip frequently during his ownership. After the Forest Service acquired the property the airstrip was closed. Bud Stangel is the last known pilot to land a plane here using a Piper Cub.[230] More modern Forest Service maps now refer to the location as the Blankenship Ranch.

ARAM PLACE

Schroeders Buy

The 1,000' runway built by Ned Schroeder in 1993.

Ned and Susan Schroeder built this airstrip, located between Wolf and Quinn creeks. Schroeder, originally from Redmond, Oregon, moved to Lewiston in 1978 after practicing medicine in Helena, Montana, for three years. Early on, Ned and his twin brother Ted enjoyed spending time in the Idaho backcountry. The two hunted annually on the Middle Fork of the Salmon River and generally chartered with Dick Williams of Salmon Air Taxi in Salmon, Idaho.[231] Always wanting his own piece of backcountry paradise, he and his wife bought the 1,920-acre Wolf Creek property containing the old Aram Place from Jack and Peg Marek in April 1993.

Early History – Arams and Johnsons

Peg Marek's parents Slim and Mary Johnson purchased the land in 1942 from the Aram family. James and Phebe Aram were early homesteaders on the Joseph Plains. Aram's first in-holding in the Joseph area was on Getta Creek (for more information see Getta Creek).

In a roundabout turn of events the Johnsons bought the Aram's Getta Creek Ranch from the bank and ultimately bought out the other land they had accumulated during the 1930s. Under the Johnson ownership they used what was referred to as the

Slim Johnson and Louie Wimer with Wimer's early model Piper Cub at the Aram Place.

"Aram Place" in the summers from 1942 to 1948. The old farmstead buildings were no longer used once the Johnsons purchased the Dobbins land above Soldiers Home (tributary to Getta Creek) in 1948. The actual building complex saw little use from then on. The Johnson's youngest daughter Peg and her husband Jack Marek purchased the Aram Place and the associated acreage from her father's estate. The main house still stands, but the barn burned accidentally in the 1990s.

The lengthy horse pasture stretching between the footprint of the former barn and the now abandoned house was occasionally used as a landing area for airplanes. Louie Wimer of Cottonwood was one of the first pilots known to land in the pasture in June 1948. Wimer's visit was caused by a Johnson family emergency. The Johnson kids were playing a game of rodeo, where the older children acted as horses and the younger as the riders. Peg, the smallest of the clan broke her arm after being "bucked off a horse." Her brother Pete, who had been acting as the horse, panicked and ran inside the house for help. He then sprinted back outside, approached his bawling sister with the "z-shaped arm" and in effort to fix his wrongdoing tried to straighten it. Clearly needing medical attention Wimer flew in and took the injured rodeo rider to the hospital and then flew her back to the ranch after the bone was properly set. Remembering the story sixty-some years later, Peg commented, "I really thought I was a big shot because I got to ride in an airplane. The pain almost went away. It was my first airplane ride and I just loved it. After my arm was put in a cast, I was given my first lollipop. It was a pretty good day . . . Many years later Louie flew Jack to the Spokane hospital after a bad horse accident . . . even then he remembered my broken arm as a little girl."[232]

More on the Schroeders and an Airstrip

Schroeder was first introduced to the Joseph Plains area through friend and Idaho boat builder Darell Bentz of Lewiston. Soon after the papers were signed for the property, Schroeder consulted with Darell's brother Rusty about designing an airstrip. Rusty, a well-recognized backcountry pilot of the lower Salmon and Snake rivers, was happy to help. The runway was oriented northeast-southwest to take advantage of the prevailing winds and to enable landing approaches from both directions. Schroeder hired Musselman equipment operators from Orofino for the excavation work. Due to the rocky geology of the ridge a grader and roller were required. As the project progressed Schroeder sped his Ford pickup back and forth on the 1,000'-runway to see if it was smooth enough. Satisfied he then hired Rusty, who owned a hydro seeding business, to seed the strip. Later in the summer of 1993 while the Schroeders camped on the property they spotted Rusty's red Cessna 185 flying overhead. Before they had time to think much about it, Rusty unannounced swung down and made the first landing. As Rusty climbed out of the plane with a big smile he explained that he just happened to be in the area and thought he would give the runway a try.[233]

Throughout the next twenty years many friends came and went using the strip. Bill Fate, a Lewiston eye doctor and Ned's flight instructor for the majority of his pilot ratings, visited several times flying a Cessna Hawk XP. The Schoeders owned a Cessna 206 and a pair of Super Cubs. The latter airplanes became their primary access to the backcountry getaway. After the construction of a roof over their camp trailer, along with a tool shed, Schroeder designed a solar power system. The installation of the solar system was meticulously planned out, or so he believed. Making an extensive list and inventory prior to departing for the weekend, he thought he was set. As he got into the project he realized he was missing things – one part here, one part there. Before the panels were operating he had made multiple flying trips back and forth to Lewiston.[234]

The Schroeders became actively involved in Idaho aviation. Susan, a registered nurse, took to flying and eventually obtained a commercial license. She occasionally ferried airplanes for people and at one point flew fire patrol for the Clearwater-Potlatch Timber Protective Association. Susan was killed while landing a Piper PA-18 (N82591) on a gravel road near a friend's ranch outside Frenchglen, Oregon, in March 1994.

Ned and his second wife Carole carried on the tradition of flying to the special property until health issues forced Ned to stop in the spring of 2004. They then parted with the airplanes, but continued to enjoy the backcountry. Retired and wanting to further simplify their lives, they sold the old Aram Place in September 2013 to the Wilks brothers of Texas (see Hitchcock Ranch for more information).

FLYING U RANCH

Oren Hollandsworth built this 1,800'-airstrip on the upper end of Wolf Creek circa 1970. Hollandsworth and his wife Grace obtained the land from her mother Alberta Morrow.[235] Alberta ran the ranch with the help of her two daughters after her son Floyd died in 1937 and her husband Clyde died in 1943. The Morrow's Flying U Ranch, which extended toward the Snake River down Birch Creek was originally homesteaded by the Oscar Canfield family.

The Hollandsworths planned on subdividing part of the acreage and built the airstrip to make the land more attractive to potential buyers. However, with the nearby main road the airstrip saw little use and the subdivision never fully materialized.

Hollandsworth did sell one small parcel to pilot Ralph Reynolds who hauled in a mobile home for living quarters and occasionally visited the property via airplane. J. P. Seubert of Cottonwood used the airstrip for a short time as well, when his company Seubert Excavators had an active rock crushing operation close by the property. The material was used to supply family-owned companies such as Clearwater Concrete and Valley Paving. Seubert enjoyed flying and linked his passion for aviation to business every chance he could. Seubert was killed in his Cessna 185 flying from McCall to Cottonwood in 2001.

The Hollandsworths sold the land and airstrip to Delos Robbins of Missoula, Montana, in about 1974. Robbins was a cattle rancher who also owned Missoula (Robbins) Livestock Auction. His son Dave acquired the parcel when his father died in 2010. He sold it two years later to the Wilks brothers. While part of the runway could potentially be used, a fence was built across the airstrip during the Robbins ownership and no planes have landed there since.

Christmas Creek

Early Years

The Christmas Creek Ranch — 2014. Note the shed obstructing the downstream end of the runway.

Supposedly, early cattlemen Jim Tryon and Lou Knapper brought their sheep to winter at the location on Christmas Day 1888. The reference to the holiday stuck. Jim and Elvarre Dorrance bought the location from Homer Hayes in 1927. The Dorrance's used the ground for winter rangeland and summered near Lord Flat. When their two children, Jimmy and Phyllis became of school age they moved to Enterprise and sold the ranch in 1943 to Frank Wilson of Somers Creek.[236] Max Johnson and his brother Oakley, who owned a ranch on Deep Creek, took over the Christmas Creek operation and ran it through the late 1940s. Max was briefly a son-in-law to Wilson.[237] During most of the Johnson tenure they housed Basque sheepherder employees at the ranch.[238]

Longfellow, Wilson, Airplane Use

Ralph Longfellow, a rancher with headquarters in Council, bought the Christmas Creek place from Johnson and combined it with two other homesteads located at Deep Creek and Little Deep Creek. He continued to use the place, mainly to house employees. To access the property Longfellow generally drove down the Van Pool's Dry Creek Road. At the end of the road he kept a boat so he could then cross the river to his ranch. Lem Wilson (no relation to Frank Wilson) bought the entire acreage from Longfellow circa 1967.[239]

In roughly 1955, Longfellow contacted Ted Grote about the possibility of flying supplies to Christmas Creek. After some discussion the two decided a landing could be made parallel to the river in a hayfield upstream from the confluence of Christmas Creek and the river. Approximately a 600' area became designated for aircraft and was used regularly by pilots flying Cubs, such as Grote, Stangel, and Lem Wilson. The use of the airstrip was eventually eliminated when the Wilsons built sheds over the location in the late 1960s. The materials for these sheds were trucked down the road to the Van Pool Ranch. Lem and his sons then boated the material across the river to Christmas Creek.[240]

Portions of the short landing area still remain visible from the air. The property and house are now part of the NRA.

Friends of Hells Canyon NRA

After sitting vacant for many years the Forest Service placed the Christmas Creek dwelling on the Recreation Rental Program. The program allows the public to rent federally owned facilities for recreational uses. The cabin slowly fell into disrepair and was delisted. A group of Hells Canyon outdoor enthusiasts, consisting of Rusty Bentz, Pat Garrett, and Bill Venosdel, worked with the Forest Service to form Friends of Christmas Creek, a nonprofit, to help save the historic ranch. The volunteers later changed the name to Friends of Hells Canyon NRA to encompass a broader spectrum of future projects in the area. The organization has rebuilt and preserved much of the historical integrity of the turn-of-the twentieth century home at Christmas Creek through volunteer efforts. While the group's primary focus began with the Christmas Creek project, they also have the goals of protecting the overall history of the canyon, preventing noxious weeds, planting and fostering the growth of native plants, shoreline protection, and encouraging responsible use of the area.[241]

VAN POOL RANCH (HITCHCOCK RANCH)

Early Years – Van Pools

Looking upstream at the former Van Pool/Hitchcock property and lower airstrip – 2014.

Several early settlers made an effort to homestead on various portions of this 18,000-acre area. In the last hundred plus years this vast landscape has commonly been known as the "Van Pool Ranch" and later the "Hitchcock Ranch." Besides a number of flat benches, two primary-landing locations have become well-established places for airplanes to land.

David Van Pool was born near Jefferson City, Missouri. He married Sarah Buzan at Versailles, Missouri, in 1879. The couple had nine children. Around 1905, they pulled up stakes with the five youngest children still living at home and moved west. They spent one year in Sterling, Colorado, before arriving in Grangeville, where David ran a general store for four years.[242] Eventually the Van Pools made their way to the Snake River at the mouth of Dry Creek in about 1911. They proved up on their first parcel of land in 1919 and subsequently added several more patented homesteads as their children became eligible to apply for land entries. Additionally, they bought out other neighbors.

David and Sarah retired from the ranch in 1934 and moved to Lewiston. David died at age ninety-five in November 1952. He is buried in the Lewiston Normal Hill Cemetery.[243] Sarah died shortly thereafter. Son Harold received homestead approval for 589.36 acres the same year his parents decided to retire. In the end Harold inherited the entire ranch, and built it up to about 18,000 acres. Harold married Alta "Tuppy" Tupper in May 1938. Within two years of their marriage the upper home located near the head of Big Sulphur Creek burned. The summer ranch operation was then moved to Pick Chamberlain's homestead site, to the northwest toward Joseph Plains. By the early 1950s Chamberlain's house was torn down and replaced. The living situation on the river portion of the ranch was also improved. While they kept

Homesteaders David and Sarah Van Pool [left] standing with son Harold and grandson Ron in the mid-1940s.

(top) The Pick Chamberlain homestead prior to the Van Pool's construction of a more modern summer home.
(bottom) The Van Pool home on the lower ranch that was built circa 1940. Notice the Cub and Cessna 170 tied down above the airstrip.

Harold's original homestead cabin, the Van Pools designed a modern house for the site circa 1940. At the time of this writing the house still serves as the main living quarters for the ranch during the winter. Concurrently Tuppy's sister Amy Taylor and her husband built a nearly identical house in Lewiston at 1118 10th Street. After World War II a new barn, bunkhouse, and several outbuildings were added to the lower ranch.[244]

Harold and Tuppy had one son, Ron. Beginning in 1949, the family spent part of the year in Lewiston so he could attend school. From the end of June through Thanksgiving the Van Pools lived at the upper ranch and the remainder of the time was spent at the river ranch. Tuppy and Ron migrated back and forth while Harold lived in the backcountry most of the year. The Van Pools sold the entire ranch to White Swan Lumber Company, owned by Maurice and Katherine Hitchcock for a reported $800,000 in 1968. Harold and Tuppy retired to Lewiston.[245]

Harold was an avid reader on days when the weather forced him to be housebound at the ranch. He never read books per se, but enjoyed stories of adventure and mystery, and regularly subscribed to magazines such as *True: The Man's Magazine* and *Saga: Adventure Stories For Men*. However, Harold's favorite reading material was *National Geographic*. It was through this publication that he could travel to far-off places from his armchair along the remote river. And when he retired he did travel to some of the places he read about. Before his wife Tuppy died of cancer in 1971, they took a world cruise. After her death, he continued to travel. On one of his trips he met Erma Schaefer, whom he married in 1973. Harold died at age ninety-one in the Moscow Care Center on May 2, 1993.[246]

After graduating high school in 1961 Ron attended the University of Washington, married his wife, Jackie, and then earned an MBA from Berkeley. He landed a job with Weyerhaeuser and lived various places around the country while raising a family before settling permanently in the Seattle area. He has returned twice to the ranch since his parents sold to show his kids where he grew up. In addition to his visits he has flown over it several times with childhood friend and pilot Bill McCann Jr. of Lewiston.[247]

Landing Areas, Pilots, and Aircraft of the Van Pool Era

Aviation became an important link to the outside world for the Van Pools. The only way in or out of the ranch was on the weekly mail boat, horse, or by airplane until the road was built down the Left Fork of Dry Creek circa 1957–58. Even then the road was not open year-round. Due to the various living locations on the ranch, aircraft used four landing areas, two on top for summer access, and two on the river in winter. The first upper landing patch was at the head of Big Sulphur Creek in a hayfield about a half-mile from the house. This was a nice smooth and well-drained location. It had enough regular use beginning in about 1940 that a windsock was installed. While the home burned at this site, the landing area was used through the early 1960s at times when the lower fields were too wet or

(top) Landing at the Lower Bar airstrip.
(bottom) Looking downstream on the Lower Bar airstrip.

137

planted with crops. The second upper landing area was developed at the Chamberlain homestead about a hundred yards below the 1950s-era house.[248]

The river ranch near the mouth of Dry Creek had two designated landing areas, dubbed "Lower Bar" and "Upper Bar." The Lower Bar is the site of the current airstrip and is closest to the main ranch house. The Upper Bar field was located upstream between Dry Creek and Wolf Creek and was actually a more suitable site, but less favored because of the distance from the house. Pilots landed parallel to the river at both places. For the Van Pools aircraft moved passengers, either family or employees, to and from town during the winters, and in times of emergency.[249]

Zimmerly Brothers – First Recorded Landing

The first recorded airplane landing in the entire middle Snake River occurred February 2, 1937 on the Lower Bar runway. The need for rapid air transportation arose after neighbor Floyd (Dwight) Morrow was thrown from his horse and fractured his skull. His parent's Clyde and Alberta ran the Flying U Ranch upstream at Birch Creek and the nearest air access point was at the Van Pools. Word reached Zimmerly Air Transport in Lewiston requesting help. Brothers Fred and Bert Zimmerly flew their Zenith Z6B (NC935Y) to the Van Pool Ranch as quickly as possible and brought the injured boy out to the Lewiston hospital. The round-trip flight only took one hour and ten minutes. Other than the flight time and destination, Fred's only other notation in his logbook was, "Ambulance up Snake River."[250] Morrow did not survive the head trauma.

Although the first aircraft did not land until 1937, one year earlier the Zimmerlys advertised scenic flights over the middle Snake River in the *Lewiston Morning Tribune*. The ad from the May 3, 1936 edition boasted, "If you want to really see this section of Idaho – take one of our scenic airplane trips . . . trips over the Grand Canyon of the Snake; see Seven Devils, Buffalo Hump, the Salmon River and historic Elk City."[251] The two brothers had established the company two years earlier in March 1934 as the first commercial air operator in the area. The Zimmerlys migrated to the Lewiston-Clarkston Valley from Vancouver, Washington, after hearing

of possible flying opportunities available with the expansion of both the Forest Service in central Idaho and mining companies in the remote stretches of the Salmon River. The start of their business did not come without its woes. Early on Fred did the majority of the flying as Bert was still building time to earn his commercial license and could not legally carry passengers for hire. In October 1934, Bert wound up in trouble with the Bureau of Air Commerce (now the FAA) after crashing a Student Prince airplane near Elk City, Idaho, while trying to outmaneuver poor weather and fog. The accident attracted regional attention, as passenger Marshall Dana was an editor with the *Oregon Journal* newspaper. Increasing Dana's public profile was his position as the northwest director of the Public Works Planning Board, organized by his personal friend President Franklin D. Roosevelt to spur economic development. On this particular trip Dana was looking into the growth of mining districts. Returning from the exploration trip the plane crashed ten miles east of Elk City where pilot and passenger abandoned it and walked to town. It appeared to the authorities that Zimmerly was illegally carrying a passenger for hire and his license was temporarily suspended.

The little hiccup turned out to be nothing compared to the Zimmerly's great accomplishments and influence on the aviation advancements of the region. In 1938, Bert took over flight operations and Fred went to work for Northwest Airlines. Around the same time Bert moved the business across the river from Lewiston to Clarkston. From the new location the company capitalized on the opportunities provided by World War II and started a CPTP. The Zimmerlys expanded backcountry recreational opportunities by offering clientele a place to hunt and fish at a remote fly-in lodge with guided trips from the Moose Creek Ranches located deep in the Selway-Bitterroot Primitive Area. They also focused on establishing air routes that connected major cites in Idaho as well as Spokane.

When the war ended Bert shifted his business efforts toward developing scheduled air service. By 1946, he earned approval from the Civil Aeronautics Board (CAB) and created Zimmerly Airlines, which was later renamed Empire Airlines. The same year, when stock options were created, he was forced out. However, he continued to grow his original company – Zimmerly Air Transport. On February 17, 1949, at age forty-one, Bert was killed when his Cessna Airmaster hit high terrain near Pullman. He was flying in low visibility on a return flight from Spokane

(top) Fred Zimmerly in 1937.
(bottom) The Zimmerly's Zenith Z6B. This is the first airplane known to have landed in the middle Snake River country. The plane was designed as the ultimate mountain airplane. Notice the open-air cockpit and separate enclosed cabin for passengers.

(top) The wreckage of Bert Zimmerly Sr.'s Student Prince [NC893K] near Elk City in October 1934.

(bottom) A 1935 panoramic photograph taken from the Horse Heaven Fire Lookout tower. The image clearly shows the mountaintop meadow used by Bert Zimmerly Sr. in 1939.

(top opposite) The lines added to this modern photograph indicate the landing site used by Zimmerly during the rescue mission. Granite Creek is the major drainage in the background. The log Horse Heaven Lookout cabin is still standing [center].

(bottom opposite) Looking north-northeast at the landing area [marked by line] used by Zimmerly at Horse Heaven on the southern end of the Seven Devil Mountain Range.

B. ZIMMERLY JR.

USFS

Bert Zimmerly Sr. and wife Edna in 1938.

to Lewiston. The aviation community was shocked by the loss. Two days after the wreckage of his Airmaster was discovered *The Spokesman-Review* still voiced disbelief, "Noted for his skill and daring as a pilot, he achieved the reputation of having almost a 'charmed life.' He had brushed close to danger many times in the past, but always managed to escape without serious injury. The popular pilot was famous for the many mercy missions he had flown in to the north central Idaho wilderness. By landing in remote pastures and along ridges he brought many an injured or sick person to Lewiston and Clarkston for hospital treatment. His plane was a familiar sight skimming through Hell's Canyon of the Snake river [sic] this winter dropping mail, food and other supplies to snowbound ranchers."[252]

One of the more daring and impressive rescue missions of Bert Zimmerly's career occurred on July 31, 1939, about ten years prior to his death. The Forest Service asked for his assistance in trying to save the life of Lawrence Howard, the seasonal fire observer stationed at the Horse Heaven Fire Lookout. Word reached the Nez Perce NF office in Grangeville that Howard had discovered three tick bites on himself upon returning to his post after a few days off. A severe case of Rocky Mountain spotted fever ensued. Forest officials feared for Howard's life. While men had reached Howard via horseback, they worried he could not make the fifteen-mile trail ride by horse to the nearest road. Zimmerly knew the terrain and thought he could land on the west side of the 8,200' mountaintop, about a quarter mile from the lookout building. Howard's caregivers were contacted by telephone and instructed to clear the field of obstructions and outline the best landing site with sheets of canvas.[253]

With a solidified plan, Zimmerly flew to Grangeville the following morning at first light in a Travel Air 6000 (NC9844) and picked up Dr. J. P. Weber for medical assistance.[254] Back in the air, Zimmerly climbed over the 9,000'-plus peaks of the Seven Devils. Arriving on the south end of the jagged range they circled the Horse Heaven Lookout. The ground crew had done as instructed and Zimmerly effortlessly set the big plane down on the roughly 1,000' grassy clearing. With about a twelve percent slope to the top of the mountain he was able to stop right before the main pack trail below the lookout station. The crew carried Howard to the plane on a stretcher and loaded him in.[255] Ensuring a safe takeoff, Zimmerly left Dr. Weber behind and speedily delivered the patient to the Grangeville hospital.[256] Arriving back in Lewiston after the heroic three-and-a-half hour air mission Zimmerly spent the remainder of the day flying from Lewiston to Boise and back in a Cessna Airmaster – revealing he viewed his actions as just another day.[257]

In spite of the loss of Bert, brother Fred continued flying the remainder of his life, becoming a chief pilot for Northwest Airlines. Fred died in May 2004 at age ninety-four. The two brothers are well remembered in Idaho and the surrounding region for their early aviation achievements. The company trained thousands of pilots for World War II, made incredible air rescues, and groomed many of the greatest Hells Canyon and lower Salmon River commercial pilots. Pilots influenced by the Zimmerlys are endless – a few related to the latter region include: Ivan Gustin, Don Schumacher, Arnie Brandt, Jerry Wilson, Stan Hepler, Clyde Martin, Don Wolfe, Jack Houston, Frank Borgeson, Bud Richardson, Fred "Chris" Christensen, Glenn Shannon, and of course Bert Zimmerly Jr. Bert Jr. grew up in the aviation business and took his first commercial job flying for Abe Bowler of Orofino in the mid-1950s. His career led him to corporate aviation where he retired at age eighty in 2014 with 25,000 hours of flight time.

After the emergency trip to the Van Pool Ranch in early 1937, ranchers in the remote region of Hells Canyon and the lower Salmon River took notice, and so did the Zimmerlys. The ability to reach the lower sections of the river during the winter when the upper roads/trails were closed by snow could often mean life or death in an emergency. The Zimmerly's entrance into the market was slow because most middle Snake River residents primarily relied on the weekly mail boat for goods and services. But the airplane did have its place, especially when the mail boat could not get through due to ice or mechanical malfunctions. The most noted air rescue missions to the river inhabitants were in the tough winter of 1948–49. In December of 1948, the water flow of the Snake River dropped to extreme levels – so much that the weekly mail boat run by Kyle McGrady could not get up the river. Worsening the situation came a record-breaking winter that froze the middle Snake solid for a month. McGrady's boat was immovable for over fifty days. Many of the ranchers had not finished stocking up on supplies for the winter and were caught without enough feed for their livestock. Coming to the rescue were the Zimmerly pilots. The company made countless airdrops to ranches up and down the river and parachuted in over fifty tons of hay.

After Bert's death his widow Edna became the president of the company. With the help of Chief Pilot Clyde Martin, the business continued its postwar winter air route, servicing customers each Tuesday along the middle Snake and lower Salmon rivers. It was not an official airmail route and clients could use the service on a per-call request or sign up for a full winter contract. When Zimmerlys sold out, former employee Don Schumacher took over the route with his own company Schumacher Ag-Air. The route was primarily flown with Stinson 108s, Cubs, and Cessna 180s.

Post Zimmerly Years – Ivan Gustin

By the early 1950s, the Van Pools flew exclusively with friend and pilot Ivan Gustin. Gustin was no outsider to the area. He was born in Montana and moved to Lewiston with his family as a youngster

Pilot Ivan Gustin – 1950s.

R. GUSTIN

– graduating from Lewiston High School in 1933. Four years later he began taking flying lessons with Zimmerly Air Transport under the tutelage of Harland Tyler. Within less than two months he soloed on New Years Day 1938. Gustin earned his many ratings and stayed with Zimmerly until late 1945 when he and three partners started Hillcrest Aviation, the first postwar business on the new Lewiston airport.[258]

The other three men involved with the startup were Jack Houston, Tom Duffy, and Howard Melcher. The latter two ran the business and supplied the funds, while Gustin and Houston did the flying. Hillcrest began with several Stearmans, a Cessna Bobcat, and a fleet of Aeronca Champions for flight instruction. With success they then bought out Zimmerly Air Transport in 1953. The purchase brought them several other aircraft – Stinsons, an Airmaster, and a Travel Air 6000. More airplanes meant more pilots and more work. Six years later Gustin merged with Jerry Wilson of Orofino, who

143

Ivan Gustin and son Ron pose with a Hillcrest Aviation Aeronca Champion in Lewiston after a deer hunt in the 1950s.

In late June 1958, Idaho Power began testing the newly constructed Brownlee Dam. When the experiments started they withheld large amounts of water, and overnight the river dropped three feet. The drawdown caused problems for river goers and grounded the *Wenaha*, a tourist boat that parked for the evening at Cap Creek. The next morning when eleven passengers were to return to Lewiston the boat was high and dry. Boatman Dick Rivers ferried the stuck customers to the Van Pool Ranch where Gustin shuttled them back to Lewiston by airplane.[261]

Gustin was the last person to fly Ron Van Pool out of the ranch in the early 1960s. In fact, the lower landing areas were too wet for the heavily loaded airplane. After several failed takeoff attempts, Gustin instructed his passengers to unload and get a ride up to the old Big Sulphur airstrip where it would be dryer. Sure enough Gustin was able to pull the larger load right off the Big Sulphur site with no problems.[262]

A few years prior to the previous incident, Ron Van Pool and his wife-to-be, Jackie, chartered Gustin to fly them to the ranch on their spring break from college in 1961. Gustin decided it would be best to shuttle them in two separate trips with a Super Cub. Jackie, more oriented to big cities, had never met Ron's parents, been in a small airplane, or roughed it at a remote ranch. She was to go first. By the time Ron was flown in, Jackie had hit her forehead on the leading edge of the airplane, met his parents, and saw a cow give birth.[263]

had acquired Abe Bowler's Bowler Air Service in 1956. The two immediately hired a helicopter pilot with an instructor rating and learned how to fly the machines. They invested heavily in creating a helicopter business, but kept a fixed-wing service as well. By 1968, Gustin and Wilson sold Hillcrest Aviation. After some thorny business dealings during the sale, Wilson ultimately reinstated his involvement with the company. Hillcrest then became solely a helicopter operation. Wilson died in 2000. The company is currently run by his son Gale and Keith White. Gustin retired after the business sold. Although he lost his medical due to heart problems, he kept his hand in aviation by rebuilding a Piper PA-12 and a Cessna 182 at his son Ron's aircraft maintenance shop – Gustin Aviation in Lewiston. Ivan died in January 1989.[259]

During Ivan Gustin's career he spent a lot of time flying back and forth to the ranch for the Van Pools. Occasionally flights were picked up by some of his employees such as Mel Daily. One spring Gustin even made several trips between Lewiston and the river spraying crops on the ranch. Gustin also flew emergency missions from the Lower Bar airstrip.[260]

Vernon Speer – Speer Bullets

While the airstrips served as a lifeline and a utility purpose for the ranch, the Van Pools also received social visits from friends with airplanes. Vernon Speer and his wife Ruth were friends who flew in regularly for visits. The couple lived two houses apart in Lewiston and loved to come to the ranch to hunt as well as attend the annual New Years Eve party.[264]

Speer was a noted machinist who moved to Lewiston in 1944 and founded Speer Bullet. He refined the reprocessing of rimfire casings, developed Hot-Core bullets, and made the first mass-produced jacketed handgun bullets for reloaders. His brother Dick, a machinist as well, left his position with Boeing and started manufacturing ammunition cartridges, also in Lewiston. Dick's former business is now Cascade Cartridge Inc. (CCI).

Although Speer was most noted for revolutionizing bullet manufacturing, he was also a noted pilot. As a young man he built his own five-cylinder aircraft engine from scratch and hung it on a Waco 10. He had plans of mass-producing the engine, but could not find enough investors. In the meantime, he flew the airplane regularly before donating it to a high school mechanics class. During World War II he was a chief ground school instructor at a Nebraska flying school. For most of his adult life he was an avid flier and owned several aircraft, including an Aeronca Sedan, a Cessna 170A, a Cessna 170B, a Cessna 180, several Cessna 182s, and four different Cessna 310s. His son Ray was also a pilot and they enjoyed flying together.[265]

Vernon was commonly found working on airplanes in his backyard or at the Lewiston airport. Speer built a long row of hangars on the northeast side of the Lewiston field and was often consulted for his machine work and built custom aircraft parts for friends such as Ivan Gustin. He loved flying the Idaho backcountry and visiting friends that owned remote ranches. Again, his expert machinist skills were often tapped at these places, as he was well versed in developing hydropower plants. On the Salmon River he helped Paul Filer at the Shepp Ranch design his dam and hydro generator. At Moose Creek Ranches near the Selway River he helped his Lewiston friends revamp the hydro system located on East Moose Creek.[266] At the Van Pool ranch he relaxed a little more by hunting and testing the company's latest bullets. The bullet testing was particularly popular with Tuppy since she was a competitive shooter while attending the University of Idaho. Son Ron noted, "She was an incredibly accurate shot – the best in the family."[267]

No known airplane accident occurred at the ranch during the Van Pool ownership. However, in one close call, Speer, flying a Cessna 180, turned final for the Lower Bar runway, landing to the west and did not notice the old telephone line strung between the bar and the river. Most pilots knew it was there and avoided it by making a close-in approach. At the last second, Speer saw the wire out of the corner of his eye and pitched the airplane forward, narrowly missing it. The elevation loss, however, forced his landing gear into the brush off the end of the hayfield.[268]

Hitchcock Years

Part of the allure of the ranch to the Hitchcocks was the available timber. Maurice grew up in the

Harold Van Pool and Vernon Speer at the lower airstrip with a Cessna 170.

logging trade. His father Charles became involved with the Oregon timber industry near Deschutes at a mill near Lapine in 1929. He later started his own company in Redmond and another in Sisters, and in time brought in his sons Philip and Maurice. The latter expanded the business to Washington, taking up residence in White Swan near Yakima. Brother Philip also became drawn-in with logging operations and served one term (1948–54) as a senator in the Oregon legislature.[269]

As Maurice continually grew the White Swan Lumber Company, he acquired and operated mills in Idaho at Juliaetta, Kooskia, and Tamarack. Always looking for timber to supply the operations, he appointed Willis Spoo, a distant relative and employee, to look for a ranch that had sustainable logging opportunities in addition to good grazing and recreational values. The search was concentrated in the central area of Idaho. As the prospects narrowed on the old Van Pool Ranch, son Bob joined a professional forester on an inspection trip of the property in late 1968. The two used a pair of snowmobiles for the survey work and found the timber and grazing to be very promising. By the spring of 1969 the documents were signed. On paper the new purchase was sometimes called "Evergreen Cattle," but within the family it became known as the "Flying H Ranch."[270]

Logging began right away. Other than the narrow road built from Sugar Loaf to the lower ranch the property was relatively roadless and therefore difficult for log transport. Over the next several years fifteen miles of roads were constructed, allowing annual harvests of five million board feet through 1974. As intended, the timber paid for the initial cost of the place many times over.[271]

While logging defined much of the Hitchcock use, the property was also kept as an active cattle ranch. From the beginning a full-time manager was hired to keep this end of the operation functioning. Family friend Richard Anderson from White Swan filled this role for nearly ten years until starting is own outfit near White Bird. On top of logging and cattle, the ranch was used extensively for hunting, fishing, and relaxation. After Maurice married Katherine in June 1930, the couple had five children: Richard, Sam, Kathleen, Robert, and Maureen (Molly). All five kids worked in various capacities for the family company. Sons Richard and Bob cottoned to the ranch and spent an immeasurable amount of hours keeping it going and enjoying it with their own families. Bob and his wife Elaine moved to McCall in 1974 where he could better manage the Idaho operations. Living closer to the ranch also allowed him to spend more time there. In 1980 the Hitchcocks built a modern four-bedroom home on the old Chamberlain homestead and turned the former Van Pool summer residence into the manager's house.[272]

Maurice died in 1984, and Richard and Bob ended up with majority shares of the property. Eventually Bob bought Richard out and became the sole owner for many years. He sold it to the Wilks brothers in November 2010.[273]

The Hitchcocks and Aviation

Maurice learned to fly at age thirty-one in 1939. He looked at aviation as a valuable business

HITCHCOCK FAMILY

Maurice Hitchcock at the lower ranch house in August 1983.

The summer residence built by the Hitchcocks at the old Pick Chamberlain Place in 1980.

tool. The following year his wife also picked up flying. While living in Sisters the husband and wife pilots had their backyard transformed into a runway, which is now the current Sisters airport. Brother Philip was also a pilot and served as the president of the Oregon State Aviation Council starting in 1945. In Sisters when not flying for work, Maurice actively volunteered with the Civil Air Patrol.[274]

Maurice added several ratings to his pilot's license after moving to White Swan, including a multiengine instrument, an ATP, and eventually a type rating for a Learjet in 1976. Katherine also furthered her aeronautical knowledge by obtaining a multiengine instrument rating before hanging up her wings after 10,000 hours of flying. The two owned dozens of airplanes: a Piper J-3, a Fairchild 24, a Navion, a Cessna 185, a Cessna 195, a Cessna 337, a Cessna 340, an Aero Commander, several Beechcraft 18s, several Beechcraft Barons, several Beechcraft King Airs, several Aero Commanders, and two Learjets. Maurice retired from flying with about 14,000 hours of flight time. All five of their kids took some kind of flying instruction. Richard earned his first license in the early 1960s, followed by Bob in 1966.[275]

As aviation was a primary focus in their business and personal lives it also became a focus of accessing their Snake River ranch. Initially when they bought the place the family was busy working in various places throughout the West and in order to enjoy the ranch they flew larger twin-engine

airplanes to Grangeville. From Grangeville Frank Hill would fly them on the last leg over Joseph Plains to the ranch.[276] On one of Hill's early flights with the Hitchcocks one of the rear side windows in his Cessna 180 shattered when a huge rock was kicked up as the right man wheel hit the ground on landing. No one was hurt, but it sure scared them.

As logging carried on during the first year of ownership, the road building crews also extensively modified the original Lower Bar landing site to its present 950'-runway. Additionally a completely new airstrip was laid out near the summer residence. The following year the 2,500' east-west strip, now commonly referred to as "Upper Hitchcock," was finished. Pleased with the work on both of these airstrips Maurice toyed with the idea of building a third runway on Sugar Loaf Ridge that would measure at least 4,000' to accommodate his first Learjet. The dream never materialized. Much of his flying career was documented by author Margaret Elley Felt in the biography *Maurice G. Hitchcock: The Flying Lumberjack!* that was published in 1985.[277]

The Hitchcocks did not allow any commercial flights on their airstrips, but they did not restrict the use to private individuals either, especially neighbors. Lem Wilson of Pittsburg and landowner across the river from them stopped by regularly flying one of his many Super Cubs. Wilson and Maurice, both self-made men who believed in outright hard work, hit it off from the beginning. When Wilson's ranch became besieged with condemnation proceedings

HITCHCOCK FAMILY

(top) Katherine and Maurice Hitchcock with a Learjet at their home in White Swan.
(center) The Upper Hitchcock airstrip.
(bottom) Looking west down the 2,500' Upper Hitchcock airstrip.
(top opposite) Todd, Katherine, Elaine, and Bob Hitchcock with a Beechcraft King Air.
(bottom opposite) Todd Hitchcock with a Fairchild Republic A-10.

HOLM

HOLM

and court battles concerning appraised land values, Hitchcock lent a hand testifying on his behalf.[278]

Bob usually used a Cessna 182 to access the ranch from McCall. Like his father he had several airplanes linked to the business for travel ranging from Piper Cheyennes to Beechcraft King Airs. Professional company pilots generally flew these larger airplanes. Growing up around the large aviation oriented family, one of Bob's two sons – Todd instantly took to flying. He earned his private license in the family 182 during high school from instructor Lyn Clark of McCall. In fact, his parents allowed him to fly the 182 to and from Pullman while he attended school at Washington State University.[279]

Upon finishing college Todd became employed with the family business. Working for the company allowed him to pursue his aviation interests as he built time flying personnel and parts to and from the various sawmills. A majority of the Hitchcock mills had private or municipal airstrips close by. Two of these more obscure private airstrips are still visible, but inactive – White Swan (southwest of Yakima at HITCH intersection) and Tamarack (west of New Meadows). The runway at White Swan was a paved airstrip capable of handling small jets. The Tamarack runway was a lengthy sod strip that paralleled US Highway 95 and often accommodated Beechcraft Barons.[280]

Todd joined the Idaho Air National Guard in 1989, but continued to work for the business. With the guard he flew various models of the F-4 and the A-10. When the family sold White Swan Lumber Company in 1999, he dedicated two years of full-time work with the guard. In 2001 he hired on with United Parcel Service (UPS) flying 757s, 767s, and MD-11s. He retired from the guard in October 2013 with the rank of Lieutenant Colonel. His career with the military took him on five deployments to Iraq and one deployment to Afghanistan.[281]

Unable to immerse himself enough in aviation, Todd and fellow commercial pilot friend Willy Beebe started Hitchcock Aviation LLC as a sideline in 2008. The company brokers aircraft and is a distributor of aircraft parts and accessories specific to backcountry operations.[282]

From the time Todd learned to fly until the selling of the ranch, he frequented the place using various airplanes ranging from Piper Super Cubs to Cessna 182s and a turbo Cessna 206. While he has owned many airplanes over the years his all time favorite is a Cessna 195 (N3898V) that he currently owns. The plane has immense history in Idaho and the backcountry, as it was the former state of Idaho airplane. In more recent years he has passed the Hitchcock flying legacy onto his son Blake. Blake picked up flying as a high school student. Separating him from other young student pilots is his father's background and knowledge with the military, which allowed him to obtain most of his early flight training in a Beechcraft T-34.[283]

The Wilks Brothers

Dan and Farris Wilks of Cisco, Texas, purchased the place from the Hitchcocks in 2010 and renamed it "Wilks Ranch." The duo grew up in a blue-collar family – their father Voy was a factory worker who eventually learned the masonry trade and started his own company. When his sons were old enough they too joined the business, taking jobs across Texas and Oklahoma.[284]

Ever the entrepreneurs, the brothers entered the energy industry and founded Frac Tech in 2002, a company specializing in hydraulic fracturing, which is the process of utilizing fluids under pressure to cut through rock layers to extract fossil fuels. The technology was the first in the field to allow access to pockets of once-thought-to-be inaccessible shale gas reserves. Less than a decade later the brothers sold their sixty-eight percent interest in the company for 3.2 billion dollars. With their financial success and interest in fly-fishing and hunting, the Wilks have concentrated on acquiring massive tracts of remote lands in Texas, Kansas, Montana, and Idaho. The first big land purchase was the N Bar Ranch in Montana for forty-five million dollars.[285]

Since buying the old Van Pool Ranch from the Hitchcocks the Wilks have also acquired several other adjacent ranches. The Wilks brothers are rarely at their Snake River holdings, but when they do visit, they arrive in a personally owned helicopter. Generally, the Wilks fly to their Montana property via jet and then hop a ride in a copter to Idaho. The brothers are very active in their hometown, particularly Farris, who founded a Christian church, the Assembly of the Yahweh 7th Day, where he serves as pastor.

DUG BAR

Early History

Looking downstream at the 1,900' Dug Bar airstrip.

HCNRA

The bar is named for Thomas Douglas, an early settler of the site in the late 1870s. Douglas constructed a small cabin on the bar and eked out a living prospecting and running cattle. George Craig obtained the location by the 1880s. In the spring of 1887, the men who committed the well-known Chinese massacre at Deep Creek occupied his cabin while he was busy moving cattle off the winter range to the Wallowa Valley.[286] R. Gregory Nokes has written an extensive historical account of this incident in the book *Massacred for Gold: The Chinese in Hells Canyon.*

The Tippetts and the Nez Perce Crossing

Since Craig, the bar has been owned by several people including: Hi and Colonel Graves, Sam Litch, Leonard Johnson, Ivan Simmons, and James H. "Jidge" Tippett. The Tippett family relinquished ownership when the NRA was created. Shortly thereafter the Forest Service erected the sign indicating the historic crossing of the Nez Perce above the bar at Big Eddy in June 1877. In desperation the Nez Perce fled the US Army to reach safety across the Canadian boarder. Their efforts were hindered with defeat in the Bear Paw Mountains of Montana.[287]

Tippett purchased the place toward the end of World War II. Tippett originally moved to Wallowa County at age four. His parents homesteaded on a place near Enterprise. When he was old enough he began working as a sheepherder and eventually established his own ranch in the Grande Ronde area. In about 1919, he expanded his operation and bought 720 acres from Roy Lukes on Joseph Creek, which became his headquarters. From here the Tippetts raised six children, four boys: Jack, Bob, Donald "Biden," and Doug, and two girls; Betty and Barbara. At about the same time he pushed his cattle

rangeland to Dug Bar he also bought ground along Jim Creek.[288] After the war, Jidge worked with his four sons and sons-in-law and formed Tippett Land Company. Their enterprise consisted of more than 20,000 acres, much of which was made up from parts of the old Dobbin and Huffman Sheep Company and eight other ranches. They held grazing permits on 50,000 acres and owned 3,500 acres of irrigated land.[289]

Author Rafe Gibbs highlighted the Tippetts and their way of life in the March 1953 *Popular Mechanics Magazine* article, "Cattle Ranch in a Canyon." In the exposé Gibbs compares Jidge to Zane Grey's heroic character Jim Lassiter from the novel *Riders of the Purple Sage.* Building on the fact that they are both tough cattle ranching cowboys who live in remote canyons, Gibbs draws the line there, as Jidge is "the real-life counterpart," not just fiction. Gibbs further concludes, "Jidge is a cattleman from the tip of his pointed boots to the crown of his broad-brimmed hat . . . He [Jidge] sums up their life in the canyon this way: '[T]he canyon has been a good place for the cattle – and us Tippetts.'"[290]

When the Tippetts obtained the Dug Bar property, several outbuildings remained usable. They added several more. In the winter of 1946–47, Bob and Biden constructed the pumice-block house. All the building material for the project was freighted up the river from Lewiston via boat. Bob mainly managed the Dug Bar property during this time. By the end of the 1940s, Bob added a barn and updated the corrals. Since then several more structures have been added to the complex. The location of the present day airstrip had long been established, dating to the late 1930s. Throughout the Tippetts time little work was done to improve the field. Doug Tippett commented, "It was a naturally good spot as it had been farmed for decades so there were no rocks to speak of and the ground was good and leveled. . . it was one of the best landing places in the canyon."

The Tippetts contracted with a logging company to build a road down to the bar from Imnaha in 1951. Even though the road allowed for greater access, the airstrip continued to be used regularly. Bob took up flying and came in and out of the ranch frequently. Throughout his flying career he owned four different airplanes. His first was an Aeronca and the last a Cessna 210.[292]

The Tibbett Land Company dissolved in about 1954 and the family diversified to various means of income. Bob moved out of the canyon and ended up in the insurance business. Biden bought the family's rangeland associated with Jim Creek. Jack acquired the original ranch on Joseph Creek where he remained until 1974, when he sold it to the Washington Game Department.[293] Doug, the youngest son, purchased the Dug Bar Ranch from the family in 1957 and he continued to run cattle. However, he and his wife Janie also started an outfitting and guiding business where they entertained fisherman in the spring and summer with their boat and guided hunters in the fall. Doug and Janie continued this seasonal routine for several years after they sold out. Then retired permanently to Joseph.

Steens Wilderness Adventures

Jim and Connie Steen followed the Tippetts as the outfitter from Dug Bar, starting in the early 1980s. Jim's son Shawn and his wife Shelly now operate Steens Wilderness Adventures from the location. The Steens built their own cabin amongst the former Tippett buildings and lease it on a year-to-year basis from the Forest Service. The husband and wife team offer big game hunts from Dug Bar and for about a six-year period in the mid-2000s also

ran a branch of their outfitting business from Minam Lodge.[294]

Shawn Steen grew up in an aviation family. Both maternal and paternal grandfathers were pilots. Grandfather J. Wilson Steen even had the privilege of flying an F-111 while serving a term as an Idaho state senator. Shawn's father Jim took up flying in his mid-twenties as a means to compete in more than one rodeo on a given day, and his older brother Jim Jr. "Rowdy" was also a pilot. Following in their footsteps, Shawn began flying from the co-pilot seat as a young kid with his dad or Rowdy in the left seat. By age fourteen he took his first official lesson with Rowdy, who had recently earned his certified flight instructor (CFI) rating. By 1980, Shawn soloed a Cessna 170 at the Joseph airport. He gleaned as much as he could from his family pilots and took formal lessons with Gary Holmes. At the same time Shawn earned his private pilot license, Rowdy hired on as a commercial pilot in Salmon flying for Salmon Air Taxi. Rowdy's first season with the company ended when he was killed flying a Cessna 207 on a mission to Indian Creek on the Middle Fork of the Salmon River. While the family mourned the loss they continued to enjoy flying the backcountry of northeastern Oregon. During Shawn's career as an outfitter he used a Cessna 170, a Cessna 180, a Super Cub, a Bushmaster, a Maule M-5, and a Maule M-7 in conjunction with his businesses at Dug Bar and Minam Lodge.[295]

Bill Duncan – Alaskan Bushwheels Inc.

Overlapping with the Steens early years at Dug Bar were Bill and Dianna Duncan, also of Joseph. Don Hubbard, who held the Forest Service grazing permit for the area, hired the Duncans as ranch foremen. The husband-and-wife team ran the ranch for a number of years in the late 1990s. Duncan, a pilot, used a Pacer and Maule regularly to access the property. His interest in aviation stemmed from his youth while he grew up in the East.

Toward the end of their tenure at Dug Bar, the Duncans bought the Alaska Tire and Rubber Company of Alaska, in 2000. The company specialized in the production of customized off-field airplane tires mainly for small light aircraft. Duncan moved the company to Joseph and renamed it Alaskan Bushwheel Inc.

and manufactured the products in a hangar at the Enterprise airport. Within a few years Duncan and his team learned and developed new techniques and slowly upgraded the technology, rubber formulas, testing, and overall tire construction. The company soon produced all of its tires with Radial construction and re-enforced sidewalls. After growing and expanding the business, Duncan sold it to Airframes Alaska of Chugiak, Alaska, in January 2014.

The Duncan's daughter Nicole and her husband Wup Winn helped to manage Alaskan Bushwheel Inc. Winn, a native Oregonian, had his own connections to Dug Bar, as it became the destination of his first small aircraft flight. It also became the site of his first off-pavement landing after he earned his license with instructor Joe Spence. Lastly, Winn can trace direct bloodlines to ancestors such as Chief Joseph who used the bar frequently as part of the Nez Perce Crossing.[296]

Wallowa County Pilots Association and Bill Ables

After the Duncan's occupancy at Dug Bar, Hubbard sold his ranch, cattle, and grazing permits. The new permit holder of the Snake River portion of the former Hubbard Ranch failed to keep it valid. With the disappearance of the cattle, the proximity of the runway and bar became fairly overgrown.

The Wallowa County Pilots Association, formed in 2009, took notice of the deteriorating airstrip and proposed a plan of action to the Forest Service. Needing guidance to better work with the agency, the association approached the IAA about becoming partners. With the help of IAA Director Jim Davies and two former Idaho directors of Aeronautics, Bill Miller and J. V. DeThomas, the Wallowa pilots were granted their own out-of-state chapter in 2011. Bill Ables was appointed the director of the chapter. The following year physical work began on maintaining the Dug Bar airstrip. The Idaho Division of Aeronautics even donated a Ford tractor to help keep the 1,900'-runway mowed.[297]

The three-way partnership between the Wallowa pilots, IAA, and the Forest Service has gained traction in the last few years and is helping to preserve general aviation access to backcountry airstrips in the vicinity of Hells Canyon. The Dug Bar project served as an excellent example of what can be done when a group of like-minded people rally together with a common goal. The success here has spread to other airstrips in the region – Memaloose, Sluice Creek, Big Bar, Lord Flat, and Salmon Bar.[298]

Ables is one of key players in successfully maintaining these airstrips. Prior to his volunteer efforts, Ables served twenty-five years as a fish and wildlife officer for the Oregon State Police. His jurisdiction covered the four most eastern Oregon counties. During his term he spent uncountable hours patrolling the Hells Canyon region by horseback, jet boat, and airplane. The last fourteen years of his job, as a supervisor, he persuaded the state to allow him to fly his own aircraft for the job to cut down on travel costs to many of the remote parts of the region.[299]

Ables obtained his private pilot license while living in Ontario in 1975. When he moved to Enterprise the next year he joined the Chief Joseph Flyers. Retiring in 2001 he bought a Cessna 170B. As an employee with the state police he regularly flew with their Baker City-based pilots in a Cessna 180. One of the more memorable flights over Hells Canyon occurred after Roy Phanter picked him up in Enterprise at midnight. The goal of the flight was to track the activity of poachers spotlighting bobcats from jet boats along the middle Snake River. The night, of course, was pitch black. After an exorbitant amount of time passed and not seeing the massive Snake River, the two questioned just where they were. Running some calculations placed them nearly at Grangeville. As they turned back, the moon began to emerge, guiding them to the canyon. The poacher's lights were easily spotted and the criminals were eventually apprehended.[300]

Jim Zanelli – Innovative River Entrepreneur and Pilot

Jim Zanelli was another outfitter who frequently used Dug Bar as part of his river rafting operation. Zanelli created one of the most unique outfitting adventures offered in Hells Canyon and possibly Idaho. His Oxbow-based business, Hells Canyon Navigation Company, offered multi-day trips that started within an hours drive below Hells Canyon Dam. Depending on the length desired, customers boated to Pittsburg Landing, Dug Bar, Heller Bar, Rogersburg or Hells Gate Marina in

Lewiston. Setting Zanelli's operation apart from any other rafting business on the Snake River was the way he returned his clientele to their vehicles that had been shuttled to Eagle Bar (parking area about a mile and a half above Hells Canyon Dam). Unlike other companies who used a combination of automobiles and maybe wheeled aircraft, he incorporated a floatplane. While he regularly staged gear and pick up points from the remote airstrips of the canyon, he also had the option of using any relatively flat water on the entire river to retrieve customers and employees.[301]

Zanelli believed the airplane flight back upriver gave people a whole new perspective of the canyon – an entirely different dimension from the landscape they had just experienced while rafting and camping. The view offered by floatplane was indeed a fantastic selling point, but it was also very practical and cost-efficient.[302] Even other outfitters took notice and began abandoning their time and cost-consuming shuttles and simply hired Zanelli. Friend and outfitter George Hauptman of Canyon Outfitters commented, "It worked perfect to fly with Jim especially for small groups. He was a good pilot, no doubt about it, especially to do what he did with that airplane."[303]

Zanelli first came to the Snake River with friends in the late 1960s. At the time he owned a machine shop in La Grande. Completely taken by the beauty of the place and needing a change, he and his wife Doris moved their family to Oxbow and by 1972 bought a dwindling outfitting business. Tying an airplane to the business came naturally as he had longed to become a pilot since his time as a young man in the US Navy. Following his dream with a little money in his pockets he began taking flying lessons at the Baker City airport in 1975. Three years later he purchased his own aircraft a 1964 Cessna 172 (N8230U) and later upgraded it to a 210-horsepower Franklin engine. He kept the plane in Baker and used it as much as possible.[304]

After a year of ownership he consulted with friends Vern and Jack McClure, both pilots with float flying experience in Alaska, about equipping the 172 with floats. Based on their suggestions he purchased a pair of floats in Seattle and flew the plane there to have them mounted. Vern worked with Zanelli on his single-engine seaplane rating and then sent him back to Oxbow. Zanelli cautiously honed his float flying skills and adapted them to the more uncommon water of the Snake River. By the 1978 boating season, he had fully integrated the plane into his business.

He even rigged a small dock system and trailer to store the plane at his home just below the town of Oxbow.[305]

On a routine flight hauling passengers back to Oxbow from a rafting trip, Zanelli, his wife, and two passengers were killed on July 14, 1982. The accident occurred while he was landing in front of the Zanelli house. The exact cause of the crash is unknown and in fact the NTSB accident report fails to mention the airplane was even on floats. It is most widely believed that he saw something in the water as he was landing to the north and then attempted a go-around. Usually when he made a go-around after rejecting a landing in this direction he flew under a series of power lines that crossed the river. However, in this case he attempted a hard left turn short of the power line and stalled the airplane into the driveway of his home.

Steve, the oldest of the Zanelli's five children, carries on his parents' passion for Hells Canyon and the outdoors. As a youngster he was being groomed to eventually take over the family business. At age six he tagged along on raft trips and by the time he turned eleven he learned to run his own boat by following his father down the river. Steve modestly explained, "The outfitting and outdoor business was in my blood." His career did not lead him directly on a path of operating his own outfitting business as he once hoped, but he did end up making a living working in Hells Canyon. Employed with Idaho Power as a water resource specialist, Steve's job allows him to do a little of everything from hydrology to engineering to surveying equipment. In recent years he has accumulated historical research regarding the relicensing of dams and has been instrumental in collection of sediment data that helps monitor the health of the river below Hells Canyon Dam. Additionally, the company utilizes his expert jet boat piloting skills on the Snake; the part of the job he enjoys most.[306]

Zanelli, too young to takeover the family business at the time of his parents' deaths, the estate sold the business and house to Gary Armacost and his wife. The Armacosts turned the home into a bed and breakfast and continued to run a jet boat service. Armacost unluckily had an accident with a power tool while working on a boat, cut his femoral artery and died. His son Bret ran the business until about 2000. Mark Yates, the son of Council commercial pilot Clint Yates, then bought the boating part of the business and renamed it Hells Canyon Adventures.

Jim Zanelli and his float-equipped Cessna 172 on the middle Snake River.

Spencer Ranch

The Spencers

The Sugar Loaf (Upper Spencer) airstrip.

Craig Spencer and his son John slowly built up a cattle operation together, starting in the late 1920s. They combined most of the property that makes up the current Spencer Ranch in 1936. In the 1920s, John and his first wife Fay lived on portions of the ranch during the warmer seasons, but wintered some near Grangeville and in Seattle. John moved permanently to Idaho, outside of Grangeville, in 1929. He later remarried to wife Carm. The couple's son Craig took over the family business in 1971. John remained active in the ranch until the mid-1980s and died in 1988. Craig and his wife Jane now own and operate the ranch with their kids.[307]

John Spencer, George Foster, and Aviation

John had a keen interest in aviation as a young man and took flying lessons. As he prepared for his final check ride his father threw a fit. Apparently his father was unable to understand why they worked so hard to put the ranch together only to have his son taking unnecessary risks. With his father's disapproval he hung up his wings. In spite of the elder Spencer's opinion of flying it became in important part of winter operations at the ranch for over sixty years.[308]

After World War II Spencer became acquainted with George Foster, who moved to Grangeville in late 1945 looking to start a commercial flying business. Originally from Miles City, Montana, Foster had a background in ranching and was a noted bronc buster. Following his service with the navy during World War I he took up flying. He married Alvera Erikson in Wallace, Idaho, in 1922. The couple moved to Pasadena, California, where he worked as a salesman for the Shell Oil Company until hiring on as an airline pilot. As a professional pilot he flew a scheduled route between Los Angeles and San Francisco. During World

War II the Fosters relocated to Washington, where George mainly served as a flight instructor at a CPTP in Spokane. With the end of the war, Foster was out of a flying job.[309]

In Grangeville, Foster started Grangeville Air Service. Besides one airplane, his finances afforded him some land and a military surplus Quonset Hut that was modified into a hangar. In need of more airplanes he approached Spencer about investing in the company. Spencer, a forward thinking businessman, was intrigued by Foster's ambitions and could see the benefits of bringing air commerce to the quaint community. He could also envision the potential of the airplane for accessing his ranch in a timely manner from town and during the difficult months of winter.[310] Of course he had longed to be a pilot years earlier, and perhaps he saw this as an opportunity to accomplish multiple things, including a chance to become involved with aviation. To further persuade Spencer, Foster took him on scenic flight of his property. Commenting about the experience Spencer wrote in his personal diary on July 5, 1945, "Took my first flight over the Snake River ranch and it was very thrilling."[311] With no expectation of financial gain, Spencer loaned Foster $3,200. For the next several years Spencer's diary entries disclose his enthusiasm for the local aviation scene and somewhat silent partnership with Foster.

George Foster standing in front of his Grangeville hangar in 1948.

Many entries reveal the scouting of potential landing sites, the building of airstrips, and the acquisition of new airplanes. With the initial loan money in place by September 1945, Foster arranged for the two of them to look at a pair of Curtiss Robins. One of the planes was flown to Grangeville by well-known Alaskan pilot Noel Wien and the other by a Mr. Jenkinson from Twin Falls. Writing about the event Spencer remarked, "Foster has decided to take one of the Robins . . . This is a mountain plane that seems to be what George needs here."[312]

Two Airstrips

Within the first year of business, Foster and Spencer, with the help of many Snake River ranchers in the Joseph Plains area, improved and created many landing sites used for winter access. In June 1946, Spencer decided to build an airstrip near his Sugar Loaf Butte ranch headquarters.[313] This portion of the ranch was a conglomeration of land homesteaded by John Alles (1910), Conrad Alles (1911), Henry Alles (1911), Christopher Knorr (1916), and Robert McCulley (1919). The majority of the current airstrip sits on the old Knorr and Alles places.[314] The Knorrs likely constructed some of the Spencer's dwellings and when the latter acquired the parcel it contained a well-built house, barn, and several log structures. Jack Brust, Clarence Hardin, and Cecil Lyda used a motorized grader to build the strip. Foster made the first flight from the runway on June 15, 1946. By August the next year the strip was extended to its current length of 1,600'.[315]

In general the Sugar Loaf portion of the ranch was used from spring until late fall. Once the cattle were moved to the lower winter ranges the ranch foreman migrated with them to the Poole Place located on the north side of Divide Creek. T. McCann built the first cabin known to exist on the site circa 1907. Albert Poole homesteaded the 160 acres in May 1920.[316] When the Spencers obtained the acreage they sometimes utilized the existing dwellings built by previous occupants and added on as needed. Charlie Williams, a Spencer Ranch cattle foreman,

(top) The Spencer Ranch building complex [lower center] located near Sugar Loaf Butte in September 1958. The airstrip is above the structures, situated left to right, with a small shed on the upper end.

(bottom) Pilot Randy Lorentz landing his Champ at the Sugar Loaf airstrip in the 1980s.

(top opposite) The Lower Spencer airstrip is located in the center of the photograph, below the towering terrain, slightly to the right of the small knob.

(center opposite) An airborne view of a Super Cub landing at Lower Spencer.

(bottom opposite) A Super Cub landing at Lower Spencer.

HOLM

HOLM

HOLM

159

lived at both the upper and lower places with his wife Geneva for seventeen years. In the beginning the Williams split their time during the winter, living between the two sites. By the early 1950s they had begun riding horses over to Flynn Creek on the Salmon River from the Poole Place, where supplies were occasionally flown in.[317]

The need for the Williams's occasional journey to either Flynn Creek or Sugar Loaf was eliminated in 1955 when the old trail to the lower ranch was widened into a road. Owen Smith operated the dozer for the project. Once the road was punched toward the Salmon River, a discussion occurred between Spencer and Foster about a possible landing site on the east side of Pot Creek. With an airstrip, winter supplies could almost be delivered directly to the lower residence.[318]

The shallow landing patch under debate was near "Pot Corral" situated in the upper breaks of the Salmon River above Blue Canyon. It was nothing more than a short, naturally smooth steep bench. The little promontory jutting out from the high rim of the canyon wall was highlighted by sheer drop offs on three sides, falling into Pot Creek and the turbulent Slide Rapid on the Salmon. Foster thought it could be done. With no work performed on the surface of the site, Foster discussed a trial landing with one of his pilots, Frank Hill. On March 17, 1955, Spencer casually wrote in his diary, "Sent Frank Hill in with the Cub to try out the new landing strip at the upper Pot Corral. It turned out to be feasible and with a little work can be a fair strip."[319] Four months later Spencer jotted another note about the precariously placed runway, "Flew to Salmon River [Flynn Creek] after lunch to inspect the bulldozer work. Vern, Foster and I drove to the Poole place and found the dozer starting into Belnap. He had finished the road to the Pot airstrip after a hard struggle. Foster made some suggestions for improving the new airstrip, which we will do next week."[320] The improvements to the 750'-runway were indeed completed.

Several years later Smith's road was used to construct a series of high-tension power lines that now run above the road and airstrip against a looming rock wall. The line extends east to west and provides a link to the Snake River dams.

Frank Hill, the first pilot to land and takeoff on the airstrip, used it the remainder of his career, hauling winter supplies to the Poole Ranch for the Spencers. He considered the approach and landing to this airstrip as one of the more difficult in the Snake and lower Salmon area. Although he started out

with a Cub at the strip he graduated to regularly using Cessna 180s and 206s. The strip is rarely used anymore and over the years has been referred to as the "Pot Airstrip," the "Poole Place," and "Lower Spencer."

Frank Hill, Lower Spencer Airstrip, Relatives, and the End of an Era

Legendary backcountry pilot Frank Hill began flying for George Foster at Grangeville Air Service in 1952. With a flying background that began in the navy during World War II and spread to include ag flying in Enterprise for famous aviatrix Bessie Halladay after the war, Hill fitted right in at Foster's operation. By the end of the decade he and his wife Joanne purchased the business and lived in a home at the Idaho County Airport where they raised four kids: Rose, Beverly, Greg, and Becky.

George Foster died at age sixty-four in August 1961 not long after selling the business to the Hills. All of the pallbearers at his funeral were pilots and or former students – Frank Hill, Sid Hinkle, Lou Fortin, Jim Mitchell, George Crea, and Abe Bowler.[321] Foster's wife died seven years later. They are both buried in the Grangeville Prairie View Cemetery.

While Foster, who also served as the airport manager for years, could not be replaced, Hill became the go-to pilot of the greater Grangeville area. He did just about any kind of flying that came through the door. He flew supplies and contracts for the Forest Service, performed ag work for local growers, taught dozens of locals to fly, and hauled supplies for ranchers. One major advantage he had over competitors was his central location. At arms length was the River of No Return to the south, the Selway-Bitterroots to the east, the Snake River to the west, and out his backdoor were crops to spray.

The middle Snake and the lower Salmon River country particularly kept Grangeville Air Service busy in the winter months as local ranchers moved their base of operations to lesser elevations along the rivers, following the cattle to the warmer temperatures. Due to high snow accumulations along the Joseph and Doumecq plains, the ranches were only accessible by air. Hill created a weekly route flying mail, supplies, and passengers for roughly thirty years. Stops along the route varied, but often encompassed: Flynn Creek, Billy Creek, Spencer

Frank Hill at the Poole Place in 1987.

Jay Cawley at the Upper Spencer airstrip in the mid-1980s.

Ranch, and Wapshilla. The route was flown with a variety of aircraft from ski-equipped Super Cubs to Cessna 206s.

While Hill mainly flew the winter route himself, he hired seasonal pilots depending on the workload. A few pilots that worked for Grangeville Air Service over the years included: Travis Wadley, John Moberly, Ty Edling, Roger Ferguson, George "Buzz" Kopczynski, Tom Gearing, Mike Miller, Michael D. Miller, Dave Kelsey, Steve Kelsey, and John McKenzie.

Hill taught two of his kids and his wife how to fly. Son Greg earned his private license on his sixteenth birthday and later joined the navy. In 1980, he returned to Grangeville and joined the family business. Greg was killed in an airplane shortly after takeoff from Moose Creek Ranger Station in the fall of 1986. After the accident, Hill's son-in-law Jay Cawley began flying for the company. Cawley came to Idaho flying Beech 99s for Cascade Airways. While working for his in-laws he flew charter flights

around the state, with a primary focus on backcountry work. At one point Cawley considered taking over the operation, but in late 1992, Hill was offered a substantial amount of cash for the business. Jim VanDyke of Sacramento, California, and a partner took possession of Grangeville Air Service and all of its assets in January 1993. Hill and Cawley continued to fly for the company for a short time. The VanDyke ownership quickly became troubled with a string of accidents, badly damaging five airplanes. One accident claimed the life of veteran Idaho pilot Don Schumacher's son Colby in 1995. Within roughly five years of Hill selling his historic business it was run into the ground and liquidated.

The first accident under the new VanDyke ownership occurred on February 3, 1993, when Cawley was dispatched on a flight with a Cessna 206 (N2837J) to haul supplies to the Lower Spencer Ranch. Following standard procedures Cawley slowed the airplane down and overflew the airstrip to insure no cattle or game were on the runway before committing to the approach. Circling over the strip into the top of Divide Creek, Cawley made a tight left turn up against a rock wall near the ridge top. This maneuver positioned him for a downhill run over the airstrip in the direction of the Salmon River to buzz the runway if needed or to enter a wide approach to turn back upstream for final. However, in the apex of the turn he hit a wire within a series of overhead power lines. On impact, one of the lines broke free and wrapped around the propeller, causing the engine to quit, but not before collapsing the nose gear. The ranch crew waiting on the ground at the strip saw a shower of sparks as the 206 clawed its way out of the entanglement. Not believing what was happening they watched Cawley then maneuver the crippled plane back toward the river. Cawley, somewhat along for the ride, continued to pitch the machine for best glide speed and aimed for the strip. The plane skimmed over the runway, hit the ground, and skidded to a halt. The ranch crew immediately showed up on the scene to help. Cawley for the most part escaped the accident uninjured. The ranch hands returned to the house with Cawley and placed a call to Grangeville to report the event.

The next morning Frank Hill and Ken Kuther flew a company Cessna 180 (N2731K) to the lower strip to retrieve Cawley. When they flew over the accident the two could not believe how close the plane was sitting to the edge of a bluff that stands 1,000' vertical from the river. Still in amazement about the accident twenty years later Kuther commented, "The plane was maybe only thirty to forty feet from the edge of the bluff . . . what saved Jay from going over was the collapsed front gear. The broken gear caused the plane to dig into the ground when it hit, instead of rolling. That saved his life."[322] Later the plane was disassembled, trucked out, and repaired.

After the accident Cawley continued to fly for Grangeville Air Service through 1994 and then made a move toward corporate flying. However, he continues to enjoy the Idaho backcountry with a Piper PA-11 and a Piper Pacer.

Frank Hill's flying legacy continued on both in Grangeville and at the Spencer Ranch, even with the closing of his business. He died in 2006. One of Hill's granddaughters, Jayci, married Chad Frei. In high school Frei learned to fly initially from his father and took formal lessons with Hill. Working his way through various ratings, Frei flew with Hill at every opportunity. As their friendship developed, Frei gleaned as much as he could from the quiet and reserved Hill and his approach to flying, especially

in the backcountry. Thinking about his time in the cockpit with Hill, Frei said, "He taught me never to be in a hurry around an airplane. You walk, you don't run." For example, one time at the Lower Spencer strip he told Frei to hop in the Cub and go through his checklist. Hill climbed in behind him. After the engine idled for a while Frei became slightly anxious. Hill, patiently finished his cigarette and remarked, "I just wanted to make sure the motor was going to keep running that good when it counts on takeoff." Frei also remembered, "You always knew when Frank was ready to go flying . . . especially in a Cub or a Champ, before he would say much from the backseat he would casually bend down and role up one of the cuffs on his pant leg for an ash tray and light a cigarette . . . half the time I was flying with him, I was just trying to see through his smoke, but he was a heck of a guy to learn from."[323]

Not by coincidence, Frei took one of his first commercial pilot jobs at McCall Air Taxi flying for Mike Dorris, one of the foremost expert backcountry pilots to ever fly in Idaho. Dorris said, "Several people told me about this young kid who wanted a job, and I kept telling them and myself he doesn't have enough hours. But the response was – just go fly with him. I did and all I have to say is he [Frei] is the lowest time pilot I ever hired. He was just a natural."[324]

Frei flew for Dorris seasonally for nine years. When not flying the backcountry Frei began working for Valley Air Service owned by Bill and Gary Hubler. Headquartered in Caldwell, the Hublers also owned a field northwest of Grangeville commonly known as "Fenn" that was started by ag pilot Lee Owens. Under the supervision of Hubler employee Tim Shamblin, Frei learned the ag aviation business and in time bought the Fenn operation in 2008 and renamed it Frei Aviation. However, with a true passion for the backcountry, he acquired a Cessna 180 (N2993C) that he flies for fun. He, like Frank Hill, has helped the Spencers fly groceries and supplies to the ranch during the winter months. Keeping the family's aviation history alive Frei's son Josh soloed his dad's 180 at age sixteen in 2013 and earned his license the following year.[325]

To date Chad Frei is the last pilot to fly for the Spencer Ranch. Since his flights, the Spencers have determined it is more cost effective to drive an ATV (four-wheeler) over Sugar Loaf Butte and down Dry Creek. At the confluence of Dry Creek and the Snake River his employees meet the Beamers' weekly mail boat that can deliver supplies when requested.[326]

Chad Frei with son Josh and their Cessna 180, the day Josh soloed on his sixteenth birthday.

SALMON BAR

Looking downstream at Salmon Bar.

The large Dobbin and Huffman Sheep Company associated with downstream Cherry and Cache creeks used the Salmon Bar site for many years. Although the company did not own the ground at the bar they erected several lamb/shearing sheds there prior to 1919. The gentle sloping terrain toward the river no doubt made it easy to load woolsacks onto boats bound for market in Lewiston.

By the 1950s, the sheds were gone and the Pacific Northwest Power Company (PNPC) moved onto the Bar. The PNPC was comprised of four private utility companies: Pacific Power and Light, Portland General Electric, Washington Water Power, and Montana Power and Light. The PNPC used the site as a base camp for crews locating and collecting core samples at the various proposed dam sites along the Snake River. Two of the closest proposed dam sites near Salmon Bar were the Nez Perce Dam,

A Cessna 180 parked at the upper end of Salmon Bar.

164

C. CONLEY

(top) The Dobbin and Huffman Sheep Company's buildings at Salmon Bar in the 1910s.

(right) Lettering was used throughout the canyon to indicate proposed dam sites. [High Mountain Sheep - Pacific Northwest Power]. The photo is particularly interesting as it shows the water level of the 1974 flood — at usual flows these markings were about twenty feet above the water surface.

(bottom) Pacific Northwest Power Company's prefabricated structures at Salmon Bar.

T. RIVERS

T. RIVERS

HMT PNP

A Super Cub [lower right] on final approach landing upstream at Salmon Bar.

HOLM

2.1 miles downstream and the High Mountain Sheep Dam 1.3 miles upriver. For decades many of the proposed dam sites remained clearly marked with orange and white paint etched on the walls of the river. Boaters on the river added their own markings by drawing large two-foot wide circles at various places on the river to indicate navigational hazards. The Forest Service viewed the circles as graffiti and worked with volunteers from the Northwest Power Boat Association to remove them in the 1990s. When the navigation circles were removed, some of the dam-site indicators were also washed off with a high-pressure hose.

Due to the increased activity at Salmon Bar, the PNPC assembled two prefabricated buildings on the upper end for housing and cooking facilities, complete with a buried septic system. In addition to the structures, the company hired Dick Rivers to haul in a small Caterpillar dozer via boat.[327] The dozer was used to level the current 750'-airstrip. The PNPC wanted air access to the remote region. The airstrip was primarily considered an access point to be used in case of an emergency because of the high-risk work performed by employees. The first to land on the strip was Grangeville pilot Frank Hill. Hill also became the first to land a larger aircraft on the small runway, using a Cessna 206.

Sometime after 1965, Rivers disassembled the prefabricated structures and moved them by boat to his Copper Creek Camp. He reassembled the buildings and modified them into guest quarters. The current operators of the camp still use them.[328] Much of the evidence of the utility company's temporary camp at Salmon Bar was washed out in the high water year of 1974. As at other sandy beaches of the middle Snake River, the frequent fluctuations in the reservoirs, have slowly eroded the beach at Salmon Bar. As the bar has worn away, parts of the PNPC's septic system are now visible.

After the NRA was created in 1975, this airstrip was kept open under emergency status only. Its designation was later upgraded to open. One of the biggest hazards of this landing location is the debris that can often wash up on the strip when the river is at flood stage. Many, many, airplane accidents have occurred here over the years. The runway is deceivingly short and has no grade to help on landing or takeoff.

CHERRY CREEK RANCH

Early History

The Cherry Creek Ranch in the 1950s with sheep grazing in the background.

William Duncan, Mike Thomason, and Jude Basin settled on the creek and built a cabin in the late 1880s. The men named their slice of paradise "Cherry Creek" because of all the chokecherry bushes that grew along the drainage. Jay Dobbin acquired the land, which formally became identified as the Cherry Creek Ranch, then sold it sometime in the mid-1940s to three of his Basque sheepherders.

The Basques

The three Basque herders, Seberino "Silver" Egana, Gus Malaxa, and Tony Martiartu, were affectionately known on the river as "the Bascos." As young men they immigrated to the United States circa 1920 from Vizcaya – one of four Basque Provinces in Spain. The group worked for the Dobbin and Huffman Sheep Company for about twenty years prior to buying the ranch.[329]

In 1953, Martiartu wanted to retire and move to Boise to be closer to his family. Joe Onaindia, who was living in Utah, bought out Martiartu's interests in the Cherry Creek Sheep Company. About three years earlier Onaindia had met Malaxa on an airplane flight from the United States to Spain. After becoming acquainted they realized they grew up very close to one another. Once in Spain they met again and began dating the Ulacia sisters. On March 17, 1951, the couples wed on the same day – Malaxa married Juana and Onaindia married Maria. Eventually Malaxa returned to Cherry Creek and Onaindia to Utah. However, the sisters did not like being separated and the opportunity occurred for the buy-in on the middle Snake River.[330]

Throughout the Basques' ownership the ranch retained its primitive character. The six-mile horseback ride from Deadhorse Spring to Cherry Creek limited the improvements they could make to the property. The ranch was fairly self-sufficient and they meticulously maintained the 25' X 40'

one-room log cabin with sleeping loft as built by Dobbin. Likewise the Dobbin-era blacksmith shop, cellar, barn, and granary were also kept in perfect condition.[331]

Three years later, the partners decided to build a road from Buckhorn Spring to the ranch in 1956, the operation was so oriented to horses and pack animals that only Onaindia knew how to even drive a vehicle. For the construction of the road they worked a deal with Boise Cascade. Part of the agreement allowed the company to log within a certain distance from the road for partial payment, since the timber was on deeded ground. The road provided easier access to the ranch from May through November until winter snows blocked the upper reaches of the canyon.[332]

Generally the men stayed at Cherry Creek most of the winter, while the women were in town with the kids attending school. The Malaxas had a daughter Mary and the Onaindias had two boys and one daughter. Joe Jr., the oldest child of the Onaindias, remembered spending summers at the ranch. His fondest memories were riding horses, helping with the pack animals, and tending to the sheep. Unlike the other kids in his generation he ended up in the livestock business, working in the Imperial Valley of California, after graduating from Oregon State University. In his youth, the three partners had about 3,000–4,000 ewes in the summer, which doubled with the yearly lambs. The sheep were run in three bands during the summer and two bands during the winter. Basque sheepherders from Spain came each season to help. These men were hired through the

ONAINDIA FAMILY

ONAINDIA FAMILY

(top) The Cherry Creek Ranch crew in spring 1966.
[standing, left to right] Bonitacio Elorieta [herder], Silver Egana [partner], Joe Onaindia [partner], Justo Mendiola [herder], Gus Malaxa [partner].
[kneeling, left to right] Jose Antionio Malaxa [herder, nephew], Rick Onaindia [son], and Eugueno Urrutibeascoa [herder].
(bottom) Maria Onaindia at Cherry Creek in the mid-1950s.

(top) Some of the Cherry Creek men enjoying
the view of the middle Snake River country
during lunch in June 1961.
[left to right] Frank Marguergiaga [herder,
Egana's nephew], Eugueno Urrutibeascoa
[herder], Celestino Eguerrula [herder,
Onaindia's nephew], and Silver Egana.
(bottom) Loading wool at the mouth of Cherry
Creek onto Dick Rivers's Idaho Queen III.

Looking up the Cherry Creek drainage from the Snake River. The landing area was located in the lower right of the photograph.

Western Range Association and worked on visas that were commonly renewed every three years. The goal of most of their young twenty-something herders was to earn enough money to buy a home so they could start a family in Spain.[333]

Silver Egana, the oldest of the partners, died in about 1964. Malaxa and Onaindia continued to run the operation well into their seventies before selling the land to the government during the preliminary creation of the NRA in 1973. When asked if the partners were remorseful about having to sell, Joe Jr., explained, "By then they were fairly old guys – at least seventy years old – who slept on the hard ground every night and rode horses everyday, all day. They also had wives who were about twenty years younger. I'm not sure my mom or aunt was ready for them to move to town . . . I was the only one who even thought about taking it over, but I was in college at that time and it is a pretty isolated way to live. I did not even speak English until I attended grade school. So, no I don't think they cared about

selling . . . the timing was about right and it was a buyer."[334]

Onaindia did not retire right a way, but worked a few seasons as a herder for Greg Johnson at Temperance Creek. Ultimately both partners retired to Enterprise. Onaindia died in 1996. Malaxa died in April 2000. Their wives, Juana and Maria, remain actively involved in the Enterprise area and are dedicated to helping preserve their Basque heritage.[335] After the formation of the NRA the original ranch buildings at Cherry Creek burned in a wildland fire.

The Airstrip

About the same year the road was finished from Buckhorn to Cherry Creek, Enterprise pilot Ted Grote began landing on the small hayfield at the ranch. To this seasoned pilot Cherry Creek was

171

A Zimmerly Air Transport airplane [top center] flying over the frozen Snake River, dropping hay to ranchers in January 1949.

R. VAN POOL

considered one of the toughest landing spots in the canyon with a roughly 550' long runway on a seventeen percent grade.[336] The approach to even get to the landing patch was tedious – requiring a low approach up the creek and a blind right hand turn to final.

The purpose for the strip was to supply the ranch with goods related to their lambing operation or in times of emergency. The only airplane considered safe to exercise at the strip by its users was a high-powered Cub. When asked about the place Grote commented, "Darn short, had to be sure to be on the ground quick . . . just put it down and get it stopped."[337] As with other strips, Bud Stangel is the last known pilot to access the locale with an airplane sometime in the 1980s.[338]

A Walk to Town
– the 1949 Air Drop

Similar to other canyon residents the Cherry Creek Sheep Company was unprepared for the harsh

winter of 1948–49 (see Van Pool Ranch). Caught without enough hay or feed for their sheep and no easy way to contact anyone for help, Gus Malaxa began a long cold walk down the edge of the frozen Snake River toward Lewiston. Once he passed Rogersburg he hitched a ride to town with a passing motorist. In Lewiston he hired Zimmerly Air Transport to airdrop hay to the ranch. Likely due to the high demand from other area ranchers, there was a feed shortage in this region.[339] Because of scarcity of hay in Idaho, it is believed that Malaxa then requested another hay drop from Bessie Halladay who ran a flight service from the Joseph airport. Frank Hill, one of her pilots, flew the mission.[340]

An Aviatrix of Hells Canyon
– Bessie G. Halladay

Bessie Gale Halladay was one of the earlier pilots to fly in Hells Canyon and the surrounding area from Oregon. Halladay arrived in Wallowa County after World War II and became the manager of the Joseph Municipal Airport, as well as the main fixed-wing operator there. She married local farmer Alfred Butterfield in October 1949. Widowed in 1973, she remained active in the Oregon aviation community until her death at age seventy-nine in January 1979.

Prior to building a reputation in eastern Oregon, Halladay had already had an impressive career in aviation. Growing up in Portland she began taking flying lessons from Lieutenant James L. Meadows of Rasmussen-Meadows Flying Service at the Swan Island airport in August 1932. She completed her private license in October 1933. A week after earning her wings she visited her brother Lloyd Gale in China for four months. Gale was an engineer who owned his own business, L. E. Gale Company, which imported Boeing and Waco airplanes to China. During her visit she became the first white woman to fly an airplane solo in the country – using her brother's Fleet Finch airplane powered with a B5 radial at the Hungjao airport in Shanghai. Upon her return to the United States she continued to fly as often as she could and became a part-time flight instructor and clerk at the Commercial Aircraft Company of Portland in 1937. The following year, after acquiring her commercial transport license, Halladay bought a Piper Cub and founded her own flight instructing business at Swan Island airport. She traveled weekly to the neighboring communities of Silverton, Woodburn, McMinnville, and St. Helens to teach students.

Besides work, Halladay found time to fly in powder puff derbies and helped to organize the Sportsman-pilots of Oregon where she served as the club's first secretary. She was also the first deputized flying policewoman and member of the National Aero Policewomen's Association in Portland. When not in the air, Halladay became a noted author and authority on aviation, writing articles for magazines and regional newspapers. Her reputation landed her a weekly column in *The Oregonian* titled "Hangar Flying." She maintained the popular editorial from 1938 to 1939. Through her writing she met many leading aviators of the era as they flew their way through the Northwest. One of the most notable was her introduction to Russian pilot Valery Chkalov who piloted a Tupolev ANT-25 from Moscow, Russia, over the North Pole to Vancouver, Washington.

During World War II Halladay transformed her business into a CPTP. Halladay's postwar career kept her busy with aviation associations and clubs. Her name continued to stay in the headlines of *The Oregonian* and other regional newspapers, which often noted her accomplishments and participation in the industry as the "only woman airport operator in the state." She hired many excellent pilots to fly for her Joseph-based company. Among the most reputable in the backcountry were Jack Cathcart and Frank Hill. On top of charter flights and ag flying Halladay sustained her old business of flight instructing. She became a dealer for Piper Cubs through Portland friend and aircraft distributor A. W. "Art" Whitaker, who was famous for designing a tandem-wheeled landing gear for the planes. To boost sales in 1948 a flight instruction package was included with every new Cub sold.

FRENCHY CREEK

Homestead and Buildings

Final approach at Frenchy Creek.

William Fountain homesteaded land along this drainage in 1921. At the time of the land survey he had constructed a well-built cabin along the creek. He and his wife Cora also owned rangeland downstream on Cave Gulch.[341] Ross Howard later acquired the Fountain property and over time leased it to several cattle operations. By the 1970s, Harold Heitstuman leased the ground including Frenchy Creek from the Howard family. During Heitstuman's tenure in the country he and his four sons built a hay barn near the creek and occasionally used the old cabin in the winter.[342] The Idaho Department of Fish & Game (IDFG) obtained the cabin, barn, and associated land in 1992 as part of Craig Mountain Wildlife Management Area (WMA) expansion.[343]

New Cabin and Landing Field

The Maloney Creek Fire of 2000 burned through the Frenchy Creek drainage and destroyed the structures. During this period the IDFG valued maintaining various cabins and cultural sites throughout the Craig Mountain WMA. At the spurring of volunteers such as Gene Majors, who donated money for some of the cabins, Regional Wildlife Habitat Manager Sam McNeill oversaw the projects. Replacing the cabin at Frenchy Creek was no exception.[344]

When McNeill secured the funding for Frenchy Creek, he hired Leading Edge of Lewiston to fly in most of the material with a helicopter. Jim Pope Jr., the owner of the company, piloted the copter for the job. Extra heavy materials such as the cement bags for the foundation were hauled in on a trailer with a four-wheeler. Rusty Bentz and Harold Alexander, who both own Cessna 185s, flew in tools, generators, and other miscellaneous supplies.[345]

The small 800' uphill landing spot to access the drainage is located northwest of the cabin on a small bench. Hillcrest Aviation owner Ivan Gustin of Lewiston first landed an airplane at the site in the 1950s. Bentz started using it in the late 1990s. As the cabin neared completion Bentz drove a backhoe in and excavated an area in front of the cabin for a porch. At the same time he also installed tie-downs at the airstrip. The outline of the runway is somewhat defined. Surprisingly, no equipment has been used to alter the field surface. As others in the area, it was once the site of a cultivated field and therefore is void of large rocks.[346]

Building the current Frenchy Creek Cabin.

Jim Creek

Early Years and Tippetts

The Jim Creek drainage and ranch.

HOLM

The creek earned its name from early homesteader Gustave "Jim" Gaillard who proved up on 114.6 acres in February 1913 about two miles up from the Snake River where the North and South Forks of Jim Creek merge.[347] The Jim Creek drainage became a part of the expansive rangeland owned by the Dobbin and Huffman Sheep Company. During that ownership the property contained a small log cabin located on the Gillard homestead site that was used by the company sheepherders. Guy Huffman sold the Jim Creek holdings to Herb Clark, who then sold it to Jidge Tippett (of upriver Dug Bar) circa 1948. Donald "Biden" Tippett then bought the land from his father in 1957.[348]

Biden married Betty Heasty in June 1948 and by fall the newlyweds moved to the Jim Creek Ranch to care for the cattle on the winter range. Construction on the road to the ranch, began on Armistice Day 1949. The logging company that the Tippetts had hired for the work finished the road from Cold Springs Ridge down Downey Gulch and north over to Jim Creek by March 1950. With better access on the ground, Biden hauled in cinder blocks and other building material for a new home that he and a general contractor completed in 1953. The new house fit the needs of the Tippett's growing family, which consisted of daughter Donna and son Tracy "Casey." In the same year in which they bought the Jim Creek Ranch from Jidge they purchased a second home in Enterprise so the kids could attend school. Over the years Biden added a hay barn, horse barn, bunkhouse, and granary to the ranch. The Tippetts lived at Jim Creek nearly year-round until they sold it to the Forest Service in 1992.[349] The couple enjoyed their retirement living in Enterprise. Betty died at age eighty-five in September 2012.[350]

Landing Locations

Even after the road was built to the ranch, it was sometimes blocked by snow or it was just more cost efficient to have things flown in. The Tippetts did receive most of their supplies during the winter via mail boat. However, to meet the boat they had to ride horseback a mile and a half down to the river. Conditions sometimes did not favor boat travel when the river iced up. For the first few years Biden kept an outboard boat at the mouth of Jim Creek to commute back and forth to the end of the road at the Grande Ronde River. But in the case of an emergency it was not a fast way out of the canyon. These drawbacks meant that airplanes played an important role at the Jim Creek Ranch during the Tippetts ownership. Planes were used for hauling in supplies, personnel, family, and in emergencies. The first landing site associated with the ranch was situated to the north near Garden Creek on a bench within the old Baldwin homestead. This airstrip, sometimes referred to as "Garden Creek," was actually located on Les Oliver's Cache Creek Ranch, but Biden was granted permission to use it whenever needed.[351] Zimmerly Air Transport pilots used it regularly throughout the 1940s.[352]

The second landing strip built in the early 1950s lay on a flat ridge between Jim Creek and Downey Creek, below the road and parallel to the river. This spot was naturally good for landing, but Biden further improved by grading it with a D4 Caterpillar. Biden remembered, "The field was

B. TIPPETT

B. TIPPETT

(top) The Tippett family home on Jim Creek in the mid-1950s.
(bottom) Longtime Snake River rancher Biden Tippett.

177

An aerial view of the Jim Creek Ranch. The former landing site is in the center of the photogragh.

nothing fancy, but with the D4 dozer, I knocked down the humps and filled in some small gullies . . . it made it pretty smooth." The 1,000'-airstrip was well laid out and provided an uphill slope for landing and a downhill slope for takeoff. The Zimmerly pilots approved of the work and used it for several years.[353]

Not long after the strip was in use, Biden's wife Betty accidently bludgeoned her hand with an axe while cutting firewood. Weighing the options of a six-hour trip by boat and car to the nearest hospital or a thirty-minute flight, they telephoned out to Zimmerlys for help. Within a short time the two met the airplane at the new airstrip and Betty was delivered to the Lewiston hospital.[354]

The only major aircraft accident to occur at the ranch happened on this southern airstrip. In the late 1950s, pilot Jack Cathcart flew Betty and Donna to Jim Creek with a Stinson 108 owned by

Ray Dunsmore. As Cathcart, an experienced and respected pilot, prepared for takeoff he revved the engine up and lifted the tail off the runway. As he released the brakes the plane dipped forward and the prop nicked the ground. When the plane became airborne, Cathcart promptly noticed a bad vibration. Thinking he had enough runway left to set the plane back down, he attempted to land the aircraft. Once the wheels hit the ground he mashed on the brakes, skidded off the end, and the plane nosed over causing considerable damage. Unhurt, Cathcart scrambled out of the plane. Biden, who watched the whole event transpire, rushed to the plane to help. Later another plane came in to retrieve Cathcart. At the same time several valuable parts were removed from the wrecked Stinson.[355]

The wreckage of Dunsmore's airplane sat at the base of the airfield for several years until a salvage

178

crew came in to haul it out. The salvagers removed the wings and strapped them to the fuselage. Then the two main tires were inflated and Tippett used a team of horses to pull it up the runway. From the top of the airstrip the horses continued to pull the plane along the quarter mile length of trail to the road. Once Tippett got it on the road the crew lifted the tail onto the flatbed portion of his truck and lashed it down. Biden noted, "With the plane perched backwards on its main landing wheels I pulled it up the rough grade to Cold Springs Ridge, just like it was a fifth wheel trailer. There the salvage crew hooked it to the hitch of their pickup truck . . . After all that work the guys got in a hurry, took a corner too fast, and wrapped the fuselage around a pine tree. That was that."[356]

By the early 1960s, the Tippetts were mainly using Bud Stangel for their flying needs. Stangel and Biden discussed the idea of landing in a field slightly downstream from the house, as it was no longer being used to grow alfalfa and would be more convenient. Stangel bounced the idea around with pilot friend Ted Grote and the two saw no reason it could not be done with an airplane such as a Super Cub. With the go-ahead from the pilots, Biden filled in several ditches and smoothed it out the best he could. The steep 650'-airfield, aligned perpendicular to the main Jim Creek drainage, was used through the late 1980s as the main landing site. Although short, the runway had nearly a seventeen percent incline, which made it very usable for small, but powerful aircraft.[357] The Forest Service has used the field for landing helicopters, but not for fixed-wing aircraft.

Forest Service Ownership

The Forest Service designated the Jim Creek property as an administrative site. Since then the ranch buildings have been used regularly for fieldwork. The agency also created an administrative range allotment that extends from the south side of Garden Creek to the north side of Experiment Creek. The allotment provides winter grazing land for Forest Service stock, which is managed from the Jim Creek Ranch. Prior to this, stock was wintered near Tryon Creek after the agency took over the Tryon Creek Ranch during the creation of the NRA.[358]

CAVE GULCH

Early Years

The Fountain Ranch on Cave Gulch in the 1950s.

This drainage earned its name from a large rock overhang that resembles a cave near the mouth of Cave Gulch Creek. Extensive mining occurred along Cave Gulch from the 1880s through about 1905.[368] As the interest in mining slowly faded, the large flat areas along the creek became homesteads. The Nature Conservancy obtained multiple tracts of lands in Cave Gulch and China Garden creeks in the 1980s. All of the parcels but one on China Garden were transferred to BLM ownership.[369]

Pete Fountain and Family

The William and Cora (Bowman) Fountain family once occupied an old homestead located on the south side of Cave Gulch about a mile above the Snake River. They proved up on this portion of their ranch in March 1927. The couple also owned tracts of land along the upstream side of the Frenchy Creek drainage. The Fountains had several children and at times even took in young relatives. One nephew, Pete, came to live with them on and off for several years in the 1920s. During his stay he helped his relatives farm on Cave Gulch, as well as other sections of the ranch on Wapshilla Ridge, located on Eagle and Deer creeks. Pete attended school with his cousins at a one-room schoolhouse on Eagle Creek. Enduring several financial difficulties on the ranch the Fountains turned to bootlegging to earn extra money. On more than one occasion they had near run-ins with revenuers.[370]

By the 1930s, Pete moved to Eugene, Oregon, and took up flying before attending the University of Idaho. While at the University he would often visit his family at the various parts of the ranch via airplane (Piper Cub) in the early 1940s. During this time he used two known landing areas – one on Cave Gulch and the other near the Moffett Place on upper Deer Creek. To familiarize himself with the unique challenges of mountain flying he took several lessons with Bert Zimmerly Sr.[371]

An Airstrip and Fountain's Aviation Career

At Cave Gulch, Fountain utilized a decent sized hayfield located on a bench about a half-mile above the ranch building complex. The landing area measured roughly 800' long. He routinely landed along the creek to the east and took off downstream to the west.[372]

After World War II Fountain married Ella Rose Larson. The two decided to settle in Moscow, which was her hometown. Fountain and his brother Walt Bowman decided to capitalize on veterans returning from the war who were able to take flying lessons using the GI Bill. Fountain and Bowman instructed from several airfields in eastern Washington at such places as Ritzville and Washtucna. Bowman moved his flying adventures to Oregon, and Fountain

Pilot Pete Fountain in the mid-1950s.

Fountain's B-1 Ryan [N7212] at the Moscow Sky Ranch in the mid-1950s. The plane was later modified into a replica of the Spirit of St. Louis *for the 1957 Warner Brothers film starring Jimmy Stewart.*

focused on developing a flight instruction program near the University of Idaho. However, the only nearby airfield to instruct from was across the state line in Pullman. Undeterred, Fountain obtained a tract of land southeast of Moscow along Paradise Ridge Road and constructed a 2,000'-runway. His original intention was to build it as a community airfield facility, but this did not materialize. The field became known as "Moscow Sky Ranch" and officially opened in 1946.[373]

Within two years of starting the flight school, Fountain decided to diversify by expanding his business to encompass agricultural spraying and some charter services. He purchased several airplanes including an Aeronca Champion with a sixty-gallon spray tank, two spray-equipped Piper Cubs, a Piper Pacer, and a normally-configured Piper Cub. The latter airplane was fitted with a Whitaker Gear (a pair of tandem wheels on each side) for backcountry charter use.[374]

Through the years Fountain Flying Service primarily became an ag operation. However, flying the Idaho backcountry remained a pastime for family recreation. The Fountains raised six children at their Moscow airfield. By the time the children graduated high school they all had received some flight instruction from their father. Four went on to earn a private pilot license and three of the four earned a commercial rating – mainly flying ag work. Sons Ron, Craig, and Steve well remember flying the Idaho backcountry with their father. Thinking back about those years, Craig commented, "Anytime dad would get a notion to reminisce about the old days of growing up on the river we would make a trip. He loved to go fly there and visit."[375] Of course several of these trips created lasting memories and his kids also came to enjoy the wilds of Idaho. Several of these lasting memories involve small airplane mishaps and now-humorous near misses.[376]

One of the little mishaps became one of Fountain's last landings at his family's old Cave Gulch homestead in the early 1970s. He decided he wanted to visit and do some target shooting. Son Craig and a friend tagged along. Fountain assured his son that their 135 Piper Pacer would make the trip just fine. However, on landing he lined the plane up just slightly too far to the left and nailed a rock as he set the plane down. The rock was something Fountain had pointed out time and time again when he checked his kids out on the strip. He knew the rock well – it was shaped like a ramp on the takeoff side and square as a box on the landing side, but some unknown force just pulled the left main wheel straight into it. Luckily no one was hurt.[377]

To recover the airplane the Fountains robbed a gear off another Pacer and hauled in other needed parts by truck. They made the necessary field repairs to ferry the plane back to Moscow. But while they had the four-wheel drive truck there, Fountain insisted on pulling the rock out of the way with a chain.[378]

For decades after the ranch was abandoned the place remained fairly untouched. However, this changed when the road was punched down the drainage. Even with road access, Fountain preferred to fly in, that is until Craig overflying the property spotted a sports car parked near the old ranch. He then convinced his dad that landing on the old hayfield was not worth the risk of damaging company equipment when he could simply drive to the location.[379]

Craig primarily took over Fountain Flying Service in 1977 and his siblings continued to work on and off for the operation over the years. His dad continued to fly for the company through 1982, but stayed active as a private pilot until 2000. Pete Fountain died in 2006. His aviation business continues to actively serve clientele in the Palouse region of the state under the management of Craig's son Pete. Pete maintains the tradition of using the family airfield in Moscow and picked up his flying skills from his grandfather. Additionally, he operates from a runway that he purchased from pilot Ralph Stout, near his home in Genesee, Idaho.[380]

Pete Fountain not only had the tie of growing up in the backcountry, but he also owned several well-known Idaho backcountry aircraft. One historically significant airplane he owned was one of A. A. Bennett's original Zenith biplanes (NC392V). Friend Dean Wilson helped convert the once-specially designed backcountry passenger plane into a spray plane. Under Fountain's ownership it was used mainly to spread dry fertilizer and often flown by friend Wayne Hughes. Joe Terteling, who owned a large private vintage aircraft collection in Boise, later obtained the aircraft. The plane was then purchased by a private collector and restored. It is the only Zenith known to exist today.[381]

The other historic airplane Fountain owned was a Ryan Brougham B-1 (N7212) that he bought from Abe Bowler, an Orofino-based backcountry pilot. Paul Mantz a noted movie stunt pilot, who worked with major movie studios for films involving aircraft and aerial work, approached Fountain about buying the airplane. Mantz needed the B-1 to fulfill a contract with Warner Brothers for the filming of *The Spirit of St. Louis* (1957), starring Jimmy Stewart. Since the actual *Spirit of St. Louis* owned by Charles Lindbergh was a one-of-a-kind Ryan, Mantz was forced to find similar looking models that could be modified and used for the film. Fountain initially hoped he could lease the airplane to Mantz and perhaps even fly it for him. However, Mantz was only interested in buying it outright. In the end Fountain sold it. The plane was one of three B-1 Ryans used in the movie and was rumored to be the main airframe appearing in the final cuts of the film.

CACHE CREEK

Early History

Looking downstream at the Cache Creek property and airstrip [lower center].

Native Americans lived along the creek. Early Euro-Americans discovered their caches at the mouth of the drainage. Purportedly the Indians regularly cached dried salmon in a chalky place, preventing it from absorbing moisture. The bar also served as a main crossing for Native Americans coming and going from Lapwai, Idaho.

Jon Shoemaker and Captain Forester worked a placer claim along the creek in the 1880s. Other men also tried to mine the bar, but the gold was too fine to placer, and was not worth the cost of labor.

Homesteaders and Sheep

Multiple families homesteaded the vast, steep, but open benches in the vicinity of Cache

Jay Dobbin and wife Etta in the late 1940s.

184

Creek. Baldwin, Kernan, Blanc, Gaillard, and Brown are just a few of the early settler names associated with the area. The Dobbin and Huffman Sheep Company eventually acquired most of the homesteads on the Oregon side of the river, ranging from the mouth of the Salmon River through Cache Creek. The business owned by Jay Dobbin and brother-in-law Guy Huffman was one of the largest ever in the Snake River country. The partnership was dissolved in the 1930s after a successful twenty-plus years of business. Huffman moved to California and invested in feedlots. Dobbin held onto much of the river property and continued sheep operations until the mid-1940s. He sold various land parcels and the remaining sheep mainly to Basque employees. Dobbin died at age ninety-one in 1961.

Other Owners and Walter "Bun" Purcell

Sheep-man Les Oliver acquired the main Cache Creek property from Dobbin. Oliver sold it to cattle operator Glen Hamilton, who then sold it to Leo R. Beard in the late 1950s. Walter "Bun" Purcell then obtained the place from Beard in about 1967. After the original purchase, Purcell slowly gathered other land over the years until he owned 6,556 acres. Of the acreage, an incredible four and a half miles lay along the Oregon side of the Snake River. One year before Purcell died in December 1992, he sold the Cache Creek Ranch to Trust For Public Lands.

Purcell, a businessman, entrepreneur, and old-time logger was known as a gentleman's gentleman. He was born in Chehalis in 1907 and attended Washington State College. Purcell migrated to western Oregon where he did well in the logging and timber industry. He owned several logging companies, but found the most success in manufacturing plywood. His main manufacturing facility was in one of the all-wood-constructed blimp hangars that were once a part of the former Tillamook Naval Air Station in Tillamook.

His accomplishments in the timber industry allowed him to invest in real estate and pursue his passion for breeding and racing thoroughbred horses. Most of his horses were kept and trained at a large farm he owned in Battleground, Washington.

A few of his racehorses did well at the regional level. His most decorated animal, Sporting Event, won the Portland Meadows Mile in 1979. Many of the names for his thoroughbreds were creatively derived with the help of family and friends. He even named one successful horse "Captain Rivers," after middle Snake River boatmen Dick Rivers.

Beyond his Battleground farm he and his wife Evangeline "Van" and their two daughters, Kay and Candace spent time at another piece of property in eastern Oregon known as the "Beard Ranch." Purcell's life came full-circle when he realized Leo Beard, from whom he bought the Oregon ranch, owned more acreage on the middle Snake River. This particularly interested Purcell as he had worked for Jay Dobbin one summer while attending college in Pullman. When Beard revealed he was going to sell his Snake River ranch at Cache Creek, Purcell bought it.

With several old homesteads to choose from for their living quarters, the Purcells selected the one settled by Joseph Brown at the mouth of Cache Creek. Brown had moved to the location around the turn of the twentieth century. When the land was surveyed in August 1908 Brown had already built two houses and a shop on the north side of the creek. He received homestead approval for 152.09 acres in January 1912.[359] The Purcells chose to keep the place rustic and only added necessary improvements. When in residence they lived in the main house, built circa 1940, which is now used by the Forest Service as the main river check station.

Another fairly complete farmstead located south of this complex along Coon Hollow was also fixed up. In the beginning the Coon Hollow place was used to house caretakers or managers of Purcell's cattle. Starting in 1979, Purcell leased the Coon Hollow buildings to Clarkston friends Frank and Carrie Hoyt, who were avid jet boaters and used the place for recreation. It was a win-win for both parties, as Purcell liked having people look after the property. Hoyt, a longtime employee of The Lewiston Tribune, leased the buildings for ten years. As Purcell was arranging the sale of the property to the Trust for Public Lands, he and Hoyt were working on a separate sale for just the Coon Hollow structures and associated land. However, the Hoyts backed out due to the restrictive scenic easements.[360] These historic buildings burned in the Cache Creek Fire of August 2012.[361] Reminiscing about Purcell, Hoyt wrote, "Bun let Carrie and me pick fruit from the ranch orchard and she made the best pies on the old wood stove in the cabin. Yum! We got a kick out of Bun and his annual elk hunt with his friends – lots of big bulls. However, he would only allow 3 to be shot, then tell his pals, 'that's enough for this year boys.' Bun was a great guy."[362]

The Airstrip

Visiting Cache Creek was not easy for Purcell living in western Oregon. In January 1966, before purchasing the somewhat inaccessible Cache Creek property, he invested in buying a 1965 Piper Aztec (N5834Y) for business travel. When looking for the new airplane and potential pilots to fly it, he became acquainted with Norman "Swede" Ralston through mutual friend Axel Erickson. Erickson and his family were moguls in the Oregon logging/timber industry and, like Purcell, owned a World War II blimp hangar in Tillamook. He used it for storage and production. Erickson had several airplanes and used the services of Ralston's Aero Air Inc. based in Hillsboro, Oregon.[363]

Ralston too was a tycoon of his industry. Early on he managed and taught flight instructing at the Rankin Air Academy in Tulare, California. After World War II he became a professional air show pilot. One of his more famous maneuvers was flying an AT-6 Texan through one of the Tillamook blimp hangars. He became well known in the aviation community while running Aero Air at the Hillsboro airport where he offered everything: crop-dusting, flight instruction, corporate flying, maintenance, and sales. He was an innovative guy. For example, he was the first person in the world to buy military surplus TBMs, single engine World War II torpedo bombers, and convert them in to aerial fire tankers. Through the years he became a certified dealer for various aircraft, but he is best remembered for having a Rockwell International dealership and selling the versatile Aero Commanders. Prominent Aero Commander test and stunt pilot Bob Hoover was a frequent visitor to Ralston's business.

Ralston's right-hand man (1958–85) was none other than Bert Zimmerly Jr., the son of the late pioneering middle Snake River pilot. When Purcell came onboard as a charter client, he and the young Zimmerly instantly hit it off. With Purcell's ownership of Cache Creek and Zimmerly proud of his family's aviation roots in western Idaho and the rugged area of Hells Canyon it was instantly something they had in common. When Purcell bought the Aztec it was Zimmerly who picked it up new in Seattle.[364]

Shortly after the purchase of the ranch, Ralston flew Purcell to Cache Creek in the Aztec to scope out a landing site. Upon arriving at the ranch Ralston amazingly decided to set the twin-engine plane down on a ridge far above the main building complex, along the river on a bench near Garden Creek. Although Zimmerly Air Transport pilots had used the bench in the 1940s and early 1950s, it was an amazing feat, considering he was flying a low-wing Aztec! Based on several observations Ralston designed the current Cache Creek airstrip for Purcell. Purcell certainly had the resources through his logging and timber businesses to build the suggested airstrip, but the problem was getting the equipment to the ranch.[365]

In order to bring in a dozer big enough to carve out the bank and slope of the purposed strip, Purcell hired a crew to punch a steep rough fifteen-mile road into the property. The thoroughfare constructed with a D8 Caterpillar extended from Spring Ridge down to the mouth of Cache Creek.[366] Once the airstrip was completed Ralston walked it and determined that Purcell was going to have to upgrade his airplane. Due to the eleven percent downward slope on the 1,300'-runway he felt the brakes on the Aztec were not strong enough. Plus, the low wing did not provide enough landing clearance above the cut-bank to avoid hitting the starboard (right) wingtip of the plane. Ralston pitched Purcell on buying an Aero Commander. Aero Air sold Purcell their relatively new 1968 demonstration model (N5009E). By the following year Ralston and Zimmerly were making regularly flights in and out of Cache Creek with the Aero Commander. A few years later Purcell upgraded his airplane when he bought the Erickson's Turbo Commander (N512JD). This plane was used regularly to reach the ranch through the mid-1980s.[367]

An upstream view of the 1,300' Cache Creek runway.

HOLM

NOTES

1   Jerry Hughes, Personal Communication, 4 April 2013.

2   Tim Palmer, *The Snake River: Window to the West*, (Washington, DC, 1991, Island Press), 201.

3   Greg Johnson, Personal Communication, 29 October 2013.

4   Andrew Funk, BLM General Land Office Records.

5   Bill Wilson, Personal Communication, 4 December 2013.

6   B. Wilson, Personal Communication.

7   B. Wilson, Personal Communication.

8   B. Wilson, Personal Communication.

9   B. Wilson, Personal Communication.

10 Mike Wilson, Personal Communication, 20 May 2014.

11 M. Wilson, Personal Communication.

12 M. Wilson, Personal Communication.

13 Bruce Womack, Personal Communication, 12 June 2014.

14 Gerald Tucker, *Historical Sketches of the Wallowa National Forest*, (Baker, OR: 1954, Wallowa-Whitman National Forest – reprinted February 1981), 196–201.

15 Gerry Weaver, "Airports in National Forest Urged: Projects Studied by Oregon Board," The Oregonian, 9 August 1936.

16 Weaver, "Airports in National Forest Urged: Projects Studied by Oregon Board."

17 Weaver, "Airports in National Forest Urged: Projects Studied by Oregon Board."

18 Tucker, 206–07.

19 Jim Vincent, "Hellitack – Go Like Hell While Fire Is Still Small," *The Oregonian*, 8 September 1971.

20 Womack, Personal Communication.

21 Leverett Richards, "'Long, Hard Fight' Expected to Control Eastern Oregon Fire," *The Oregonian*, 22 August 1973.

22 "Forest Blaze Explodes Into Fierce Firestorm," *The Oregonian*, 21 August 1973.

23 "Flight Control Added to Forest Fire Crews," *The Oregonian*, 9 September 1973.

24 Ray Kresek, *Fire Lookouts of the Northwest*, (Fairfield, WA: Ye Galleon Press, 1998), 101.

25 "Hat Point," *Union-Bulletin*, 18 November 1956.

26 Johnny Carrey, Cort Conley, and Ace Barton, *Snake River of Hells Canyon*, (Cambridge, ID: Backeddy Books, 1979), 209–10.

27 Clem Marks, BLM General Land Office Records.

28 Florence E. Smith, *Snake River Daze*, (Self-published, 1985).

29 Walter A. Winniford, BLM General Land Office Records.

30 John F. Winniford, BLM General Land Office Records.

31 Smith, *Snake River Daze*.

32 Smith, *Snake River Daze*.

33 Smith, *Snake River Daze*.

34 Fred Zimmerly, Pilot Logbooks.

35 Greg Johnson, Personal Communication, 17 June 2014.

36 Mark Yates, Personal Communication, 31 March 2014.

37 Yates, Personal Communication.

38 Yates, Personal Communication.

39 Carrey, Conley, and Barton, 213.

40 Carrey, Conley, and Barton, 214–15.

41 "Ralph Ace Barton" (obituary), *The Lewiston Tribune*, 8 September 2014.

42 Ivan Gustin, Pilot Logbooks 1937 to 1946.

43 Clark Hanson, *Interview with Floyd Harvey - Oregon Historical Society*, 22 October 1999.

44 Art Seamans, Personal Communication, 6 December 2013.

45 William Ashworth, *Hells Canyon: The Deepest Gorge on Earth*, (New York, NY: Hawthorn Book, Inc), 145.

46 Ashworth, 144–49.

47 Boyd Norton, Personal Communication, 7 January 2014.

48 Ashworth, 144–49.

49 Brock Evans, Personal Communication, 12 January 2014.

50 Norton, Personal Communication.

51 Ernie Heimgartner, Personal Communication, 1 February 2014.

52 Heimgartner, Personal Communication.

53 Russ Mager, *HCPC – I and Citizen Action*, (Hells Canyon Preservation Council), 2006.

54 Jim Pope Sr., Personal Communication, 5 February 2014.

55 Ernie Heimgartner Hells Canyon Files.

56 Ashworth, 163.

57 Walter J. Hickel, *Who Owns America?*, (Englewood Cliffs, NY: Prentice-Hall, Inc., 1971), 149.

58 J. Pope Sr., Personal Communication.

59 Heimgartner, Personal Communication.

60 Hickel, 150.

61 Ashworth, 163.

62 Ernie Heimgartner Hells Canyon Files.

63 J. Pope Sr., Personal Communication.

64 Ashworth, 164.

65 Ashworth, 189.

66 Seamans, Personal Communication.

67 Ashworth, 189.

68 "$1.75 Million Damages Due," *The Spokesman-Review*, 5 May 1977.

69 "Perjury Case Trail Scheduled In Idaho," *The Spokesman-Review*, 19 April 1978.

70 "Idaho Man Acquitted of Perjury," *The Spokesman-Review*, 4 May 1978.

71 *Hells Canyon Excursions, Inc. v. Oakes*, 111 Idaho 123, 721 P.2d 223 (Ct. App. 1986).

72 Gerald J. Tucker, *The Story Of Hells Canyon*, (Self-published, 1977), 72.

73 Carrey, Conley, and Barton, 241.

74 Walter S. Brockman, BLM General Land Office Records.

75 Carrey, Conley, and Barton, 242.

76 Greg Johnson, Personal Communication, 29 October 2013.

77 G. Johnson, Personal Communication.

78 G. Johnson, Personal Communication.

79 G. Johnson, Personal Communication.

80 G. Johnson, Personal Communication.

81 Butch Brown, Personal Communication, 15 April 2014.

82 Jerry Hughes, Personal Communication, 25 June 2014.

83 Carrey, Conley, and Barton, 225–29.

84 Matilda H. Hall, BLM General Land Office Records.

85 Kathy Poston, Personal Communication, 11 June 2014.

86 John McKenna, Personal Communication, 13 April 2014.

87 George Hauptman, Personal Communication, 27 March 2014.

88 Hauptman, Personal Communication.

89 Bud Stangel, Personal Communication, 9 November 2013.

90 Stangel, Personal Communication.

91 Victor L. Coggins, Personal Communication, 10 July 2014.

92 Coggins, Personal Communication.

93 Coggins, Personal Communication.

94 Carrey, Conley, and Barton, 245.

95 Teri Murphy, Personal Communication, 4 December 2013.

96 Bob Black, Personal Communication, 4 December 2013.

97 Murphy, Personal Communication.

98 "Death Plane Remains," *Spokane Daily Chronicle*, 24 July 1964.

99 Black, Personal Communication.

100 Black, Personal Communication.

101 Black, Personal Communication.

102 Clyde Hanson, Personal Communication, 14 January 2014.

103 Hanson, Personal Communication.

104 Ted Grote, Personal Communication, 11 November 2013.

105 Grote, Personal Communication.

106 Grote, Personal Communication.

107 Grote, Personal Communication.

108 Grote, Personal Communication.

109 Grote, Personal Communication.

110 Grote, Personal Communication.

111 Grote, Personal Communication.

112 Grote, Personal Communication.

113 Joe Jordan, Personal Communication, 22 March 2014.

114 Jordan, Personal Communication.

115 Jordan, Personal Communication.

116 Jordan, Personal Communication.

117 Donna Matschke, Personal Communication, 17 June 2014.

118 Matschke, Personal Communication.

119 Matschke, Personal Communication.

120 Grote, Personal Communication.

121 Matschke, Personal Communication.

122 Matschke, Personal Communication.

123 Carrey, Conley, and Barton, 276.

124 Mike Thomason, BLM General Land Office Records.

125 "Snow Responsible Two Plane Upsets," *Idaho County Free Press*, 29 January 1942.

126 Vince Welch, *The Last Voyageur: Amos Burg and the Rivers of the West*, (Seattle, WA: The Mountaineers Books, 2012), 234.

127 Welch, 234–35

128 Ivan Gustin, Pilot Logbooks 1937 to 1946.

129 Welch, 235.

130 "Two More River Explorers Due," *Lewiston Morning Tribune*, 29 September 1944.

131 "Photos Obtained of Hell's Canyon," *Spokane Daily Chronicle*, 22 August 1947.

132 Doris Wilson, *Life in Hells Canyon: A Private View*, (Middleton, ID: CHJ Publishing, 2002), 11–25.

133 Ray Wilson, Personal Communication, 4 April 2014.

134 D. Wilson, 175.

135 R. Wilson, Personal Communication.

136 D. Wilson, 218–31.

137 D. Wilson, 232.

138 R. Wilson, Personal Communication.

139 R. Wilson, Personal Communication.

140 R. Wilson, Personal Communication.

141 R. Wilson, Personal Communication.

142 R. Wilson, Personal Communication.

143 R. Wilson, Personal Communication.

144 R. Wilson, Personal Communication.

145 R. Wilson, Personal Communication.

146 D. Wilson, 180.

147 "McGrady Youth Still Unsighted In Snake Canyon," *Lewiston Morning Tribune*, 25 May 1948.

148 Bert Zimmerly Sr., Pilot Logbooks.

149 Carole Simon-Smolinski, *Hells Canyon & The Middle Snake River: A Story of the Land and Its People*, (Lewiston, ID: Confluence Press), 282.

150 D. Wilson, 219.

151 Carrey, Conley, and Barton, 289.

152 Frank P. Somers, BLM General Land Office Records.

153 D. Wilson, 55.

154 Jim Renshaw, Personal Communication, 5 May 2014.

155 Renshaw, Personal Communication.

156 R. Wilson, Personal Communication.

157 Joe Spence, Personal Communication, 25 March 2014.

158 Gary Willett, Personal Communication, 9 July 2014.

159 Willett, Personal Communication.

160 Willett, Personal Communication.

161 Willett, Personal Communication.

162 Calvin Henry, Personal Communication, 10 June 2014.

163 Henry, Personal Communication.

164 Henry, Personal Communication.

165 Henry, Personal Communication.

166 Henry, Personal Communication.

167 Henry, Personal Communication.

168 "Forest Service Closes Six Lord Flat Roadways," *The Oregonian*, 5 September 1985.

169 Katy Nesbitt, "Court Ruling on Lord Flat Trail Goes in Favor of Forest Service," *The Observer*, 28 January 2010.

170 Grote, Personal Communication.

171 Grote, Personal Communication.

172 "Oregon Flier Sure Plane Out of Fuel," *Spokane Daily Chronicle*, 24 March 1969.

173 Bob Longfellow, Personal Communication, 9 May 2014.

174 James W. Tryon, BLM General Land Office Records.

175 Tucker, 103.

176 Charles J. Crader, BLM General Land Office Records.

177 Mary Ann McLaughlin, Personal Communication, 2 June 2014.

178 Grote, Personal Communication.

179 Stangel, Personal Communication.

180 Calvin Henry, Personal Communication, 27 March 2014.

181 Henry, Personal Communication.

182 Henry, Personal Communication.

183 "Mrs. Addie Smith (obituary)," *Spokane Daily Chronicle*, 18 December 1972.

184 Anita Smith, Personal Communication, 19 May 2014.

185 Randy Lorentz, Personal Communication, 16 March 2014.

186 Youngdahl, 38–41.

187 Youngdahl, 157.

188 Youngdahl, 179.

189 Peggy Marek, Personal Communication, 14 March 2014.

190 Polly Hollandsworth, Personal Communication, 27 May 2014.

191 Peggy Marek, Personal Communication, 9 May 2014.

192 Marek, Personal Communication.

193 Hollandsworth, Personal Communication.

194 "Flying rescues – one mile down in Hell's Canyon (Chevron advertisement)," *Flying*, February 1956, 13.

195 Grote, Personal Communication.

196 "Search Copter Crashes in Idaho; Pair Unhurt," *Spokane Daily Chronicle*, 27 June 1968.

197 "Bodies Taken From Plane Crash Scene," *The Spokesman-Review*, 29 April 1969.

198 Simon-Smolinski, 168.

199 Simon-Smolinski, 209.

200 Simon-Smolinski, 209.

201 Dennis Albers, Personal Communication, 20 November 2013.

202 Tim Rivers, Personal Communication, 18 November 2013.

203 T. Rivers, Personal Communication.

204 Simon-Smolinski, 288.

205 D. Albers, Personal Communication.

206 T. Rivers, Personal Communication.

207 Joe Rivers, Personal Communication, 21 November 2013.

208 Carrey, Conley, and Barton, 295–98.

209 "Gustin Lands Plane on Rocky Hill to Aid 83-year-Old Exhausted Prospector," *Lewiston Morning Tribune*, 5 July 1959.

210 J. Rivers, Personal Communication.

211 J. Rivers, Personal Communication.

212 J. Rivers, Personal Communication.

213 D. Albers, Personal Communication.

214 T. Rivers, Personal Communication.

215 D. Albers, Personal Communication.

216 Wally and Myrna Beamer, Personal Communication, 30 June 2014.

217 Beamer, Personal Communication.

218 Guy K. Russell, BLM General Land Office Records.

219 Elben F. Dotson, BLM General Land Office Records.

220 Tucker, 104.

221 Dick Hammond, Personal Communication, 30 June 2014.

222 McLaughlin, Personal Communication.

223 Gary Bledsoe, Personal Communication, 2 June 2014.

224 McLaughlin, Personal Communication.

225 Grote, Personal Communication.

226 Stangel, Personal Communication.

227 Grote, Personal Communication.

228 John Skow, "Farewell to Hells Canyon," *Saturday Evening Post*, 1 July 1967.

229 McLaughlin, Personal Communication.

230 Stangel, Personal Communication.

231 Ned Schroeder, Personal Communication, 3 March 2014.

232 Marek, Personal Communication.

233 Schroeder, Personal Communication.

234 Schroeder, Personal Communication.

235 Hollandsworth, Personal Communication.

236 Carrey, Conley, and Barton, 300–01.

237 Hammond, Personal Communication.

238 Ron Van Pool, Personal Communication, 22 May 2014.

239 R. Wilson, Personal Communication, 15 April 2014.

240 R. Wilson, Personal Communication.

241 Rusty Bentz, Personal Communication, 2 June 2014.

242 "Leading Idaho Stockman Dies," *The Spokesman-Review*, 6 November 1951.

243 "Leading Idaho Stockman Dies," *The Spokesman-Review*, 6 November 1951.

244 Ron Van Pool, Personal Communication, 2 April 2014

245 Van Pool, Personal Communication.

246 "Harold Van Pool" (obituary), *Moscow-Pullman Daily News*, 6 May 1993.

247 Van Pool, Personal Communication.

248 Van Pool, Personal Communication.

249 Van Pool, Personal Communication.

250 "Injured Youth Flown to Care," *The Spokesman-Review*, 8 February 1937.

251 "Scenic Airplane Trips," *Lewiston Morning Tribune*, 3 May 1936.

252 "Routine Flight Kills Zimmerly: Daring Idaho Mercy Pilot Crashed Near Pullman," *The Spokesman Review*, 19 February 1949.

253 "Tick Victim Is Air Passenger," *Lewiston Morning Tribune*, 1

August 1939.

254 Bert Zimmerly Sr., Pilot Logbooks.

255 Sister M. Alfreda Elsenshon, *Pioneer Days In Idaho County Volume II*, (Cottonwood, ID: The Idaho Corporation of Benedictine Sisters, 1971), 318.

256 "Tick Victim Is Air Passenger," *Lewiston Morning Tribune*, 1 August 1939.

257 Bert Zimmerly Sr., Pilot Logbooks.

258 Ron Gustin, Personal Communication, 17 July 2014.

259 Gustin, Personal Communication.

260 Van Pool, Personal Communication.

261 "Boat Stranded As River Falls," *The Spokesman-Review*, 27 June 1958.

262 Van Pool, Personal Communication.

263 Van Pool, Personal Communication.

264 Van Pool, Personal Communication.

265 Ray Speer, Personal Communication, 7 April 2014.

266 Speer, Personal Communication.

267 Van Pool, Personal Communication.

268 Van Pool, Personal Communication.

269 Bob Hitchcock, Personal Communication, 6 June 2014.

270 B. Hitchcock, Personal Communication.

271 B. Hitchcock, Personal Communication.

272 B. Hitchcock, Personal Communication.

273 B. Hitchcock, Personal Communication.

274 B. Hitchcock, Personal Communication.

275 B. Hitchcock, Personal Communication.

276 B. Hitchcock, Personal Communication.

277 B. Hitchcock, Personal Communication.

278 B. Hitchcock, Personal Communication.

279 Todd Hitchcock, Personal Communication, 7 July 2014.

280 B. Hitchcock, Personal Communication.

281 B. Hitchcock, Personal Communication.

282 B. Hitchcock, Personal Communication.

283 B. Hitchcock, Personal Communication.

284 Edwin Durgy, "The Forbes 400's Newest Undercover Billionaires: The Wilks Brothers," *Forbes Magazine*, September 2011.

285 Durgy.

286 Tucker, 111.

287 Tucker, 111–13.

288 Donald "Biden" Tippett, Personal Communication, 4 June 2013.

289 Doug Tippett, Personal Communication, 18 December 2013.

290 Rafe Gibbs, "Cattle Ranch in a Canyon," *Popular Mechanics Magazine*, March 1953, 278.

291 D. Tippett, Personal Communication.

292 D. Tippett, Personal Communication.

293 B. Tippett, Personal Communication.

294 Shawn Steen, Personal Communication, 3 June 2014.

295 Steen, Personal Communication.

296 Wup Winn, Personal Communication, 7 July 2014.

297 Bill Ables, Personal Communication, 7 July 2014.

298 Ables, Personal Communication.

299 Ables, Personal Communication.

300 Ables, Personal Communication.

301 Steve Zanelli, Personal Communication, 22 January 2014.

302 Zanelli, Personal Communication.

303 Hauptman, Personal Communication.

304 Zanelli, Personal Communication.

305 Zanelli, Personal Communication.

306 Zanelli, Personal Communication.

307 Craig and Jane Spencer, Personal Communication, 5 January 2014.

308 Spencer, Personal Communication.

309 "Rites held Tuesday For George Foster," *Idaho County Free Press*, 31 August 1961.

310 Craig and Jane Spencer, Personal Communication, 5 May 2014.

311 John W. Spencer, Personal Daily Diary Notes Concerning Ranch Airstrips and Aviation. Accumulated by Jane Spencer and provided to author.

312 John W. Spencer, Personal Daily Diary Notes Concerning Ranch Airstrips and Aviation. Accumulated by Jane Spencer and provided to author.

313 John W. Spencer, Personal Daily Diary Notes Concerning Ranch Airstrips and Aviation. Accumulated by Jane Spencer and provided to author.

314 Christopher B. Knorr, John Alles, Conrad Alles, Henry Alles, and Robert McCulley, BLM General Land Office Records.

315 John W. Spencer, Personal Daily Diary Notes Concerning Ranch Airstrips and Aviation. Accumulated by Jane Spencer and provided to author.

316 Albert J. Poole, BLM General Land Office Records.

317 Craig and Jane Spencer, Personal Communication, 6 June 2014.

318 Spencer, Personal Communication.

319 John W. Spencer, Personal Daily Diary Notes Concerning Ranch Airstrips and Aviation. Accumulated by Jane Spencer and provided to author.

320 John W. Spencer, Personal Daily Diary Notes Concerning Ranch Airstrips and Aviation. Accumulated by Jane Spencer and provided to author.

321 "George Foster" (obituary), *Spokane Daily Chronicle*, 28 August 1961.

322 Ken Kuther, Personal Communication, 2 February 2014.

323 Chad Frei, Personal Communication, 31 January 2014.

324 Mike Dorris, Personal Communication, 3 January 2014.

325 Frei, Personal Communication.

326 Frei, Personal Communication.

327 T. Rivers, Personal Communication.

328 T. Rivers, Personal Communication.

329 Joe Onaindia Jr., Personal Communication, 16 July 2014.

330 Onaindia, Personal Communication.

331 Onaindia, Personal Communication.

332 Onaindia, Personal Communication.

333 Onaindia, Personal Communication.

334 Onaindia, Personal Communication.

335 Onaindia, Personal Communication.

336 Grote, Personal Communication.

337 Grote, Personal Communication.

338 Spence, Personal Communication.

339 Onaindia, Personal Communication.

340 "Woman Flyer Slates Flight," *The Oregonian*, 16 February 1949.

341 Cora Bowman Fountain, BLM General Land Office Records.

342 Harold Heitstuman, Personal Communication, 13 March 2014.

343 Gary (Sam) McNeal, Personal Communication, 13 March 2014.

344 Rusty Bentz, Personal Communication, 11 March 2014.

345 Bentz, Personal Communication.

346 Bentz, Personal Communication.

347 Carrey, Conley, and Barton, 364.

348 Donald "Biden" Tippett, Personal Communication, 3 June 2014.

349 B. Tippett, Personal Communication.

350 "Betty Charlot (Heasty) Tippett" (obituary), *Wallowa County Chieftain*, 7 August 2012.

351 B. Tippett, Personal Communication.

352 "Plane Dusts Field With Fertilizer," *Lewiston Morning Tribune*, 23 April 1949.

353 B. Tippett, Personal Communication.

354 B. Tippett, Personal Communication.

355 B. Tippett, Personal Communication.

356 B. Tippett, Personal Communication.

357 Stangel, Personal Communication.

358 John Hollenbeak, Personal Communication, 28 May 2014.

359 Joseph J. Brown, BLM General Land Office Records.

360 Frank and Carrie Hoyt, Personal Communication, 2 December 2013.

361 Eric Barker, "Fire Destroys Hells Canyon Landmark: Cache Creek Fire Grows, Takes Out Coon Hollow Cabin," *The Lewiston Tribune*, 24 August 2014.

362 Frank Hoyt, Personal Communication (Letter to Author), 9 December 2013.

363 Bert Zimmerly Jr., Personal Communication, 29 May 2014.

364 Zimmerly Jr., Personal Communication.

365 Zimmerly Jr., Personal Communication.

366 J. River, Personal Communication.

367 Zimmerly Jr., Personal Communication.

368 Simon-Smolinski, 110–12.

369 Gary (Sam) McNeal, Personal Communication, 24 February 2014.

370 Craig Fountain, Personal Communication 24 February 2014.

371 C. Fountain, Personal Communication.

372 C. Fountain, Personal Communication.

373 C. Fountain, Personal Communication.

374 C. Fountain, Personal Communication.

375 C. Fountain, Personal Communication.

376 C. Fountain, Personal Communication.

377 C. Fountain, Personal Communication.

378 C. Fountain, Personal Communication.

379 C. Fountain, Personal Communication.

380 C. Fountain, Personal Communication.

381 C. Fountain, Personal Communication.

The Wapshilla Creek drainage and airstrip.

Chapter 3

LOWER SALMON RIVER
(AMERICAN BAR TO THE SNAKE RIVER)

This will not be a complete history – nor a literary masterpiece. It will contain some history, some biography, and perhaps a sprinkling of "blarney."

–John A. Platt (lower Salmon River homesteader)
Whispers From Old Genessee and Echoes of the Salmon River

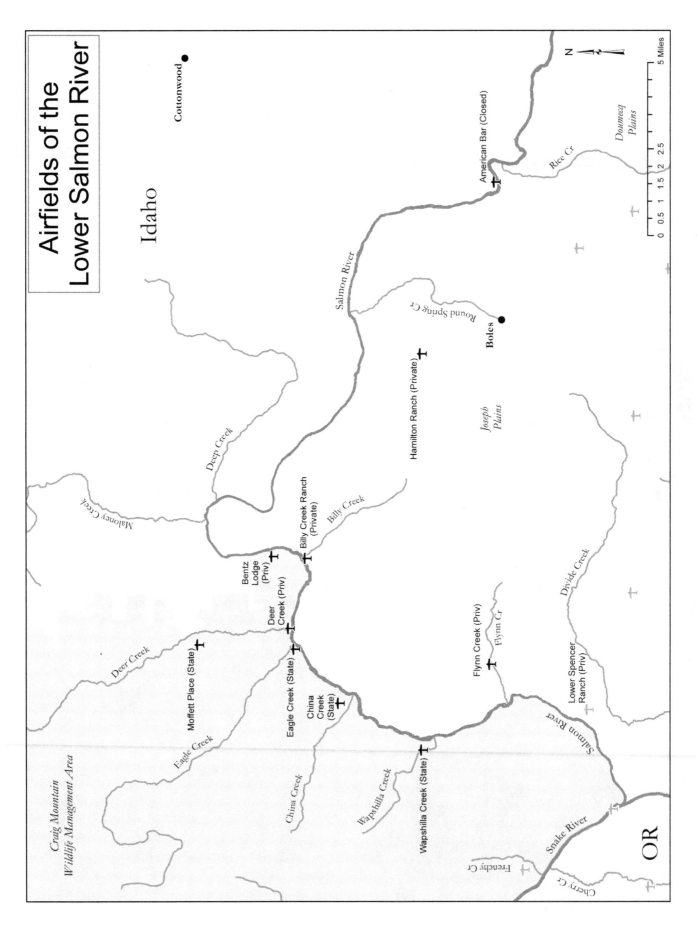

Airfields of the Lower Salmon River

Idaho

Cottonwood

Craig Mountain
Wildlife Management Area

Maloney Creek

Deep Creek

Deer Creek

Moffett Place (State)

Bentz Lodge (Priv)

Deer Creek (Priv)

Eagle Creek (State)

Eagle Creek

China Creek (State)

China Creek

Wapshilla Creek (State)

Wapshilla Creek

Billy Creek Ranch (Private)

Billy Creek

Hamilton Ranch (Private)

Salmon River

Round Spring Cr

Boles

Joseph Plains

Flynn Creek (Priv)

Flynn Cr

Divide Creek

Lower Spencer Ranch (Priv)

Salmon River

Snake River

Frenchy Cr

Cherry Cr

American Bar (Closed)

Rice Cr

Doumecq Plains

OR

N

0 0.5 1 1.5 2 2.5   5 Miles

A cockpit view of the rocky lower Salmon River.

The history of aviation in the lower Salmon River began immediately after World War II. Zimmerly Air Transport of Lewiston pioneered the majority of the landing patches in the region, primarily with the intent to provide services to out-of-the-way-ranches. For this chapter, I documented the individual histories of airstrips located along the river and associated drainages from American Bar to the Snake River – a section most unaffected by major roadways.

While a good portion of the land along this stretch of the Salmon River is administered by the BLM, particularly the river corridor, it is also checkered with several parcels of private land that contain airstrips. The majority of the south side of the river climbing toward the Joseph Plains is largely privately owned. On the north side of the Salmon, below the distinctive Oxbow is the Craig Mountain Wildlife Management Area (WMA). Most of this acreage was once a part of the former Howard Ranch, which had multiple airstrips to access the remote locales. The 115,000-acre wildlife area is managed by both the IDFG and the BLM. The portions from the old Howard Ranch were obtained in 1992 by the Bonneville Power Administration to help mitigate habitat losses associated with the Dworshak Dam above Orofino. The wildlife area extends westward to the Snake River and slightly farther north than the scope of this book to Redbird Creek.

The Craig Mountains or Craigs Mountains are named for Colonel William Craig. Some historians not only believe Craig to be the first white settler in Idaho (circa 1846), but also credit him with naming the state. This high plateau contains five named peaks; the highest is Craig Mountain with an elevation of 5,341'.

197

All pilots flying in this area should educate themselves on the location of power lines in this section of the lower Salmon River. While I have already clearly stated that this publication is not a how-to-book or a guidebook, the power lines here present a significant enough hazard that I feel compelled to note the minimum locations with which every aviator ought to become familiar: (1) the line that crosses the river below the Rice Creek Bridge at Maze Rapid, (2) the line on Eagle Creek that crosses just above the Eagle Creek runway, (3) the line that crosses Wapshilla Creek above the Wapshilla Ranch and airstrip, and (4) the line that crosses the lower Salmon in the vicinity of Slide Rapid, four miles above the confluence with the Snake. This is not a complete inventory of the hazardous power lines, but just a few that must be given significant attention.

AMERICAN BAR

HOLM

An aerial view of American Bar — the 1,100' landing area is sandwiched parallel and between the road and the river.

This small bar contains the outline of a 1,100'-airstrip that was used from the 1960s through the 1980s.[1] The landing area was located on an 18.80-acre mining claim. Lula M. Lancaster Unzicker withdrew the claim in May 1944. Channel Lumber Company of Craigmont, Idaho, acquired the land in the early 1960s under their land holding enterprise of H and R Land Company. When the company dissolved, Merle L. "Bud" Herr, a partner in the business, retained the claim. Herr sold the property to Key Brothers of Grangeville. The land was then traded to the BLM in 1991 for parcels of timberland.[2]

Herr had intended to build a small outfitting business with cabins at American Bar, but the plan never materialized. He and his friends called the property "the Snake Farm" due to the amount of rattlesnakes at the site. When he became involved with the property in the 1960s many pilots had already landed on it, and he granted permission to pilot friends to do the same. It was a great place for friends to gather during the spring to eat, play baseball, and enjoy the outdoors. Herr loved the property and commented, "It had some of the best fishing on the entire river . . . Hay Hole, one of my favorites, had great steelhead."[3]

Jerry Harlan of Harlan Aerial Application based in Craigmont made one of the more memorable landings at the Snake Farm flying a Stearman PT-17 in the mid-1980s. Harlan had just returned from a several-week spray job near Walla Walla, Washington. It was Easter Sunday and all of his friends and family were having a big picnic on the river, so he decided to fly down and meet them. It was something none of them forgot. Harlan later sold the airplane to Jack Cawley, a crop duster in Nezperce, Idaho, after having some engine trouble during a takeoff.[4]

HAMILTON RANCH

Early Owners

Jim and Janet Pope's emblem for the ranch featuring the original homestead cabin built by Thomas O'Hern.

Thomas O'Hern first settled this location, at the head of Mahoney Creek, around the turn of the twentieth century after emigrating from Northern Ireland at age twenty in 1897. He built a modest log cabin and received homestead approval for 160 acres in March 1918. O'Hern later proved up on additional acreage in 1921 and again in 1926. A stockman by trade, O'Hern left Joseph Plains and worked for Wade Humpherys's sheep operation near Yellow Pine, Idaho, from roughly 1930 through 1940. He then made his way back to northern Idaho, living at Graves Creek near Cottonwood. O'Hern never married, and he died in January 1960. O'Hern is buried in the Cottonwood Catholic Cemetery.

Grace Hamilton bought the ranch some time after her husband George was killed at age fifty-two in a logging accident near Hayden Lake, Idaho, in November 1933. She and son Robert, "Bob," moved from Coeur d'Alene to the ranch, mainly to run sheep. He inherited the ranch in 1950 after her death. Bob married Ruth Schlstrom in 1944, and the two raised three children: Barbara, Allen "Buddy," and Lynn. Bob made a living primarily as a sheep rancher, but he also worked as a sawyer for Robinett Logging and founded a fencing business. He took on large scale fencing projects, including many jobs for neighbors on the Joseph Plains.

By the mid-1980s, Bob decided to sell most of the land including the section containing the main building complex. He retained a few small land parcels for himself and his children on what is known as "Nesson Field," named for a previous resident. In his somewhat retired life, he and Ruth wintered in Culdesac, Idaho, and summered in the high country.

DeVlieg and Pope

Janet DeVlieg of Detroit, Michigan, purchased the 1,300-acre ranch from Hamilton in September 1981 while on a visit to Idaho with a friend. She had no intention of buying property in the state, let alone a remote historic ranch. However, when she saw the place for the first time, she absolutely fell in love with it. After signing the papers, she returned to Detroit and her city life, but kept thinking about the Salmon River. Tired of Michigan and ready for something different, she made a major life decision and moved to Lewiston in 1985, so she could spend her free time at the ranch, which she calls the DeVlieg Ranch or the Salmon River Ranch.[5]

She gutted the interior of the original O'Hern Cabin, which had been remodeled by the Hamiltons, using milk carton paper painted in hues of pink, turquoise, and yellow. She turned it into a very livable space and finished it with tongue and groove pine. Janet was very fortunate in her early stays at the ranch to become acquainted with Bob Hamilton who lived nearby. Janet recalled, "He was a wonderful man and a great storyteller. Bob drove me around and introduced me to all the neighbors . . . it was very fascinating to me the way people lived and worked in the country. Many did not think I would last long, but here I am twenty plus years later."[6] When Bob died in 1995 Janet and Ruth spread his ashes at the Nesson Place.

In the midst of settling into the western lifestyle and landscape, Janet hired helicopter pilot Jim Pope Sr. to fly her and a friend to the ranch along with some supplies. Pope grew up in the Lewiston-Clarkston area and received his first airplane ride

Thomas O'Hern — Hamilton Ranch homesteader.

from legendary Hells Canyon pilot Bert Zimmerly Sr. As a high school student he worked for Hillcrest Aviation, where he returned after flying helicopters in the Air Force. He then started his own company, Valley Helicopter Service based in Clarkston. The private facility called "Pope Field" has a helicopter landing area and a 1,300'-runway.[7] Janet married Pope in 1992. The two even planned a surprise wedding at the ranch by inviting their families to the place for the weekend. Once everyone arrived, Pope flew out and brought a judge in to officiate.[8]

Pope also knew Hamilton and often airlifted material for him. While working together in the 1970s they became well acquainted. Pope has numerous fond memories of Hamilton and the ranch. One of the more humorous stories occurred when Pope first started flying for Hamilton. Apparently Hamilton's kids were not familiar with helicopters, and the first couple of times Pope landed at the ranch the kids would run and hide. Hamilton was also known for his homespun concoction of both whiskey and wine. While Pope never tried any of the whisky, the Elderberry wine was delicious. Pope even continues to make the wine, using the Hamilton recipe.[9]

Not long after Pope became involved at the ranch he laid out an airfield to the east of the building complex on a ridge between Mahoney and Round Spring creeks. An equipment operator from Grangeville was hired and used a large grader to level the ground for the runway. Once the preliminary excavation was done, Pope finished the airstrip using a Cat and later seeded it to prevent erosion. The final north-south runway measured 1,350'. Since Pope's aviation business competed for various fire suppression contracts, he saw potential for basing small fixed-wing air tankers at the strip. But the 1,350'-runway would not have been adequate, so he built an additional 1,000' extension to the north. To date, the extension has not been used. The extra runway remains visible between a corner section of a fence and the rim of the canyon. While Pope is a helicopter pilot, he and his family generally used a Cessna 206 (N1065N) when they flew to the property.[10]

The Popes spend as much time as they can at the ranch. In more recent years, they have completely restored the O'Hern Cabin and placed it on a concrete foundation, built a log garage, rebuilt a pond, and added a small log residence near the river called the "Cougar Point Cabin." John and Richard Burkinbine and Keith Coppernoll carried out the extensive log work on the upper buildings. Fran Leighton of Kamiah built the lower place over the course of one winter.[11]

DeVlieg Foundation, Taylor Ranch, And Wilderness Research

When Janet moved to Idaho she continued her involvement with the DeVlieg Foundation, a non-profit foundation started by her grandfather Charles and father Charles "Bud" in 1961. Her grandfather, with the help of her father, created and patented the first bed type-milling machine in the machine-tool industry. Wanting to offer better access to higher education, these men with only the equivalent of a high school education created the charitable organization to provide scholarships for mechanical engineering students.[12]

Influenced by her husband's work as a backcountry helicopter operator she inquired with the University of Idaho about how she and the foundation could become involved in wilderness research. Janet contacted Dr. Jim Peek, a professor with the College of Natural Resources. Peek was well tied to the University's Taylor Wilderness Research Station, located in the River of No Return Wilderness. Impressed, Janet met others connected at Taylor Ranch and expanded the scholarships of the DeVlieg Foundation to encompass the natural resource field, particularly those related to wilderness research. Janet could think of no better way to honor her father's love of the outdoors. Through her involvement with Taylor Ranch, she became well acquainted with former station researcher Dr. Maurice Hornocker and managers Jim and Holly Akenson. Jim Pope Sr. and Hornocker had a history together as Pope had flown some of the earliest wildlife research studies linked with a helicopter in the then Idaho Primitive Area.[13]

After the Diamond Point Fire of 2000 burned several of the structures at Taylor Ranch, Janet arranged for the DeVlieg Foundation to provide funding to rebuild new living quarters and restore the original Dave Lewis homestead cabin. She and her husband were on the ground helping. Pope arranged for Panhandle Helicopters to airlift the material and logs with a Huey helicopter from the Corn Creek area on the Salmon River. To honor the efforts of the foundation, the modern building was named the "DeVlieg Cabin."[14]

Bob Hamilton, longtime ranch owner.

BENTZ LODGE

The Early Years, Spaulding, and an Airstrip

The homestead cabin in the 1990s.

Gilbert G. Wayne proved up on this large river frontage area in January 1939. Ozzie Johnston then acquired the property. Everett and Effie Spaulding of Lewiston leased this property from Johnston starting in the late 1960s.[15] Spaulding ran an outfitting and guiding business from the location and dubbed the place, "Horseshoe Bend Lodge." The Spaulding's business offered float and powerboat trips, as well as fishing and hunting excursions.

Spaulding, a grocer from Eugene, began running Oregon rivers in the 1940s and by the end of the decade was introduced to the rivers of the Salmon River country by the Helfrich family, also of Oregon. In fact, Dave Helfrich, the son of river boatman pioneer Prince, became good friends with Spaulding and they had many fun adventures together in addition to helping guide Horseshoe Bend Lodge clientele. One of these escapades involved helping Metro-Goldwyn-Mayer collect whitewater footage for the film *How the West Was Won* (1962). Six weeks of filming was done on the Rogue and McKenzie rivers in Oregon. The film had an all-star cast with names such as: Carroll Baker, Walter Brennan, Andy Devine, Henry Fonda, Karl Malden, Gregory Peck, John Wayne, Agnes Moorehead, Jimmy Stewart, Debbie Reynolds, and Richard Widmark. While the two river runners never met any of the famous actors, they did double for them as stunt people in river scenes – all of which totaled about four minutes on the big screen. Helfrich doubled as Agnes Moorehead (wearing a long blond wig) and Spaulding as Karl Malden. For Helfrich's efforts he was paid $50.00 per day, combined with the use of his Rogue River Longboat powered by a 1960 Mercury outboard.[16]

Within ten years of Spaulding's first trip down the Middle Fork and Main Salmon rivers, he started his own business with the help of outfitter Ralph Smothers. Spaulding eventually married Smothers's sister, Annie, and the two based their operations from Lewiston. He and Annie divorced after a few years, and Spaulding married Effie in 1964. Proving the operation worked, Spaulding bought the Horseshoe Bend Lodge property from Johnston with the help of Herb Robbins. Robbins owned a large lumber company in Eugene and served mainly as a financial backer.[17] Spaulding's reputation in the outfitting world grew and earned him mention in several books about the area including author Bill Gulick's works and Verne Huser's *River Reflections: A Collection of River Writings*.

Spaulding joined The Flying Club of Lewiston in the spring of 1978 and began taking flying lessons. His ambition was to link an airplane to the outfitting business. With this in mind, he approached Dan Forsness, the owner of the club's airplanes, about building an airstrip at Horseshoe Bend Lodge. Forsness had a background as an equipment operator and put Spaulding in touch with Flying Club member Gene Gerkie who owned a construction company in Asotin. The three men designed the airstrip carving it out with a D7 Caterpillar. The final north-south airstrip measured 1,500'.[18]

Forsness was the first person to land on the strip

SEE HELLS CANYON AND SALMON RIVERS BY TWIN-JET BOAT

Confluence of the Snake and Salmon Rivers at the entrance to Hells Canyon, fifty miles upriver from Lewiston.

SCENIC - EXCITING
TRIPS IN SAFE, MODERN
TWIN-JET BOATS CAN
BE ARRANGED FOR ANY
LENGTH OF TIME

EVERETT SPAULDING
(One of the Northwest's leading guides and boat operator)

LICENSED OPERATOR IN SALMON RIVER AND HELLS CANYON SINCE 1946

BE SAFE — TRAVEL TWIN JET

(left) Everett Spaulding in about 1950, during his early years of outfitting.
(right) A 1960s brochure advertising Spaulding's outfitting services.

Everett Spaulding [third from left] and Dave Helfrich [far left] with some friends on the Rogue River while filming How the West Was Won *in 1961. Spaulding is dressed as a double for actor Karl Malden.*

The 1,500' north-south airstrip.

before it was finished with The Flying Club's Citabria (N2684Z). While Gerkie and his employees were building the airstrip, men and supplies were flown in using the club's aircraft. Since Forsness could not always handle the flying demands, area pilots were contracted for the work. Contract pilot Bob Cline often flew for the job using the Citabria. However, Gerkie initially refused to fly with Cline because he thought his hair was too long and hailed him as a hippie. However, their relationship changed one day when Cline helped Gerkie with a piece of broken equipment.[19]

For the next year, Cline continued to fly support for the lodge, mainly transporting caretaker Joseph Heinz in and out to Lewiston. By the fall of 1979, Cline had the opportunity to move on from flight instructing and contract work. Yet, he did not want to leave Spaulding and Forsness without a replacement. Therefore, he gave John Black a checkout at the strip. Black was one of his higher time students whom he had recently helped with a CFI rating. Black, a schoolteacher in Lewiston, had

just returned to college as a full-time student pursuing an engineering degree. Flight instructing allowed him to earn some extra money on the side.[20]

With Cline's approval, Black was assigned his first flight to Horseshoe Bend Lodge on October 2, 1979. Flying the club's 1959 Cessna 182 (N8489T), he made a successful landing regardless of some soft areas in the runway. As he turned around in preparation for takeoff, one of the main wheels became stuck in a hole. Unable to break the tire loose with raw horsepower, Spaulding began pushing on a strut and decided to switch sides. Known to be short tempered and often in a hurry, he ran forward to get around the airplane instead of behind.[21] As he came around the front of the airplane, Spaulding was struck by the wheeling propeller, first in the face and then in the groin. Black caught Spaulding out of the corner of his eye and pulled the mixture control as fast as possible to shut the engine down, but it was too late.

Men at the scene immediately rushed to Spaulding and attempted to stop the bleeding,

(left) The Horseshoe Bend Lodge in 2014.
(right) The Vogels have kept much of the Horseshoe Bend Lodge history intact. Former owner Everett Spaulding posted this sign for visitors, which still hangs near the main entrance.

focusing on the femoral artery. Spaulding was loaded into the back of the airplane in hopes of getting him to the Lewiston hospital (approximately a twenty minute flight), as his friends were only able to slow the bleeding. Dusk began setting in as Black prepared for takeoff down the unlit runway. With the navigation and landing lights on, Black poured the coals to the Cessna 182. The plane accelerated down the runway. Nearing rotation the aircraft hit a bump that momentarily dimmed the landing lights – the main source of illumination. The fleeting loss of light caused Black to unknowingly veer to the left. When the lights flickered back on he recognized he was too far left of center. With too much airspeed and no time to correct the takeoff roll, he forced the plane into the air off the side of the strip toward the river and made his way out of the canyon. As soon as possible, Black made contact with the Lewiston airport tower to arrange an ambulance to meet him at the ramp. Despite these efforts, Spaulding died.

As a friend and good flight instructor Cline drove out to the Lewiston airport to see how Black did on his first solo trip to the property. As he pulled onto the ramp he was surprised to see the Cessna 182 tied down and no one around. As Cline drove closer he saw a noticeable amount of blood on the airplane. Dumbfounded he walked over to the plane and looked inside. Blood was everywhere. Reasoning through the scene the best he could, Cline concluded that a hunter must have tried to load an improperly dressed deer into the plane without Black's permission. The whole site struck him as odd. Concerned, he located a phone and called Black, who told him the horrific story.[22]

New Owners

The Spaulding family and Robbins sold the lodge, along with twenty acres on the northeast end of the property, to Dave Bream. In 1981, longtime backcountry enthusiasts Darell and Rusty Bentz purchased the other 100 acres of land containing the airstrip.

Initially, for housing, the brothers poured a 20' X 24' concrete slab. On three sides of the slab, block walls were erected above ground level and then framed in over the top. In time this became the foundation and daylight basement for the present day lodge. For many years it contained two rooms and a bathroom for living quarters. Log work began on the upper levels in 1993. The first batch of logs hauled in for the project was trucked to Rice Creek. From Rice Creek the logs were floated to the property. However, these logs did not cure properly, and a second shipment of logs was trucked down the south side of the river to Billy Creek. The Bentzes pulled the logs from Billy Creek upriver behind jet boats.

Bream and Vogel

Along with the lodge, Bream's parcel also contained the homestead cabin, which he allowed friends to use for many years while they ran cattle in the area. The cabin was later burned in the Maloney Creek Fire of 2000. Bream obtained Spaulding's outfitting privileges and named his business S & S Outfitters. Early on in his outfitting career he hosted Jack Hemingway and Jack's daughter Mariel on a chukar-hunting trip at the lodge. In honor of their trip, the room they stayed in was dubbed the "Star Room." Bream's main source of income was through his job at CCI Speer (currently ATK), a Lewiston-based ammunition manufacturer. At work Bream became acquainted with fellow employee Don Vogel. The two became friends and Vogel ended up running a jet boat for Bream's outfitting business when he needed extra help. After eighteen years of lending a hand, Vogel and his wife Vicki bought Bream out in 1999. By the time Vogel acquired the place, Bream had sold eighteen acres of land to the BLM, along with the scenic easement for the two acres he kept. Vogel renamed the outfitting business, Vogel Outdoor Adventures, and has done extensive rehabilitation to the original Spaulding lodge and associated facilities.[23]

The Bentz Brothers

Darell and his younger brother, Rusty, were raised on the Bentz Brother Ranch situated on White Bird Creek, near the town of White Bird. A long ridge at the headwater of the drainage now bears the family name. Their father, Ross, was born on the ranch in 1900, and his older brother received homestead approval for the acreage in 1898. Darell and Rusty attended school in White Bird through the eighth grade, then each finished high school in Grangeville.[24]

Rusty and Darell Bentz with Rusty's Cessna 185 at the lodge airstrip in March 2014.

B. BENTZ

While on summer break from college in the summer of 1966, the Bentzes discovered a sunken plywood jet boat on the North Fork of the Clearwater River. Earlier that spring, the Potlatch Corporation lost the new boat during a log-drive. One person died in the accident. The boat was chalked up as a loss because of the large amount of logs rushing down the river combined with high water levels. However, on a float trip in late August, the Bentzes stumbled across various pieces of the boat about ten miles below the Beaver Creek Bridge. With a little ingenuity, they returned to the site and recovered the motor and jet pump, and with these few pieces the brothers decided to build a plywood jet boat. Thus started their infatuation with running rivers.[25]

When Darell graduated college in 1968, he and his wife decided to move to Lewiston where he took a job with Lewiston Grain Growers. The job was not the main motivation for settling in Lewiston. Rather it was the access to the rivers. Rusty followed two years later and started Bentz Fence Company. The next year Darell joined Rusty in the business, and the two expanded the company to include swimming-pool construction and maintenance. Shortly thereafter, they split the business. Rusty kept the fencing portion and Darell the pool business.[26]

Darell and Rusty continued to tinker with building boats and running rivers. Most of it was trial and error, but they also gathered information from others in the industry such as Bruce Oakes and longstanding Salmon River boat operator, Paul Filer, of the Shepp Ranch. In 1972, the two built a boat for their father Ross, who had plans of starting an outfitting business with it. He used the boat for many years, but his dream of guiding fishing trips never completely materialized. After he died in 1978, Darell further developed Ross's outfitting idea under the name of Intermountain Excursions. This outfitting business became an integral part of their Salmon River lodge operation. Rusty now primarily runs it under the name Bentz River Exploration.[27]

As the years passed, Rusty and Darell became more and more entrenched in Idaho rivers and the backcountry. By the end of the 1970s, Darell grew his boat building abilities into a full-time business. The Lewiston-based company, Bentz Boats, manufactures and sells high-end aluminum jet boats all over the world to both commercial and private operators. Darell's son Bryan currently manages the company. Author Richard Ripley has completed an in-depth biography of Darell's life.

The entire Bentz family has a profound interest in backcountry history. Starting in March 2010, they put together a gathering at the lodge of friends and people interested in keeping the history of the backcountry alive. The annual spring event became known as "The Old-Timers' Trip." It is certainly a "who's who" of the Idaho backcountry, especially in the outfitting community.

Bentz the Pilot

While the 1970s marked the beginning of Bentz Boats, it also marked the start of Rusty's flying career. Rusty's first flight in a small airplane was with pilot Jim Mitchell in 1964. Rusty hired Mitchell to fly him to the Chamberlain Ranger Station where he wanted to look over a possible trail contract job. Grangeville pilot Sid Hinkle later flew him out. Although Rusty was taken with mountain flying, eleven years passed before he began taking flying lessons. Wanting to obtain his private license, he and friend John Scott bought a Cessna 140 (N89537). He received some early instruction from Lewiston pilot Jim Maxwell. After earning the license, Rusty wanted to move into flying the backcountry and unloaded the 140 for a Cessna 180 (N6424X). This plane was damaged in a mishap at the Buffalo Hump airstrip in 1978. Two years later, Rusty replaced the 180 with a Cessna 185 (N2303Y). He has flown the 185 thousands of hours in the backcountry, both for pleasure and in connection to the Bentz Lodge.

Many people consider Rusty the foremost authoritative pilot and historian on the lower Salmon River airstrips. While researching for this book I heard countless comments of praise about him. Common remarks from people I interviewed included: "Have you talked to Rusty Bentz? If anyone knows it's him." Or "I've flown with Rusty to places I'm not sure are even airstrips, he has landed on every open spot an airplane can land in that country [lower Salmon River]." Or "Rusty is the only pilot I know to land there [Frenchy Creek] . . . it's just incredible." Or "Have you talked to Rusty? The guy is a walking encyclopedia of aviation in the canyon [Hells

D. BENTZ

(top) The 802 Air Tractor that ditched in the Salmon River during the Maloney Creek Fire of 2000. (bottom) Airlifting the Air Tractor from the river on August 13, 2000.

D. BENTZ

Canyon]." And finally, "Rusty's one of the best pilots you'll ever see as far as backcountry. Best you'll ever see!"

I came to realize the observations of Rusty are undoubtedly all true. Rusty indeed has an immense knowledge of the history around the area. And his command of an aircraft is admirable. He has also made several of the first and only landings at certain locales in this country.

Two Fire Accidents

During the horrific Maloney Creek Fire of 2000 a single-engine air tanker (SEAT) crashed near the Bentz Lodge boat ramp on August 11.[28] Jim Pope Sr., helicopter pilot and owner of the Hamilton Ranch, was working the same fire as the 802 Air Tractor (N76159F) and heard the pilot report engine trouble. It was later discovered that a blown compressor caused the failure. With a dead engine and gliding down the river, it was suggested that he try and make the Bentz's airstrip. By this time Pope had maneuvered the copter behind the crippled airplane and watched him abandon the idea of reaching the airstrip. Instead, he landed in the water nearly hitting a group of river rafters. The plane hit the river and flipped. Pope immediately landed as close as he could to the upside-down airplane, and his passenger prepared to dive in to rescue the pilot. But just then the pilot popped up from the aircraft. Pope gave him a quick check and then flew him directly to the Grangeville hospital, where he was released uninjured. Two days later, the SEAT was airlifted out of the river by a helicopter and flown to Cottonwood.[29]

On July 10, 2001, another SEAT crashed involving a recovery effort by the Bentzes. Pilot Doug Gilbert was called to make a drop run on a wildfire burning on the south side of the lower Salmon River. Piloting a Thrush (S-2R-1200) (N4947X) owned by Craigmont Air Service, he aborted the initial mission due to low visibility caused by smoke. On the second trip to the river he attempted to make a drop run, but came in too low, and his wheels clipped a sub ridge slightly downstream and on the opposite side of the river from the mouth of Deer Creek. The impact ripped the gear off the airplane and caused it to crash about 300 yards down the ridge, instantly killing Gilbert. Prior to the accident, Craigmont Air Service had been sold to Nyssa Air Service of Nyssa, Oregon. Short on pilots, Buck Erickson, the former owner, returned to help. He was killed three days after Gilbert while spraying near Nezperce in a Thrush (S-2R) (N5011N).

In a strange set of circumstances the motor from Gilbert's Thrush separated from the airframe and landed directly in the middle of the Salmon River. The gear also ended up in the river and was found near an island. The radial engine proved difficult to find. After several failed attempts to locate the engine, Rusty happened to spot it from the air in late July when the water dropped. The Bentzes boated down to the site and marked it so boaters would not hit it. They were then hired by the insurance company to retrieve it. Rusty, along with Russ Story, a local insurance agent, and Don Vogel boated in to the site. Darell drove in from Lewiston with a truck and trailer and met them at the boat tie-up area. The Bentzes rigged their boat with a special lift and were able to pull the radial motor onto the boat and get it to shore.[30]

Don Vogel's son Scott with the salvaged radial engine from pilot Doug Gilbert's Thrush.

BILLY CREEK RANCH

Early History

A current upstream view of the Billy Creek Ranch and lower airstrip.

This drainage was originally referred to as "Capt. Billy Creek." The name is derived from Salmon River Billy, a Nez Perce Indian who called the place home. Billy's son Luke Billy ran cattle from the location before selling out and moving to Lapwai.[31] Richard P. Nash homesteaded 179 acres on the lower end of the creek in 1919.

Shroyers

George and Helen Shroyer of Philomath, Oregon, purchased the 30,000-acre Billy Creek Ranch from Portland attorney Fred Youngberg in 1953. The couple was looking for an investment and saw the ranch advertised in *The Oregonian* newspaper. After one look at the property, the Shroyers had to have it.[32]

Shroyer grew up as a logger working for Rex Clemens Logging before starting his own business, George Shroyer Logging in 1945. In addition to his logging operation, he thoroughly enjoyed raising cattle and owned several cattle ranches in Idaho and Oregon. The Billy Creek Ranch was special, as he acquired it with the intent to make it his retirement home. The only problem with Shroyer's plan was that he loved work and never retired. In 1999, Joyce M. Hall and Lee Wood published a complete biography of Shroyer entitled *An Oregon Logging Pioneer.* A year later, he died at age eighty-eight.

The Billy Creek Ranch remains in the family.[33]

Since Shroyer was busy with his logging operations in western Oregon through Canada, he hired a series of foremen to run the ranch. A few of the people that held this position include: Rene and Lenora Myers of Grangeville, Bob Carothers, Denny Davis, Randy Lorentz, Pat and Lynette Enniking, and Ed Enniking.

Billy Creek Landing Sites

Due to the remote location of the ranch, entry by air became important to haul supplies and people in and out, especially in the winter months when the main access roads were impassible. The primary airstrip located at the confluence of Billy Creek and the Salmon River (on the downstream side) is still visible and used occasionally. This 800'-airstrip was likely active during the Youngberg ownership, starting in the 1940s. The Shroyers referred to this airfield as "Lower Billy," because the large ranch had several landing patches that were occasionally used. It is believed that the large hayfields directly across Billy Creek from the lower strip were also landing sites, as well as another spot about two to three miles up the creek on the east side. One other known airfield was located on top of the ridge at the head of Billy Creek and was referred to as "Upper Billy." The Upper Billy strip was used frequently in the early 1960s when disease was discovered in the cattle herd. Blood samples had to be flown out to a local veterinarian for testing. The pilot transporting the blood used a ski-equipped Super Cub.

Over the years, the Shroyers hired several different commercial operators at the ranch, including Don Schumacher and Frank Hill. This era of pilots genuinely disliked landing on the lower strip, as it was always wet. These soft conditions made it difficult to stop and generally covered the airplanes in mud. The yearly planting of alfalfa created the soft conditions, and regardless of the requests by pilots to leave the field uncultivated, planting continued. Hill had a few dicey landings here. One of the last times was in a Cessna 180. On landing, he was unable to stop. He ended up skidding the plane over the center of the airfield, bounced down to the far end, and ground-looped it before going into the river. He decided the muddy field was too hard on equipment and was not worth it. In more recent years, neighbor Rusty Bentz has landed a 185 in a hayfield upstream along the river, which is another spot likely used decades earlier.[34]

R. LORENTZ

Randy Lorentz with his Champ at the main Billy Creek landing site in spring 1989.

MOFFETT PLACE
(DEER CREEK MINE)

HOLM

The main open area at the Moffett Place used for landing is in the foreground. The more modern IDFG cabin can be seen in the center of the photograph among the trees.

The Moffett Place sat on the south side of the ridge from the Deer Creek Mine. James Moffett built a small log cabin, which burned and was replaced with a framed structure.[35] Ranch hands running cattle in the winter used the newer building. The area burned again during the Maloney Creek Fire of 2000, and the IDFG built another cabin a few years later in approximately the same vicinity.

The hayfield/bench, on the west side of Deer Creek and downstream from the cabin sites, provided a fairly smooth landing patch for airplanes. Bert Zimmerly Sr. and his pilots first used the airfield in the early 1940s. Local pilots actively continued to land at the location through the 1970s. Bob Zehner Jr. was one of the last pilots known to use the Moffett Place field.[36]

Moscow pilot Pete Fountain used this strip regularly in the 1940s and 1950s to visit relatives on a nearby ranch. In about 1958, on a recreational trip with his son's Ron and Craig he broke the tailwheel off a Super Cub (N3679P) on landing. The strip had a slight skiff of snow, and the ground was frozen. When the tailwheel came down it hit a frozen cow pie and snapped. As Fountain assessed the situation the weather slowly deteriorated. A cowboy with the Howard Ranch, who was staying in the little cabin, invited them in. After pacing the floor a bit, Fountain decided the snow surface was crusty enough that he could takeoff without the tailwheel. He left the two kids behind and took off to check the weather in the nearby drainages to see if he could get home. A short while later, he returned. The ceilings were too low to sneak out. With nowhere to go the cowboy cracked open some whisky and the two spun a few yarns. Ron Fountain remembered, "Us kids thought it was great to be stuck in the backcountry listening to a real cowboy tell stories. It was a great adventure. My mother [Ella] was worried sick, but we got word out to where we were."[37]

With no break in the weather, the cowboy saddled some horses and took the Fountains to a ranch several miles to the north to the nearest road. As they rode out, Ivan Gustin of Hillcrest Aviation in Lewiston circled them in a Super Cub. Ella had called Gustin and asked for his help. With knowledge of their progress, Ella made the long drive to the ranch to retrieve her family.[38]

As soon as the weather cleared, Fountain returned to the Moffett Place with a new tailwheel and flew the airplane out. After returning home, he realized that he had forgotten to grab some guns initially hauled in for target practice with his kids. Now another trip was necessary. This time Alvin "Lynn" Linsay joined him. Linsay was a Moscow farmer who occasionally flew spray planes for Fountain Flying Service during the busy season. The airfield still had the same crust on the surface, but the snow conditions had softened just enough to turn it to cement. On touch down, flying the same Super Cub as the first trip, the snow grabbed one of the main wheels and flipped the airplane on its back. Unhurt, Fountain, and Linsay clambered out of the aircraft. Unlike the earlier trip, the cowboy was not in residence. The only way out was to walk.[39]

DEER CREEK

Platts – The Early Years

An aerial of Deer Creek showing the most recent lodge and 1,000' runway.

It is common in the aviation community for this site at the upstream side of Deer Creek to be called the "Rudolph Place." The confusion stems from the fact that late 1800s settler Mike Rudolph homesteaded ground nearby, at the mouth of Eagle Creek.[40] After Rudolph died, his son Bud took over the ranch and received goods and supplies flown to the hayfield located here. However, during the homestead era on the river, John Platt occupied this location at the mouth of Deer Creek.

Platt came from a Genesse homestead family. In 1895, too young to stake his own claim on recently opened reservation lands, he headed to the Salmon River country to establish himself as a cattle rancher. In the beginning, he moved to Skelton Gulch and later bought out his brother-in-law Wesley Dorchester. Dorchester had started a cattle operation on the north side of the Salmon – leading him to Deer Creek. Platt married his wife Emma in 1900. The Platts spent the next seventeen years living on the river in various homes, raising six children.[41] In June 1914, after living nearly seven years at the mouth of Deer Creek where the present airstrip is located, they received homestead approval for 150 acres.[42] The family called the place the "Deer Creek Ranch." The early river pioneer's time on the river met a sad end. The Platts were forced out of the country after a bad winter claimed most of their cattle. The land was then taken in the bankruptcy process.[43] John Platt wrote a book chronicling his early years in Idaho entitled, *Whispers From Old Genesee and Echoes of the Salmon River.* The last half of the book offers many colorful stories and accounts of his life on the river. His son Kenneth also wrote a book called *Salmon River Saga* that offers many insights to their time at Deer Creek.

One amazing remnant of the Platts's hard work at Deer Creek is the pipeline strung across the creek near the confluence with the river. The several hundred-foot suspended pipe was built in 1915 as part of the irrigation system. While it is most impressive from the ground, it is also very visible from the air.

The Airstrip and Trouble Finds Pilot Pete Fountain

Ross Howard purchased the place in the 1940s. Under his ownership, a crude 700'-airstrip was created in a hayfield perpendicular to the river with a thirteen percent slope. The airstrip granted access to this remote side of the Howard Ranch. It was primarily used to move supplies and cowboys. The first pilots to utilize the strip worked for Zimmerly, followed by those of Hillcrest Aviation.[44] The upper end of the runway was fairly steep with about a ten percent slope and contained a small turnaround area at the top. About 600' of the runway was usable for takeoff. Pilots had to be extremely careful with higher-powered aircraft not to use full throttle on takeoff because of an abrupt mound in the center of the runway. The hump had the potential to preload the landing gear, which could cause damage or kick the plane prematurely into the air.[45]

217

Hillcrest Aviation owner and pilot Ivan Gustin with a Deer Creek deer after a successful hunt.

Pilot Pete Fountain collapsed a landing gear on a Piper Cub at Deer Creek in the mid-1950s. The plane was equipped with a Whitaker Gear. This modified gear system had two smaller tandem wheels on each side replacing the normal one wheel per side. The customized gear had some advantages for rough field work, but it had the potential to create a fair amount of stress to the gear supports and mounts to the airframe. On Fountain's Cub the Whitaker system fatigued the metal where the gear bolted to the frame. The accident damaged much of the airplane, including the propeller. After several days of flying in and out to make the necessary field repairs, Fountain still needed to hang a new prop. Downstream Eagle Creek resident Bud Rudolph assured Fountain that he would keep a watchful eye on the airplane in his absence – mainly vowing to prevent horses and cows from nibbling on the fabric of the plane.[46]

Before Fountain could get back to the airfield with a prop, a large thunderstorm swept through the area, producing heavy winds. The severe winds picked the prop-less aircraft up and turned it end-over-end down the hayfield. On Fountain's return he found his little Cub scattered all over the field. Pieces of the yellow fabric hung in the barbwire fence like tumbleweeds. Of course Rudolph was apologetic, but there was nothing he could have done. The only course of action was to haul the plane out. However, there were no nearby roads at this time, so they broke the plane down into small pieces and boated it out on rubber rafts. Pete's son Ron remembered, "I can still see uncle Otis sitting in the fuselage of the airplane that was strapped to a rubber boat, just riding the rapids."[47]

The 1970s and 1980s

Bob Gregg and Don Gage of Lewiston purchased Deer Creek circa 1970. Gregg, a native Idahoan, moved to Lewiston in 1954 and over the years ran a flooring company and sold real estate. As a side job he started Three Rivers Outfitters, which offered boating, fishing, and hunting trips, mainly on the Snake and Salmon rivers. Cougar Bar, on the Snake River, originally served as his base of operations, but the site was plagued with flooding issues. The cabin he built was boated downriver and then trucked over to the Deer Creek property and used as the main lodge.[48]

Around the same time Gregg acquired the ground, he took up flying. He and friend Bob Payne bought a 1955 Cessna 180 (N9335C) from Bill Chetwood. Chetwood, a Lewiston dentist, enjoyed both flying and the backcountry and often spent weekends at the property helping his friends. Chetwood replaced the airplane with a 1959 Cessna 180 (N9115T). Gregg used his Cessna 180 in connection to the outfitting business, but he largely relied on commercial pilot Bob Stallings of Lewiston to move supplies and customers.[49]

Another friend of the group was Marvin Twilegar, who bought Gage's interest in the business. Under the Gregg-Twilegar partnership, the two doubled the size of the lodge and tried to expand the operation.[50]

Maxwell and Payne Ownership

Jim Maxwell and Bob Payne, both professional pilots from Lewiston, bought Deer Creek in 1990. Maxwell grew up having family connections to the Snake and Salmon river areas. His father Marvin was raised on the Imnaha River, and his uncle Ken Johnson owned the old Brockman Ranch at Temperance Creek. His uncle Donald "Bud" Maxwell of Joseph was also a commercial pilot who flew

seasonally for Ted Grote. Maxwell first learned to fly in Pendleton while attending college. After earning his various ratings, he worked for Bob Stallings in Lewiston as a charter pilot and instructor. Wanting to move toward ag flying, he went to work for Buck Erickson who owned Craigmont Air Service, a spray operation located in Craigmont. From Erickson he learned enough to start his own business, Valley Air Service, in his hometown of Joseph. Maxwell eventually moved the company to La Grande. He then left Oregon for a job in Guatemala, where he sprayed illegal crops for the US Department of State. After a severe aircraft accident, he moved back to the states. While owning Three Rivers Outfitters, Maxwell flew in and out of the property with a personally owned Super Cub, and enjoyed flying the backcountry for pleasure. After seven years of ownership, he sold his interest to business partner Bob Payne. Maxwell continues to fly out of Lewiston with an RV6 and a Beech Baron for leisure. The Baron allows him to commute to and from Lewiston to his various job locations across the country where he flies government air tankers.[51]

Payne bought Maxwell out of the property and the outfitting business in 1997. With the Three Rivers name gone, Payne began to merely call the place Deer Creek. Under his sole possession, Payne primarily used the ranch for recreational purposes and accessed it with a Super Cub and Cessna 206. Payne grew up in Nezperce and learned to fly at age eighteen from Wayne Hughes. He later

A group of Cubs and pilots at Deer Creek in the early 1990s — [left to right] Sis [dog], Mike Becker, Ralph Stout, Dick Reed, Brock Hill, and Jim Maxwell.

Looking upstream at the Deer Creek property with the modern lodge and airstrip. The original runway was situated perpendicular to the current arrangement in the open field.

obtained various ratings at Hillcrest Aviation and started crop dusting. He built up his own spray business named Super Cat and had branches in Nezperce, Craigmont, Lewiston, and Walla Walla. An opportunity for spraying with the US Department of State arose in 1984, and he took the job. With this position, he traveled all over the Far and Middle East, as well as Central and South America, spraying illegal crops. Payne sold the river property to Joe Scott in 2006. Scott hired Payne as a fixed-wing and helicopter pilot, as well as the general manager of the property. With Payne's help the old lodge was replaced by a bigger, more modern structure. The current lodge is situated on the bottom end of the original landing area, and a new 1,000'-runway was re-positioned parallel to the river below this structure.

Recent Years - Scott

Scott, the only grandson of Albertsons

grocery store magnate Joe and Kathryn Albertson, grew up with a great admiration for Idaho. He is a backcountry enthusiast, owning several remote properties along the Salmon River. Scott is an avid hunter, fisherman, and sportsman who enjoys accessing his properties either with his collection of aircraft or jet boats. While he employs a full-time staff of pilots through his private flight department, he also regularly flies helicopters to and from the backcountry himself.

The Deer Creek property had been on Scott's radar since the late 1980s. In fact, he had negotiated on the parcel prior to the Payne-Maxwell ownership. When he finally completed the purchase a decade-and-a-half later, he briefly brought in longtime employee Norm Close to help Payne with the property. Whether it is an aircraft pilot, caretaker, or jet boat pilot, Scott has a reputation of always hiring the best. This is unquestionably the case with Close.

Close, originally from California, moved to Boise as a manager with an automotive parts dealer called "Service Parts." Al Tice, the owner of Mackay

Bar, was a customer. One day in 1964, the two struck up a conversation about steelhead fishing as Close had a background in guiding fisherman on the Eel River. Tice offered him a job and, after some thought, he and his wife Joyce moved to Mackay Bar. During his nine-year tenure at Mackay Bar, he honed his skills on fishing, hunting, and most importantly running the river with powerboats. He picked the brains of Tice and pioneer river runner Bob Smith, but Close's expertise and skill as a boat pilot was largely self-taught. He learned the river a section at a time. In the early years he ran the river with an eighteen-foot aluminum sled powered by a single engine thirty-five-horse-prop-driven Evinrude outboard.[52]

Close always wanted to push himself to be the best. Opportunity knocked in the late 1960s, when he, along with Bob and Don Smith were hired by Harold Bolt to take a group of nine people collecting data to determine if the Salmon River was eligible for a Wild and Scenic River designation. Three boats ferried the group from Corn Creek to Lewiston and back. Close ran a twenty-two foot craft powered by twin eighty-horse Mercury outboards. On the return trip Bob thought the group should see Hells Canyon, so they detoured. For Close it was the first time he had run the lower Salmon or the Snake River.[53]

A decade later, Close was considered an expert on both rivers. After leaving Mackay Bar in 1973 he worked three years at James Ranch, then another two years at Shepp Ranch. Tired of working for someone else, he started his own outfitting business with jet boats in Riggins. Close secured several government contracts, primarily with the Forest Service. Dale George, his main contact at the agency, approached him about the government's need for a river patrolman on the Snake to enforce river permits and activity associated with the newly created NRA. Close took the job and became a regular figure to tourists, hunters, fisherman, and boaters on the Snake. As the river patrolman, Close became one of the only US Coast Guard licensed boatman to legally run a powered vessel above Granite Creek to the Hells Canyon Dam.[54] Reflecting about Close's ability on the Snake River, Art Seamans, the former NRA assistant area ranger commented, "Nobody could replace Norm. He is an exceptionally and extremely talented man on the river, and just a darn hard worker."[55]

He held the patrolman position until 1986, when Scott hired him. Scott owned a cabin at Mackay Bar and knew Close's credentials. As a young man, Scott had been on a chukar-hunting trip with his father, guided by Close from the Shepp Ranch. From the onset, Close helped Scott look for the ideal backcountry property. After a handshake deal fell through with John Crowe at Campbell's Ferry, Scott obtained China Bar. The Closes managed the property nearly year-round for seventeen years until it was sold to Jim and Jeanne Campbell. The Closes, who own a beautifully maintained turn of the twentieth century home on Cow Creek, have since taken over the management of two other ranches for Scott on Race and Elk creeks. Since the move to land-locked properties, Close's time on the Snake and Salmon rivers has slowed to a more leisurely tempo and remains one of his favorite pastimes.[56]

Norm Close at the helm of a jet boat on the Salmon River circa 1970.

221

Eagle Creek

The Rudolphs

The 850' airstrip [left] located at the mouth of Eagle Creek.

Michael Rudolph received homestead approval for 156.11 acres at the mouth of Eagle Creek in 1913. He later proved up on more acreage in 1914 and 1924.[57] Formerly of Palatine, Illinois, Rudolph moved west while working for the Northern Pacific Railroad. He arrived in the Salmon River country and settled on Eagle Creek in 1891. His main interest in the beginning was mining and some subsistence farming, but he later became a recognized cattleman.[58]

By the time he homesteaded the land he and his wife Ada Avtch had built a sizeable ranch containing a well-built cabin and barn. The Rudolphs raised two children at the remote ranch; Forest "Bud" and Louise.[59] The Rudolphs were the first to grow alfalfa on this portion of the Salmon River and had a large orchard. Friend John Platt wrote, "Of all our good neighbors, Mike Rudolph was the most helpful and unselfish . . . Being one of the old-timers, and having a cabin where hospitality was the keynote, he fed and helped all the tenderfeet."[60]

On November 5, 1951, Rudolph died in the Lewiston hospital at age ninety-five. He is buried in the Craigmont IOOF Cemetery. Ada continued to live on the ranch before her own death. Daughter Louise lived near Wapshilla Creek for many years with her husband Chester Wilson who was a miner from Oregon. After Bud graduated from Winchester High School, he slowly took over the ranch. In 1952, he married his wife Jean and started a family. They wintered at the ranch one year with their first child. Jean remembered, "There were no roads in there then. Hillcrest Aviation from Lewiston would fly in every Tuesday to deliver our mail and groceries. We had no place to land so we walked up to the landing spot at Deer Creek. It was always a welcome sight to see the plane." With another child on the way, Bud and Jean decided the ranch was too remote to raise kids and sold the property to Ross Howard in 1955.[61] The most visible remains of the Rudolph's time at the property is the chimney of the homestead cabin.

Airstrip and Road

After a few years of using the land, Wendell Mathison began to lease it along with other portions of the Howard Ranch. Soon after the Howards obtained the ground they funded the construction of the Eagle Creek Road through the place to the river. The Howards then extended the road along the river and up Wapshilla Creek to the old Reeves ranch house, which they also owned. At about the same time this road was completed, Mathison graded out the 850' Eagle Creek airstrip with an eight percent slope. The intent of the airstrip was like others on the ranch; it made for a quick and easy way to resupply ranch hands.

While no one cared one way or the other about the airstrip, the road became a huge subject of controversy. It was really the only main road that accessed this lower section of the Salmon River. As a result, federal agencies wanted to be able to use it for management purposes. The BLM and the public, such as sportsmen, started using the road. Mathison claimed that allowing access other than to his employees was causing vandalism and theft, and he gated it off in 1961. Nez Perce County commissioners ordered him to reopen it.[62] The BLM in particular wanted to use the road to access and haul out timber located on federal land. Mathison and the Howards stood their ground. By the fall of 1962, the county filed a lawsuit in the 10th District Court asking the court to determine if the road was public or private.[63] Court proceedings dragged on through 1967 and eventually the road was opened to the public.

Similar to the road, the Eagle Creek runway is now open to the public, but it is not formally maintained. The IDFG obtained the airstrip along with other portions of the Howard Ranch in the early 1990s and incorporated them into the Craig Mountain WMA.

The Rudolphs' headstone at the Craigmont IOOF Cemetery.

CHINA CREEK

HOLM

Looking down the 700' China Creek landing area that was used regularly from the late 1940s through the 1960s.

The very faint outline of this 700'-airstrip is located perpendicular to the Salmon River along the relatively flat down-sloping ridge between China and Eagle creeks. The strip now located within the Craig Mountain WMA was once a part of the Howard Ranch headquartered on Wapshilla Creek. Starting in the late 1940s, Zimmerly pilots from Lewiston began using this location to deliver supplies to ranch hands working in the area. This landing site is rarely used anymore.

In the spring of 1960, the major power lines in this area were strung along and across the lower Salmon River. The China Creek drainage and airstrip served as the base of activity for the project. A fairly large camp that contained a dining hall for the crews was hauled in using the Eagle Creek Road. Washington Water Power hired Power City Construction of Spokane for the job. Due to the remote and rugged terrain, Power City contracted with Hillcrest Aviation, which strung the lines using a Bell 47 helicopter. The new lines allowed Washington Power and Water to tie into Idaho Power's lines connected to the then new Brownlee Dam.[64]

The following article from the February 12, 1950 *Lewiston Morning Tribune* captures Zimmerly Air Transport's weekly postwar mail route on the lower Salmon River:

"You Land Where You Can When Flying Salmon River Run"

By Chad Wallin

We were over the Snake just above the big eddy and approaching Captain John when Clyde said, "There's the Seven Devils."

"Where?" I asked.

"Over there under that bunch of white clouds," he replied. "Only, you can't see them."

It didn't seem much use to look at something I couldn't see although I was obliged for the free information. I looked down instead of ahead.

From 5,000 feet the little floes of ice looked like dabs of cold grease such as popup on the gravy when it stands in the icebox. This gravy, the Snake, was dark green.

Clyde Martin and I were flying the mail into the Salmon river country. At least, Clyde, who is chief pilot for Zimmerly Air Transport [ZAT], was doing the flying. I once took flying lessons in which Clyde had a hand so, by grace of former association, I was a sort of deputy co-pilot without portfolio.

ZAT hold contracts with four Salmon river ranchers to deliver mail, passengers, groceries and assorted what-nots each Tuesday and Clyde, who splits the run, with Glenn Shannon, had asked me to make the trip. Curious to know what a flying mailman had to do to make the daily groceries, I had accepted.

The morning was crisp and still cold enough to iced a little on the car's windshield as I drove to Asotin county airport at 8:15 a. m. Clyde was waiting with the four-place Cessna 170 [NC3919V] warmed and loaded with a couple of sacks of feed in the back seat. We growled out on the recently improved airport, snored [SIC] into the air and headed south and a little east, climbing a bit all the time.

Sun Brings Magic

Up at about 4,000 feet the morning, drab and grey on the ground, suddenly came alive with magic.

The winter sun broke through the overcast and the near-at-hand Blue mountains turned into shadowed greens with the white of snow running arabesques where the shadows faltered.

In the distance the Wallowas reared, massive sapphires caught in white gold prongs where their deep-canyoned sides, ice packed, narrowed toward the square-cut summit.

Beneath the plane the fields lay, done with winter lethargy, green with the ever-present color of grass, gold where last fall's stubble lay unturned.

Only the Snake, deep in the canyon, continued sullen, its turgid rolling absorbing the light, not reflecting.

We peaked at a little more than 5,000 feet above the confluence of the Snake and Grande Ronde rivers and Clyde flipped the plane over a ridge, barren and brown with outthrust rocks. "Less snow up here than in the valley," he remarked.

Hillsides everywhere held more brown than dirty white of soiled snow.

We began to go down. The rocks jabbed up pointedly here and there. The canyons were fairly wide but nothing in which to turn a six-mule train around.

"Deer Creek," Clyde said, identifying a crease among the hundred odd creases that all looked alike to me.

"Where do we set down?" I asked.

"There."

Clyde made the left wing of the plane dip sharply. Down below, by neck craning, I could see what looked like a corral where the horses had tramped out a small, clear circle in the snow.

I had my doubts but little time to voice them. Clyde had circled while we talked, lost a bit of altitude and now he dropped down toward the landing space. (Strip does not identify it.)

Roller Coaster Field

It seemed he might have put on the brakes a bit but before there was time to suggest it we were down.

"Ka-whoomp, ka-whoomp," we went. It was my impression we had landed on the back of a homemade roller coaster. But, there we were, stopped and everything in order, with Bud Rudolph walking up to the plane, a cigarette dropping from a corner of his mouth which slow-grinned a hello.

They unloaded the sacks, I unloaded myself and the camera. They signed papers, I took a picture. Clyde and I got back in.

It seemed he might have put on the brakes a bit but before there was time to suggest it we were down.

"Ka-whoomp, ka-whoomp," we went. It was my impression we had landed on the back of a homemade roller coaster. But, there we were, stopped and everything in order, with Bud Rudolph walking up to the plane, a cigarette dropping from a corner of his mouth which slow-grinned a hello.

They unloaded the sacks, I unloaded myself and the camera. They signed papers, I took a picture. Clyde and I got back in.

"Ka-whoomp, ka-whoomp, ka-whoomp" we went down the roller coaster. On the third "ka-whoomp" Clyde lifted the little ship neatly into the air again.

We flitted around a couple of buttes. "Wapshilla creek," Clyde said of another crack in the earth. He pointed out the Ross Howard and Don and Chester Wilson Ranch homes along the creek.

"Where this time?" I inquired.

"Oh," said Clyde, "You don't see the landing strip until you are on it."

That was little enough, but cheering. At least it was there, somewhere.

We came around another butte, not very much off the ground and, there it was. It was just a little table top with sharply dropping sides. Remembering the student days when I had trouble landing on the mile-long runway at the Asotin county airport I was interested, to put it mildly.

A moment later we were down again, rolling to a smooth halt. An army truck rumbled up to the tabletop, clanked its chains cordially at the air-visitor and came to a stop.

Mr. and Mrs. Don Wilson got out of the track's cab. While Don and Clyde talked, Mrs. Wilson climbed into the airplane and I took more pictures. Then Clyde and I got in, waved to Don, and away we went off the edge of the little plateau.

Lots of Room

Next stop was at the Vern Heckman ranch on Flynn creek. We had half a cow pasture to get down in. By now it was routine and in we went, the only thing out of the ordinary being that the plane's tail got stuck in a small drift. Mrs. Wilson, a seasoned air commuter, paid no attention to it. Clyde shoved the plane's nose down, gunned the motor and the ail popped free.

A short time later we were climbing above the craggy buttes and winging home over the Snake again.

Then we were over Clarkston heights, the motor was being out and we went in on the long leg and the turn to the airport, swinging down lightly.

And the mail run was done.

It is commonplace to ZAT fliers, this taking off into a county where you land on a roughened postage stamp that has curled up a little in the damp: this taking off with almost no run because there isn't any run, but it isn't common place the first time.

Somehow it doesn't seem it ever quite could be commonplace.

WAPSHILLA RANCH

The Reeves

Homesteaders Ben [far right] and Julia Reeves [far left] at the Wapshilla Ranch with an employee [center].

Ben and Julia Reeves settled on this drainage in 1904. Reeves came to the area from Oregon in 1884 and was known as "Oregon Ben." In 1901, he married Julia Nelson of Forest, Idaho, who affectionately nicknamed him "Ole." She was twenty-four years his junior. When they first moved to Wapshilla Creek, an earlier occupant had already erected a small cabin. Over a five-year period (1913–17) they proved up on several homestead entries totaling more than 1,100 acres. From these beginnings, the Reeves acquired more neighboring land as it became available. The ranch grew into the largest cattle operation of the time on the lower Salmon River. The Reeves spent summers on Hoover Point and the remainder of the year at their home on Wapshilla Creek.

At Wapshilla the Reeves upgraded their living quarters and constructed a framed four-room house. The latter was replaced circa 1923 with a larger one-and-a-half-story house that is in use today. This luxurious home was fancy for the era in any setting, particularly the remote Salmon River country.

The main ranch house in 1947.

The structure was built atop a concrete foundation and featured hot and cold running water. Water was supplied by a well-developed spring. All the construction materials were purchased in Lewiston and transported by wagon. To navigate down the steep wagon road from the top of Wapshilla Ridge to the ranch house, the rear wheels of the wagon were taken off and replaced with skids. If extra braking was needed, dogs were tied to the back of the carriage for drag. The self-sufficient ranch had an orchard of one hundred fruit trees containing: figs, nectarines, apricots, apples, pears, plums, prunes, peaches, and almonds. The Reeves family also grew crops of grapes, dewberries, raspberries, strawberries, blackberries, and a large vegetable garden.

The Reeves had two children at the ranch; Ben Jr. was born in 1921 and Alice Margaret was born in 1924. They attended nearby one-room schoolhouses and helped on the ranch. Julia had another older son, Merritt Field, from a previous relationship, who was born in 1901.

In 1940, Ben Reeves died of cancer at age eighty-two. His wife held the operation together for another six years with the help of trusted employees. After the sale, she moved to Winchester, Idaho, and spent her last years in a Lewiston nursing home, where she died in January 1970.

Ben Jr. stayed in the country most of his life working at various ranches, counting many years for the Heckman's at Flynn Creek. He died of a heart attack while driving in 1986. Margaret went on to become a schoolteacher and married several times, living in various places throughout the West. Her later years were spent in Lewiston. In March 2011, she died at age eighty-seven. Margaret always held memories of her childhood and parent's history in the Salmon River country dear to her heart and often reminisced about the wonderful time spent at Wapshilla.

Jackson Sundown and Wapshilla Creek

The creek and associated ranch is named after the Wapshilla (also spelled Wapsheli or Wapshela) Nez Perce family that lived on the drainage. Nez Perce Indian Jackson Sundown, who later became recognized as a famous rodeo participant and expert horseman, married the family's daughter Cecilia. Jackson Sundown even worked for Ben Reeves on the Wapshilla Ranch. Sundown at age fifteen joined Chief Joseph's 1877 flight to Montana. He was among a group that escaped to Canada to evade capture. He then married a Flathead Indian and had two children. Sometime around 1910, he separated from his wife and moved to the Nez Perce Reservation and married Cecilia Wapshela. The two lived in Jacques Spur near Culdesac. It was during this time in his late forties and early fifties that he became a prominent rodeo rider, often participating in the Pendleton Roundup. He died of pneumonia in December 1923 at his Jacques Spur home. Jackson Sundown is buried at the Slickpoo Cemetery at the St. Joseph Mission near Culdesac on Mission Creek.

According to Margaret Reeves, her father spoke fluent Nez Perce and was well acquainted with many members of the tribe. Jackson Sundown worked as a ranch hand for Reeves from 1917 through 1921. Reflecting back about her parent's stories of the Native American worker in 1994 she wrote, "Jackson began his day early with a bath in Wapshilla Creek. He always built the kitchen fire, ground the coffee beans, sliced the bacon and awoke my mother. He fed the horses and cleaned the stalls, but he would not milk the cow. His primary job was 'green-breaking' the horses, or getting the rough out of them. One such horse was a tall, well-built bay . . . As a child, I vividly remember this bay horse, well-named 'Sundown.' My brother, Ben Jr. (Bennie) . . . was a sickly child that needed much attention.

Sundown's headstone at the Slickpoo Cemetery on Mission Creek.

P. CLAYTON

HOLM

(top) Ross Howard at the Wapshilla Ranch in 1947.
(bottom) The well-maintained Wapshilla Ranch buildings in 2014.

Jackson used to carry him around the yard talking softly. Jackson did one last thing before leaving the Reeves Ranch. He cut his hair. The braids, very thick and somewhat sun faded, remained in a trunk my mother had."

Howards and the Idaho Department of Fish & Game

Ross Howard, a widely known rancher, lumberman, and large landowner of his era took ownership of the Reeves in-holdings in 1947. He was born near Grangeville in 1884 and grew up on the Salmon River at Elkhorn Creek. As a young man he worked in the Marshall Lake Mining District south of his childhood home. With his background in mining, he moved to Alaska in 1907, but returned to Idaho two years later, settling in Meadows Valley. Here, he opened two butcher shops and married Golda Irwin. Before leaving Meadows he took a job with the Stanfield Sheep Company. This position eventually landed him in Lewiston in 1915. Seven years later, he remarried to Marie Walter and a year later had one son, Nelson. The couple became active investors in land, livestock, and timber and even owned a lumber mill on Craig Mountain and in the Lewiston Orchards.

Prior to his death at age seventy-four in January 1959, the Howards had expanded the original Reeves Ranch to encompass more than 53,000 acres of land. The Howards ran cattle for a number of years on the acreage, but generally during their tenure it was leased to other stockmen. Bob and Tom Ross were some of the earliest ranchers to rent the ground. An organization called the "Bar Bell Ranch," managed by Cecil Smith, took over the property in the 1950s. The company made an attempt to buy the ranch from Howard, but after a lengthy court battle the sale failed. Wendell Mathison acquired the lease in the wake of the Bar Bell debacle, and by the 1970s Harold Heitstuman leased much of the property. For all the lessees the Reeves's former Wapshilla farmstead was used to house hired hands and served as a base of operations for the ranch. When Ross Howard died, the ranch remained in the hands of Ross's wife, his sister-in-law Madeline Walter, and his son. The latter two took ownership after Marie died in 1962. The family sold the entire ranch to Penny Land Company in 1982. Three years later Aetna Life and Casualty foreclosed on the property. Aetna Life and Casualty cleared the property from their books in 1992 when Bonneville Power Administration bought it for the Craig Mountain WMA.

When the IDFG took ownership of the Wapshilla Ranch, the main ranch building was in terrible condition – cattle were taking shelter inside of it. To adhere to the cultural resource requirements of the newly developed management plan for the Craig Mountain area, the IDFG decided to rehabilitate the buildings. Under the direction of Regional Wildlife Habitat Manager Gary "Sam" McNeill, a plan was put in place and renovations started in 1997. Fortunately, McNeill recruited Ed Carr who donated about five years of full-time service to the project living on site. Carr had previously helped the IDFG rebuild parts of their Billy Creek Ranch on the Snake River. Carr was not only self-sufficient, but he could do just about anything from carpentry to horticulture. Generally always working by himself at the remote ranch, he replaced sill logs, foundations, and roofs. By the early to mid-2000s, the farmstead had come a long way.

In 2004, McNeill received an inquiry from western singer and songwriter Patty Clayton of Colorado about the old ranch. Clayton turned out to be a great granddaughter of Ben and Julia Reeves. With McNeill's help, Clayton came to Idaho and arranged for a special trip to visit her family's homestead. She was so taken by the place that she wrote a song about the experience entitled "Ben and Ole's Land."

Airplanes Arrive

Under Howard's ownership pilots began to use the hayfield above the house for a landing area. Bert Zimmerly was the first to land here with a Stinson 108 in about 1947. When the Bar Bell organization occupied the place, Hillcrest Aviation stopped regularly with supplies. The upper location was vacated by the early 1960s. When the road from Eagle Creek to Wapshilla was completed, Wendell Mathison bladed out the lower landing area below the main building complex. The airstrip is basically part of the road. Little has changed to this lower roughly 1,000' east-west runway with eight and half percent slope. Over time, several ditches were dug across the field to help prevent erosion. With the demise of the cattle operators at the ranch in the 1990s and the IDFG's lack of air access needs for administrative purposes, the runway surface became fairly rough.

In June 1999, pilot Rusty Bentz spotted fifty-five gallon barrel drums full of horseshoes at the ranch. With a background in the commercial fencing business, he had a creative idea for a fence project at his family's upriver lodge. Bentz approached his friend Sam McNeill about obtaining the shoes. McNeill was delighted someone wanted them. With permission granted, Bentz shuttled two loads of shoes out to his lodge using a Cessna 185. On the first trip caretaker Ed Carr was a bit surprised to see an airplane land. Carr then further improved the landing area by smoothing it out. Mark Parks,

another volunteer caretaker, also bettered the runway by keeping it graded for pilots such as Bentz who would fly him in and out when needed. Parks, at times, even cut the grass with a push mower!

The fence that somewhat sparked the re-activation of the airstrip is not your average fence; it is a piece of art. The fence posts are made of thirty-four evenly spaced columnar basalt rock columns vertically placed in cement. Each post weighing about 3,000 pounds, was hand picked on the river, loaded on a boat, and then put in place with a backhoe. Bentz welded approximately 3,000 of the horseshoes together and then fastened them to the posts spanning the gaps between the rocks. Most guests are astonished by the creation. Used to hearing words of praise from visitors, Bentz usually responds with comments such as, "Its one-of-a-kind for sure." Or, "I guess you'd say it's unique, there is not another one like it."

The unique fence at the Bentz Lodge built of horseshoes from the Wapshilla Ranch. The project helped to reactive the airstrip in 1999.

(top) *Final approach to landing at the Wapshilla Ranch airstrip.*
(bottom) *Rusty Bentz's Cessna 185 parked at the top of the 1,000' runway.*

FLYNN CREEK

The Early Years

The Flynn Creek Cabin in 2014.

Carl Flynn settled at the mouth of the creek that now bears his name in the late 1800s.[86] Flynn eked out a modest living, mainly through mining. Several other settlers came and went from this substantial drainage during the twentieth century. By 1907, two families were living on the lower end of the drainage – Charlie Baird and J. H. Riggles. The Riggles family lived about a quarter mile below the approach end of the current airstrip. They constructed a house and a barn and cultivated several nearby fields. A hay barn was erected on the knoll above the house to the north along with more plantings.[87] This section of the current ranch is now known as the "Bud Place," which likely references a later owner.[88]

Unlike the Riggles, the upstream Baird family successfully homesteaded 160 acres, receiving approval in 1909. The Baird's place consisted of a house, barn, and several cultivated fields.[89] The Bairds sold out seven years later.[90] The Smith brothers used the old Baird place for several years in the late 1920s as a headquarters for their sheep operation. Several homesteads in the region made an effort to run sheep in this era, but were faced with limiting factors such as available rangeland, the cost of hired hands, predators, and the distance to market.[91]

Heckman, Timber, and the Building of an Empire

Faced with the tough economic times of the Great Depression and looking for opportunity, W. A. "Eck" Heckman bought the patented acreage on Flynn Creek in 1933. He and his wife Elizabeth sold their home near Waha, Idaho, to her sister and brother-in-law. They moved in to the Baird house with their two sons Donovan (Don) and Vern. The whole family worked themselves to the bone. The first year they trailed their cattle to Cottonwood for market (four day trip) and sold twenty-seven head for two-and-a-half-cents per pound.[92]

The Heckman's hard work slowly paid off. Little by little they scrimped and saved and expanded. When old enough, the two sons joined the operation lending to the straightforward company name – W. A. Heckman and Sons. As neighboring land to the east became available, they bought it. The ranch slowly grew to contain many of the former Joseph and Doumecq plains town sites such as Fly Blow, Boles, and Joseph. The Heckmans also acquired dozens of old farmsteads and used many of them as practical arms of the operation. For example, the Anderson homestead near the Camp Thomas Spring became the transfer point between the county road and their road down Flynn Creek. Closer toward the county road from the Anderson Place, they acquired the Burnett Place, which became the Heckman's summer dwelling when the cattle were in the high country. In the beginning, they lived in one of the original homestead cabins and constructed a separate bunkhouse for sleeping quarters. In the early 1950s, Vern built a more modern home at the site that is still in use. The old Burnett building is standing to date.[93]

Timber sales made the expansion possible. Prior to this era, landowners in the area were solely cattle operators. The owners had large stands of timber, but no cost effective means to move it off the isolated "island" of the Joseph-Doumecq Plains, which is nearly bound on all sides by the Snake and

234

Salmon rivers. McCall timber baron and mill owner Warren Brown found a solution to the dilemma by constructing a road up Rice Creek. The road took one year to build.[94]

Brown, a pilot, owned a Super Cub and used it for commuting to business meetings and various job sites. In his autobiography he explained, "My Super Cub wasn't a toy. I bought lots of property after seeing it from the air. I used it to look for timber jobs. I pretty much cruised timber out of the Cub. You could pull the throttle back and put the flaps on full and it was almost like a helicopter."[95] On a trip from Spokane to McCall while flying with Johnson Flying Service pilot Bob Fogg, Brown noticed the vast timber of the Joseph Plains area. Upon further investigation, he worked a timber sale with the state, which led to the construction of the road.[96] Recalling Brown's entry to the country, Donny (Donovan Jr.) Heckman recalls, "Warren did not just blow in like some outsider. He treated people how he wanted to be treated. People around here respected him for that."[97] Once the road was in place and the state sale completed, locals began working with Brown harvesting private timber. Brown liked the area so much that he and business partner John Cook formed a modest 11,000-acre ranch and ran some cattle.[98]

With the Heckman's strong work ethic and financial help from the timber sales, the operation continued to grow. The family even expanded to bordering states. Vern put together a cattle ranch near Winnemucca, Nevada, Don put one together in Emmett, Idaho, and the two brothers co-managed a cattle operation on the leased Flying D Ranch near Bozeman, Montana. Billionaire Ted Turner now owns this ranch. The Heckman's budding success led to incorporation in 1966.[99]

With the prosperity came change. The aging W. A. and Elizabeth moved from their adored Flynn Creek ranch in 1961 to be closer to town. The couple's lives came full-circle, as they bought back the Waha property they sold in the early 1930s. After Elizabeth's death in the late 1960s, W. A. moved to Emmett where he lived the rest of his years with his son Don. Grandson Donny Heckman, a tough rancher who grew up on his family's land, nearly choked up as he described how hard his grandfather worked to make a go of the family enterprise, "He was a darn hard worker . . . an old fashioned man who did not like modern times. He often said that

he was born a hundred years too late . . . he loved Charles Russell, had a huge collection of his books and paintings and lived life in that era. He never even really learned to drive a car." The fruit trees were one of the many aspects W. A. enjoyed about Flynn Creek in his later years. Once the cherries ripened, he picked steadily for two to three days straight. Since there was no refrigeration, the cherries were loaded into containers and packed out using mules on the last day of picking. After a long early morning ride, trying to beat the heat, W. A. would meet one of his family members at the top of

W. A. "Eck" Heckman and his companion "Toots" at Flynn Creek in 1961.

235

(top) The 850' Flynn Creek airstrip. The ranch buildings are in the center right of photograph.
(bottom) Looking down the Flynn Creek airfield.

the Jeep trail. From there his cherries were taken to the nearest home directly for canning.[100]

Flynn Creek still remains an essential part of the Heckman's operation, but none of the family has lived at the homestead permanently since W. A. Following his departure, the family kept a full-time foreman at Flynn Creek from fall to late spring. The early 1900s home has amazingly escaped several natural disasters. In the early 1970s, Flynn Creek flooded. The rush of water took out the original homestead barn and washed away structures associated with the Bud Place, but somehow the main house avoided damage. In the 1980s, a terrible grass fire came within about a hundred yards of the place – yet again it was spared. No explanation can really be offered, but Donny Heckman surmised, "The house just seems lucky."[101]

Donny, along with his sons, continues to run the current Heckman operation – Heckman Ranches Inc., headquartered in White Bird. Donny has an overwhelming respect for the history of the ranch and its associated properties. Until age four he was raised on an old Fly Blow farmstead. He attended grade school in Joseph's one-room schoolhouse. Both places remain part of the ranch. The family has even made an effort to keep the schoolhouse maintained. Dozens of old homesteads dot the ranch as small

reminders of the settlers who tried to make a living in the area. One of the most interesting homesteads is that of the Qualey family. The Qualeys continue to be recognized artists in western apparel circles for their incredible creation of silver spurs, bridles, and related engraving work. Other features of the ranch include several cultural Indian sites.[102]

Air Access

Access to Flynn Creek has generally been difficult. For the first fourteen years that the Heckman's owned the property, a horse trail from Camp Thomas Ridge was the most efficient route. Even then, it was a long way to the nearest major town. This changed in 1947 when Zimmerly Air Transport pilot Clyde Martin landed at the ranch on a bench above the building complex. Martin and other Zimmerly pilots made this a routine, hauling in supplies and people.[103] Martin moved to the Lewiston-Clarkston Valley during World War II and flight-instructed for the Zimmerly's CPTP. By 1947, Bert Zimmerly appointed him chief pilot. Two years later, Martin became a corporate pilot for Potlatch Lumber Company, flying a D18S Beechcraft. Martin stayed with the company

W. A. Heckman and pilot Don Schumacher stand next to a Stinson 108 at Flinn Creek in 1953.

Frank Hill and a Cessna 180 at Flynn Creek in March 1982.

through the transition of several Learjets. He ended his career as the manager of the Lewiston airport.[104]

Use of the upper bench as an airstrip was short lived, as the site was abandoned roughly two years later for the current spot, which is actually part of a wagon road that existed in 1907. The short road granted transportation between the Riggles and the Baird farmsteads. The hand built airstrip was further improved in the early 1950s with a bulldozer. In 1949, the dozer was used to construct the narrow road from Camp Thomas Ridge down Flynn Creek. The road remains very crude, but usable. One of the most challenging aspects of building the road was dynamiting a rock bluff. Harry Tizer did the dynamite work. Tizer did not like to wear shoes and completed the job barefoot.[105]

The 850'-airstrip, with a ten percent uphill slope, remains relatively unchanged since the 1950s, with the exception of some grading. Vern Heckman occasionally tied a log to a Jeep and drove up and down the runway – in an effort to smooth the surface. The length of the airstrip is restricted by a spring on the lower end, generally indicated by a stretch of bright green grass, and a fence at the top. Air access became depended upon at the ranch,

especially in the winter months when snow restricted other access. A close relationship grew between the Heckmans and the pilots they hired. Many times the pilots helped in emergency situations and risked their own lives battling bad weather to reach the ranch. Among the pilots best remembered at Flynn Creek are: Clyde Martin, Don Schumacher, and Frank Hill. Other pilots that helped the Heckman's operation over the years were friends John Gortsema of Grangeville and Louie Wimer of Cottonwood.[106]

W. A. and Elizabeth Heckman were pleased that airplanes could land at Flynn Creek. However, they did not always know what to do with the modern convenience. For example, they subscribed to a weekly aerial route that delivered mail and other requested goods. Since they were paying for the service, pilots always stopped, even if they did not have anything to deliver. The Heckmans could not quite grasp the concept. These were people greatly impacted by the difficulties associated with the Great Depression. On occasion, as a real treat they might order fresh fruit or vegetables, but generally the cost of it made them feel too guilty, so they simply refused to order it. As a nice gesture their children and grandchildren would often call the aviation company responsible for the flights and order the Heckmans fresh goods, since they knew they would never do it for themselves.[107]

The airstrip continues to be used occasionally by friends and ranch foremen. However, it is no longer relied upon as it was from the late 1940s through the 1980s. With less harsh winters and better equipment, it is more cost-efficient to use the rough road for supplies.

Randy Lorentz

Randy Lorentz is one of the most colorful and locally recognized backcountry pilots of the lower Salmon River and middle Snake region. At present, Lorentz and his wife Nita help manage operations at Flynn Creek. A native of Keuterville, Idaho, he began working in the area as a young kid and has filled a wide variety of jobs from running cattle and ranch management to logging. Through the years, he has lived and worked at the Smith brothers ranch on Joseph Plains, Spencer Ranch, Billy Creek Ranch (Shroyer), Howard Ranch, Hitchcock Ranch, and the Heckmans (Flynn Creek).[108]

The flying bug first bit Lorentz when he was working for the Smith brothers at the head of Getta Creek. Pilot Phil Debroth, a friend of the Smiths, landed a Cessna 170 in the rough hayfield below the main buildings in 1978. Debroth offered Lorentz a ride. "Of course it was just awesome. Poor Phil later killed himself in the plane, or at least that's what his friends told me. Ran it right into a hillside near Culdesac." Lorentz's next encounter with aviation was with Frank Hill. Lorentz was working at Flynn Creek and received regular mail and freight service from him. Hill would also occasionally look for client's lost cattle. The charge was $15.00. The first time Lorentz rode along to look for cattle from Flynn Creek it was an even better experience than earlier. "Frank's 180 had lots of power. It's a short little strip. It just sucked my guts right in . . . I was hooked." From then on Hill would stop by and visit Lorentz at Flynn Creek and even took him flying when the opportunity arose. "Frank knew I was baching it there. He also could tell I really loved flying. We became good friends and of course he taught me to fly."[109]

However, it was another five years before Lorentz himself would start flying. By 1985, he

Randy Lorentz [right] stands in front of his Aeronca Champ with friend and flight instructor Frank Hill on the Sugar Loaf airstrip after soloing in July 1986.

took a job working at the Spencer Ranch. On a winter afternoon Lorentz sat down and wrote Hill a letter expressing how serious he was about wanting to learn. The two worked out a plan. Hill located Lorentz an affordable Areonca Champ (N6057C) in Lewiston owned by Bill McCann Jr. Once the sale was finalized, Hill started giving him lessons in the Champ. After six hours of flight instruction Hill signed him off for his solo flight, which he did from the Spencer's upper Sugar Loaf airstrip. From then on Hill coached him the best he could. Lorentz, recalling his early flying, nearly thirty years later admitted, "I just started flying places. I'd seen and observed Frank go in to all these places. I'd give it a try on my own – fly downriver and land. First time I went to the lower strip [Spencer], I struggled a little, but you just get the feel for the stuff eventually." Since these early times Lorentz disclosed, "Every draw and ridge I thought I could land on I did . . . over here, over there. Not long ago on a horseback ride with Rusty Bentz, I pointed out a place I landed. Rusty said, 'Well I can see that.' Of course Rusty's a thrill seeker too. He and I've landed places people would not believe."[110]

While Lorentz adores flying for fun, his airplane is primarily used as a tool. For example, Lorentz exercises the Champ to commute back and forth to his home near Cottonwood. To no one's surprise Lorentz does not land at the Cottonwood airport, but instead in a hayfield on Windy Point closer to his house. He also used the Champ at one time to commute back and forth between summer and winter camps on the various ranches. Above Flynn Creek, he even cleared a small landing patch near the summer living quarters at the Burnett Place. Although it was handy, Lorentz acknowledged that it caused unexpected consequences. "Seemed like every time I'd have my plane parked up there in the timber, a plane would start circling overhead thinking I'd crashed and report it. People would ask me, 'how in the hell do you land there?' Well you gotta do what you gotta do sometimes. It's a tight place. I pulled out a lot of saplings with a four-wheeler. But I don't use it anymore. Bob Hitchcock heard about it and he told me to just use his upper airstrip. I did. I even kept my plane there for awhile."[111]

Beyond commuting place-to-place Lorentz and his employers used the plane often for finding lost cattle. No longer did they need to hire a pilot to come help. Donny Heckman found it very practical. Reminiscing about Lorentz and his flying he remembered, "This one time I was on the ground with a horse looking for some lost cows in thick timber and here comes Randy flying over trying to tell me where to find them. I don't know how he did it, but it appeared the plane stopped in midair right above the tall timber and me. After it paused, he kept right on flying."[112]

Lorentz and fellow pilot Rusty Bentz in the backcountry with Bentz's Cessna 185.

NOTES

1   Merle L. "Bud" Herr, Personal Communication, 19 March 2014.

2   Merle L. Herr, BLM General Land Office Records.

3   Herr, Personal Communication.

4   Jerry Harlan, Personal Communication, 19 March 2014.

5   Janet D. Pope, Personal Communication, 9 May 2014.

6   J. D. Pope, Personal Communication.

7   Jim Pope Sr., Personal Communication, 10 April 2014.

8   J. D. Pope, Personal Communication.

9   J. Pope Sr., Personal Communication.

10   J. Pope Sr., Personal Communication.

11   J. D. Pope, Personal Communication.

12   J. D. Pope, Personal Communication.

13   J. D. Pope, Personal Communication.

14   J. D. Pope, Personal Communication.

15   Bentz, Personal Communication.

16   Dave Helfrich, Personal Communication, 22 March 2014.

17   Dave Helfrich, Personal Communication, 14 January 2014.

18   Bob Cline, Personal Communication, 29 January 2014.

19   Cline, Personal Communication.

20   Cline, Personal Communication.

21   Cline, Personal Communication.

22   Cline, Personal Communication.

23   Don Vogel, Personal Communication, 22 March 2014.

24   Rusty Bentz, Personal Communication, 24 February 2014.

25   Bentz, Personal Communication.

26   Bentz, Personal Communication.

27   Bentz, Personal Communication.

28   Kathy Hedberg, "Air Tanker Crashes in Salmon River: Pilot Walks Away From Wreck Near Maloney Creek," *Lewiston Morning Tribune,* 12 August 2000.

29   J. Pope Sr., Personal Communication.

30   Bentz, Personal Communication.

31   Johnny Carrey and Cort Conley, *River of No Return,* (Cambridge, ID: Backeddy Books, 1978), 299.

32   Joyce M. Hall and Lee Wood, *An Oregon Logging Pioneer: George Shroyer's Life, Work, and Humor,* (Medford, OR: Reflected Images Publishers, 1998), 201.

33   Rex Shroyer, Personal Communication, 8 January 2014.

34   Rusty Bentz, Personal Communication, 24 February 2014.

35   Craig Fountain, Personal Communication 26 February 2014.

36   Bentz, Personal Communication.

37   Ron Fountain, Personal Communication, 24, February 2014.

38   R. Fountain, Personal Communication.

39   C. Fountain, Personal Communication.

40   Michael Rudolph, BLM General Land Office Records.

41   John A. Platt, *Whispers From Old Genesee and Echoes of the Salmon River,* (Fairfield, WA: Ye Galleon Press, 1975), XVI–XVII.

42   John A. Platt, BLM General Land Office Records.

43   J. Platt, 136.

44   Arnie Brandt, Personal Communication, 3 February 2014.

45   Jim Maxwell, Personal Communication, 9 January 2014.

46   C. Fountain, Personal Communication.

47   R. Fountain. Personal Communication.

48   William Chetwood, Personal Communication, 13 January 2014.

49   Chetwood, Personal Communication.

50   Chetwood, Personal Communication.

51   Jim Maxwell, Personal Communication, 21 January 2014.

52   Norm Close, Personal Communication, 9 May 2014.

53   Close, Personal Communication.

54   Close, Personal Communication.

55   Art Seamans, Personal Communication, 23 May 2014.

56   Close, Personal Communication.

57   Michael Rudolph, BLM General Land Office Records.

58   "Michael Rudolph Taken By Death," *Spokane Daily Chronicle,* 7 November 1951.

59   "Michael Rudolph Taken By Death," *Spokane Daily Chronicle,* 7 November 1951.

60   J. Platt, 153–55.

61   Jean Rudolph, Personal Communication, 18 March 2014.

62   "Board Hears Road Dispute," *Spokane Daily Chronicle,* 2 November 1961.

63   "New Petition Lists Changes," *Spokane Daily Chronicle,* 22 June 1963.

64   "Copter Lays Difficult Cable," *Spokane Daily Chronicle,* 25 April 1960.

65   Patty Clayton, Personal Communication, 13 March 2004.

66   K. G. Cannell and N. F. Renk, *A Cultural Resource Management Plan for the Idaho Department of Fish and Game's Peter T. Johnson Wildlife Mitigation Unit.* (Cottonwood, ID: Bonneville Power Administration, 2008).

67   Cannell and Renk.

68   Clayton, Personal Communication.

69   Clayton, Personal Communication.

70   Clayton, Personal Communication.

71   Margaret Reeves Heartburg – Reeves Family Scrapbook.

72   Margaret Reeves Heartburg, Letter to Carol Austin, 1994. (Margaret Reeves Heartburg – Reeves Family Scrapbook).

73   Justin Barrett, Personal Communication, 26 January 2014.

74   "Ross Howard, Widely Known Stockman, Dead," *Lewiston Morning Tribune,* 27 January 1959.

75   "Ross Howard, Widely Known Stockman, Dead," *Lewiston Morning Tribune,* 27 January 1959.

76   Harold Heitstuman, Personal Communication, 13 March 2014.

77   "Ross Howard, Widely Known Stockman, Dead," *Lewiston Morning Tribune,* 27 January 1959.

78   Barrett, Personal Communication.

79   Gary (Sam) McNeill, Personal Communication, 13 March 2014.

80   Patty Clayton, Personal Communication, 11 March 2014.

81 Arnie Brandt, Personal Communication, 27 February 2014.

82 Bentz, Personal Communication.

83 Bentz, Personal Communication.

84 McNeill, Personal Communication.

85 Bentz, Personal Communication.

86 J. Platt, 131.

87 Charlie Baird, BLM General Land Office Records.

88 Donny Heckman, Personal Communication, 26 February 2014.

89 Charlie Baird, BLM General Land Office Records.

90 Carrey and Conley, 304.

91 Heckman, Personal Communication.

92 Heckman, Personal Communication.

93 Heckman, Personal Communication.

94 Heckman, Personal Communication.

95 Warren Harrington Brown, *Its Fun To Remember: A King's Pine Autobiography*, (McCall, ID: Warren H. Brown, 1999), 34.

96 Brown, 34–35.

97 Heckman, Personal Communication.

98 Brown, 35.

99 Heckman, Personal Communication.

100 Heckman, Personal Communication.

101 Heckman, Personal Communication.

102 Heckman, Personal Communication.

103 Heckman, Personal Communication.

104 Bert Zimmerly Jr., Personal Communication, 3 March 2014.

105 Heckman, Personal Communication.

106 Heckman, Personal Communication.

107 Heckman, Personal Communication.

108 Randy Lorentz, Personal Communication, 17 March 2014.

109 Lorentz, Personal Communication.

110 Lorentz, Personal Communication.

111 Lorentz, Personal Communication.

112 Heckman, Personal Communication.

INDEX

Author

      The author – a historian, pilot, outdoor enthusiast, and a third generation Idahoan has a profound fascination with the history of the state, especially topics related to the remote regions. After graduating from the University of Idaho in 2005, Holm has written numerous pieces related to the backcountry, including his last books *Points of Prominence: Fire Lookouts of the Payette National Forest* and *Bound for the Backcountry: A History of Idaho's Remote Airstrips*. When not collecting information for the latest endeavor, Holm resides in Boise and McCall with his wife Amy.

CPSIA information can be obtained
at www.ICGtesting.com
Printed in the USA
BVHW010213070321
601612BV00006B/201

9 780692 305065